The Reitze Family in Philadelphia

Descended from

Christopher Reitze

Born 1824 in Hesse-Cassel, Germany

The Reitze Family in Philadelphia

Descended from

Christopher Reitze

Born 1824 in Hesse-Cassel, Germany

Kathryn Chambers Torpey
Alexandria, Virginia

Kathryn Chambers Torpey is a professional genealogist and researcher. She is certified by the Board for Certification of Genealogists℠.

Other Books by Kathryn Chambers Torpey:

John Kennedy of County Donegal, Ulster, Ireland, and His Descendants - A Compiled Genealogy (Including Risk, McCoy, and Pendleton), 2006

William Kennedy of Chester County, Pennsylvania, and His Descendants - A Compiled Genealogy (Including Davis, Smith, Wallace, Russell, and McClure), 2014

Colonial and Revolutionary Kennedy Families from Southeastern Pennsylvania, 2015

The Edwards/Scott Family History - Edinburgh to Philadelphia, 2016

The Chambers Family in Philadelphia Descended from George Chambers Born c 1815 in Ireland, 2016

Imprint: CreateSpace Independent Publishing Platform

ISBN-13: 978-1978137097
ISBN-10: 1978137095

Torpey Books
5035 Domain Place
Alexandria, VA
22311-5066

In Memory of my cousin,
Josephine Thompson Marshall

Contents

Appendices

FOREWORD

This family history documents the life of Christopher and Lucy (Devlin) Reitze and their children.

The first and second parts of the narrative describe what is known about the early history of Christopher Reitze in Hesse-Cassel and his decision to leave home. The third part documents the arrival of Christopher Reitze in America. The fourth and fifth parts provide information on the lives of Christopher Reitze and Lucy (Devlin) Reitze, his wife/widow. The sixth part provides a narrative profile of the lives of each of Christopher Reitze's children who survived infancy, Christopher, Jr., Elizabeth, Charles, John, and Josephine.

The purpose of the document is to chronicle the sequence of major events in the life of the Reitze family; to bring the family back to life, albeit only momentarily; and to depict their fundamental character and outlook on life.

The first family tree was compiled by my father, William Scott Chambers, in the 1950s. It was based on oral tradition. The research was conducted in two general time frames. The original research was conducted between 1995 and 2001. The original research was updated in 2017 with respect to the origins of Christopher Reitze in Hesse-Cassel and his early life in America.

In order to compile this family history, extensive interviews were conducted with Josephine Thompson Marshall and William Scott Chambers, first cousins who descend from Christopher Reitze's youngest child, Josephine Irene (Reitze) Chambers, and with David Harrington Marshall, Jr., one of the great-great grandchildren of Christopher Reitze. Josephine Thompson Marshall also provided copies of pages from the *Reitze Family Bible* as well as pictures of Christopher Reitze, his wife, Lucy, three of their children (Elizabeth, John, and Josephine), as well as one of their grandchildren (Charles A. Reitze, Jr.). Moreover, she reviewed the final draft of the original Reitze family history in detail and provided comprehensive comments and suggestions to augment the narrative.

During the course of the original research, contact was established with three of the descendants of Christopher Reitze's oldest child, Christopher C. Reitze, Jr. Providing their recollections of the Reitze family history from their perspective were Jeanne H. Reitze, the widow of Harry E. Reitze, Sr.; her nephew, Christopher C. Reitze, III; and a cousin, Elizabeth Wray (Wilson) Lutz. Mrs. Harry E. Reitze, Sr., also provided a copy of Christopher Reitze's Naturalization Certificate and a picture of Christopher Reitze's oldest son, Christopher C. Reitze, Jr.

Contact was also established with two of the descendants of Christopher Reitze's son, John Francis Reitze. Providing their recollections of the Reitze family history from their perspective were John Joseph Page, Jr., and his brother, James George Page.

Unfortunately, the descendants of Christopher Reitze's son, Charles A. Reitze, could not be located despite extensive efforts to do so.

In conducting the original research for the Reitze family history, the following archives and libraries in Washington, D.C., were utilized extensively: the National Archives; the Library of Congress (Newspaper Room, Map and Geography Room, City Directories Room, and the Local History and Genealogy Room); the National Genealogical Society Library; and the Daughters of the American Revolution Library. Substantial research was also conducted at the Latter-Day Saints Family History Center located in McLean, Virginia. In Philadelphia, site visits were made to the following facilities: the Free Library of Philadelphia; the Philadelphia City Archives; the Genealogical Society of Pennsylvania; the Historical Society of Pennsylvania; Mount Moriah Cemetery; Fernwood Cemetery; Northwood Cemetery; and New Cathedral Cemetery. Outside Philadelphia, site visits were made to the following locations: Glenwood Memorial Gardens in Broomall;, Lawnview Cemetery in Rockledge; Sunset Memorial Park in Somerton; and Holy Cross Cemetery in Yeadon; as well as to the Pennsylvania Memorial located at the National Military Park in Gettysburg. Finally, site visits were made to the following facilities in New Jersey: the Camden County Historical Society in Camden; the Gloucester County Historical Society in Woodbury; and the New Jersey State Archives in Trenton.

A great deal of correspondence was exchanged with numerous institutions and facilities in Philadelphia including the following: the Philadelphia City Archives; the Catholic Cemeteries Office; Evangelical Manor; Girard College; Vesper Boat Club; the Grand Army of the Republic (GAR) Museum and Library; Fireman's Hall Association; St. Edmund's Roman Catholic Church; the Court of Quarter Sessions; Northwood Cemetery; Fernwood Cemetery; and Greenmount Cemetery. Outside of Philadelphia, correspondence was exchanged with the following institutions and facilities: Glenwood Memorial Gardens in Broomall; the Pennsylvania State Archives in Harrisburg; the Friends Historical Library at Swarthmore College in Swarthmore; the Pennsylvania Division of Vital Statistics in New Castle; the Montgomery County Historical Society in Norristown; Lawnview Cemetery in Rockledge; the Philadelphia Archdiocesan Historical Research Center in Wynnewood; and the Pennsylvania Department of Corrections in Camp Hill. In New Jersey, correspondence was exchanged with the following: the New Jersey State Division of Vital Statistics in Trenton; the Presbyterian Home in Haddonfield; Haddonfield Municipal Hall in Haddonfield; the Camden County Historical Society in Camden; and the Presbyterian Homes of New Jersey in Hightown. Further afield than Pennsylvania and New Jersey, correspondence was exchanged with the following facilities: the National Personnel Records Center in St. Louis, Missouri; the Social Security Administration in Baltimore, Maryland; the Golden Gate National Cemetery in San Bruno, California; and the Sonoma County Recorder in Sonoma County, California.

An attorney, Patrick J. Reardon, was engaged to petition the Chief Administrative Judge of the Court of Common Pleas to issue an order opening Elizabeth (Reitze) Collins' divorce case file.

A professional researcher, Susan Koelble of Bareroots Research Services, was engaged to obtain a copy of the Collins v Collins divorce case file and to obtain copies of several probate files in Philadelphia. Ms. Koelble was also engaged to conduct various other research assignments at both the Historical Society of Pennsylvania and the Genealogical Society of Pennsylvania with respect to this family history. Other researchers employed during the course of this research included Barbara Edwards who conducted research at the New Jersey State Archives; Lynn Jeffries who conducted research at the Genealogical Society of Pennsylvania, the Historical Society of Pennsylvania, and the Camden County Historical Society; Margaret Posehn who conducted research at the California State Library; and Sherrie Yuhans who conducted research at the Pennsylvania State Archives.

Finally, brief family histories were written of the Benner and the Douglass families as these two families are inextricably tied to the Reitze family and it was necessary to research these families for a more complete understanding of the Reitze family history. These two family histories are contained in the appendix section.

Kathryn C. Torpey
October 9, 2017

Descendant Chart for Christopher Reitze

Christopher Reitze 1824 - 1879 — **Lucy S. Devlin** 1836 - 1909

Children of Christopher Reitze and Lucy S. Devlin:

- **Christopher C. Reitze Jr.** 1855 - 1907 — **Elizabeth L. Hoffner** 1861 - 1938
  - **Elizabeth C. Reitze** 1881 - 1971 — **John A. Bustard** 1867 - 1934
  - **Margaret May Reitze** 1882 - 1959 — **Edward Taylor Burtis** 1871 - 1956
  - **Christopher Carl Reitze I** 1885 - 1942 — **Helen C. Hoenigmann** 1887 - 1923
  - **Theresa "Tess" Reimold** 1882 - 1943
- **Susan R. Reitze** 1859 - 1859
- **Henry Reitze** 1861 - 1862
- **Elizabeth M. Reitze** 1863 - 1961 — **Edward J. Collins** 1859 - 1893
  - **baby Collins** 1883 - 1883
- **Henry Grafe Douglass** 1854 - 1932
- **Charles Archibald Reitze Sr.** 1866 - 1893 — **Rachel M. Kelly** 1869 -
  - **Charles Archibald Reitze Jr.** 1893 - 1969 — **Mary Kubick** 1897 - 1964
- **John Francis Reitze Sr.** 1869 - 1955 — **Margaret Cecilia Malloy** 1873 - 1918
  - **George B. Reitze** 1896 - 1934 — **Isabel Smith** 1899 - 1978
  - **Lucy Elizabeth Reitze** 1897 - 1980 — **Joshua Leon Bach** 1890 - 1951
  - **John Francis Reitze Jr.** 1901 - 1975 — **Catherine Irene Reitze** 1903 - 1995 — **Frank John Kelly**
  - **Elizabeth Mary Reitze** 1905 - 1957 — **John Joseph Page Sr.** 1902 - 1971
- **Emily "Emma" C. Malloy** 1888 - 1951
- **Lucy (twin) Reitze** 1872 - 1872
- **William (twin) Reitze** 1872 - 1872
- **Ellen (twin) Reitze** 1873 - 1873
- **Julie (twin) Reitze** 1873 - 1873
- **Maggie Reitze** 1874 - 1875
- **Conrad Reitze** 1876 - 1877
- **Josephine Irene Reitze** 1877 - 1962 — **William Scott Chambers** 1867 - 1950
  - **Henry Grafe Chambers** 1897 - 1953 — **Mary Ann McCauley** 1892 - 1984
  - **Lucy Elizabeth Chambers** 1898 - 1918 — **William Thompson** 1891 - 1965

The Reitze Family History

Reportedly, Christopher Reitze had a bad temper. He liked doing things his way on his schedule. Often wrong, but never in doubt, his unyielding disposition extracted a heavy toll in terms of his relationship with his wife and children, and, in the end, may have cost him his life.

So, who was he? Where did he come from? When and why did he come to America? Where did he live and what did he do for a living? And, what happened to his wife and children after he died?

THE ORIGINS OF CHRISTOPHER REITZE

Little is known about the early life of Christopher Reitze. According to family legend, he was born on March 12, 1824, in Schleswig-Holstein.[1] To the contrary, his petition for naturalization and his Certificate of Naturalization both state that he was a subject of the Grand Duke of Hesse-Cassel.[2,3] The single record that substantiates his origins in Hesse-Cassel is the record of his marriage which states that he was from Bottendorf, Curhessen (sic), then located in Hesse-Cassel.[4] Today, Bottendorf appears to be part of Waldeck-Frankenberg, Kassel, Hessen, Germany. Whether Christopher Reitze was actually born in Bottendorf or in the surrounding area is unknown.

The Geography of Hesse-Cassel

The state of Hesse-Cassel was located almost squarely in the middle of Germany in the

---

[1]Conversation on September 2, 1995, with the late William Scott Chambers, 325 N.W. 95th Avenue, Plantation, Florida 33324-7021.

[2]Petition for Naturalization of Christopher Reitze, Supreme Court of Pennsylvania, September 28, 1868, Pennsylvania State Archives, Harrisburg, Pennsylvania.

[3]The original Naturalization Certificate of Christopher Reitze dated September 28, 1868, was in the possession of the late Jeanne H. Reitze (widow of Harry E. Reitze, Sr.), 6 Pinewood Trail, Concord, New Hampshire 03301-5247.

[4]Marriage Record of Christoph Reitze and Lucy Devlin dated March 3, 1855, Saint Michael's and Zion Church, Historic Pennsylvania Church and Town Records, Historical Society of Pennsylvania, Philadelphia, Pennsylvania, <<www.ancestry.com>>, downloaded March 16, 2016.

Central German Uplands.[5] The uplands consist of two partly intersecting mountain ranges with several peaks reaching elevations of about 3,700 feet. These low lying mountains contain many high plains, undulating hills, volcanic formations, troughs, and small basins.[6] Although these mountains sometimes acted as natural divides, they were not absolute barriers. This being the case, Hesse-Cassel cannot be defined solely in terms of its geography. In fact, as its history clearly demonstrates, it was continuously influenced by population migrations, the foreign interests and political alliances of its rulers as well as a variety of social, cultural, economic, and religious factors.

The Formation and Early History of Hesse-Cassel

Hesse-Cassel formally came into being in 1568 upon the death of Philip the Magnanimous (1509-1567), the Landgrave of Hessen and a prominent leader of the Protestant Reformation.[7,8] Philip the Magnanimous assumed leadership of Hessen in 1520 and declared himself a Lutheran four years later. While he did not excel in moral standards of conduct, he had a keen political vision and was an ardent supporter of the Protestant Reformation.[9] Upon his death, Hessen was divided among his four sons giving the principality of Hesse-Cassel to his son, William IV.[10]

During the late 16th Century, Protestant princes such as Prince William IV (1532-1592) were essentially agrarian landowners who derived the major part of their revenue from the management of their states. The only way they could retain control of their domains was through good management techniques and the avoidance of military expenditures. William IV, being adapt in both instances, soon became one of the best known of the Lutheran princes most of

---

[5]Karl Romer, Ulrich K. Dreikandt, and Claudia Wullenkord, Editors, *Facts About Germany - The Federal Republic of Germany*, (Federal Republic of Germany: Lexikon-Institut Bertelsmann, 1979; reprint 1989), p. 11.

[6]Romer, Dreikandt and Wullenkord, p. 10.

[7]Ernest Thode, *German English Genealogical Dictionary*, (Baltimore, Maryland: Genealogical Publishing Company, 1993), p. 145 defines landgrave as landgraf or count.

[8]Hajo Holbor, *A History of Modern Germany - The Reformation*, (Princeton, New Jersey: Princeton University Press, 1959), p. 204.

[9]Will Durant, *The Story of Civilization: Part VI - The Reformation*, (New York: Simon & Schuster, 1957), p. 449.

[10]The other three principalities were Hesse-Darmstadt, Hesse-Marburg, and Hesse Rothenfels. When the rulers of Hesse-Marburg and Hesse-Rothenfels died without heirs, their principalities were joined with that of Hesse-Cassel.

whom distinguished themselves by their wisdom and diligence in the internal administration of their states.[11]

In the early years of its existence, Hesse-Cassel was part of a loosely knit, but ineffective, federation of German states with little central authority. This federation eventually evolved into an unstable empire that was subsequently torn apart by the Thirty Years War (1618-1648). Thereafter, whatever little unity actually remained among the German states, including Hesse-Cassel, disappeared altogether.[12]

By the eve of the French Revolution, Hesse-Cassel had disintegrated into an ill-administered state governed by the notorious Landgrave Frederick II (1720-1785). Although Frederick II had transformed the capital (Kassel) into an elegant city where art and education were preeminent, court life was immoral. Also, due to his extravagances and mismanagement, he was continually in need of cash.[13] To raise money, Frederick II became Hesse-Cassel's most infamous merchant in the sale of Hessian mercenary soldiers by dispatching 19,000 men to America to serve the British during the American Revolution.[14] For some reason, despite his notoriety and his immorality, this landgrave, who had converted to the Roman Catholic faith, chose to leave his subjects' religion undisturbed. Thus, Hesse-Cassel's population remained about 80% Protestant, most of whom were Calvinists.[15]

The Holy Roman Empire of the German States

By the time Frederick II, Landgrave of Hesse-Cassel, died in 1785, Germany had coalesced into a conglomeration of many states, both big and little, all united in what was then

---

[11]Hajo Holborn, *History of Modern Germany - The Reformation*, (Princeton, New Jersey: Princeton University Press, 1959), p. 264.

[12]Hajo Holborn, *A History of Modern Germany - 1648 to 1840*, (Princeton, New Jersey: Princeton University Press, 1964), p. 22, 39.

[13]Hajo Holborn, *A History of Modern Germany - 1648 to 1840*, (Princeton, New Jersey: Princeton University Press, 1964), p. 295.

[14]Charles W. Ingrao, *The Hessian Mercenary State - Ideas, Institutions, and Reforms Under Frederick II, 1760-1785*, (Cambridge: Cambridge University Press, 1987), p. 3.

[15]Charles M. Hall, *The Atlantic Bridge to Germany - Volume 2: Part A - Hessen and Part B - Rhineland/Pfalz (The Palatinate)*, (Logan, Utah: The Everton Publishers, Inc., 1976), p. X.

known as the Holy Roman Empire of the German States.[16] The most important states in the Empire were Prussia and Austria, but there were also a large number of independent secondary states such as Hesse-Cassel, as well as city states, ecclesiastical states ruled by bishops of the Catholic Church, and independent possessions ruled by innumerable counts, barons, and knights of the Empire. In those years, German politics turned largely on the rivalry between Prussia and Austria with the secondary states aligning themselves with either Prussia or Austria as their interests demanded.

This delicate balance of power was upset in 1803 by a decree enacted by the German diet that allowed the secondary states in southern German to increase their wealth and power by annexing the tiny states within their territories. By this act, all the city states except six and all the ecclesiastical states except one lost their independence in southern Germany. When the secondary states then tried to take over the tiny principalities within their territories, the counts, barons and knights appealed to Austria for help. Austria threatened war with the secondary states in southern Germany if they went ahead with their plans. Napoleon, Emperor of France, intervened on behalf of the secondary states and war was declared between Austria and France.

Austria lost the war. As a result, she was forced by Napoleon to cede to Bavaria, Wurttemberg, and Baden all of her scattered possessions in southern Germany and to agree that henceforth the southern states should no longer be included in the Holy Roman Empire nor should they be in any way dependent upon Austria.[17] Thus, Napoleon neutralized the power of Austria. This permitted Prussia to emerge briefly as the most powerful of the German states. However, its supremacy was short lived as Napoleon subsequently conquered Prussia in 1807, destroyed it as a great power, and brought northern Germany including Hesse-Cassel under the sway of his empire.[18]

Post-Napoleonic Germany

After conquering northern Germany, Napoleon consolidated Hesse-Cassel with Hanover, Brunswick, and the territories of Prussia west of the Elbe River. These he renamed the Kingdom of Westphalia and installed his dissolute youngest brother, Jerome Bonaparte, in Kassel as king.[19]

By 1815, however, Napoleon was vanquished and sent into exile. A Congress of

---

[16]Carl L. Becker, *Modern History - The Rise of a Democratic, Scientific, and Industrialized Civilization*, (Morristown, New Jersey: Silver Burdett Company, 1958), p. 280.

[17]Becker, p. 285.

[18]Becker, p. 289.

[19]Hajo Holborn, *A History of Modern Germany - 1648 to 1840*, (Princeton, New Jersey: Princeton University Press, 1964), p. 387.

European powers was assembled in Vienna in 1815 to address the innumerable unsettled questions created by the fall of Napoleon's empire including the political organization of Germany. To establish a lasting peace in Europe, the Congress reduced the number of German states to thirty-eight, and created a national structure known as the German Confederation where Prussia and Austria were again dominant.[20] Thus, with the old autocracies restored in most states, including Hesse-Cassel, and with Prussian and Austrian influence once more predominant in Germany, the Congress believed that it had done much to safeguard Europe from the danger of revolution and radical ideas.

As a result of the actions of the Congress of Vienna, the years between 1815 and 1830 were not a period of hopefulness for most people. In those years, many people endured a miserable existence under the shadow of oppression. This included Christopher Reitze and his family who lived under the despotic and corrupt regime of the degenerate William II, Elector of Hesse-Cassel (1821-1847).[21] Everywhere in the state of Hesse-Cassel, the political opinions and activities of the people were suppressed.

In 1831, an attempt was made in Hesse-Cassel to end the oppression by forcing William II to adopt a liberal constitution and accept his heir, Frederick William I, as co-regent. Even after these drastic action were taken, nothing improved substantially in Hesse-Cassel. The mass of the people minded their own business as best they could and busied themselves making a living. Those few who had aspired to political liberty probably realized that they had very little hope of ever obtaining it. The prevailing thought of the time while Christopher Reitze was a child growing up in Hesse-Cassel was somewhat gloomy and depressed.[22]

By 1840, however, the old fear of revolution and war had quietly begun to abate in the politically powerful aristocracy and in other influential quarters in the leading German states.[23] By then, only very old people could remember the French Revolution and only the old or middle-aged could remember the Napoleonic wars. Even the dangers of war and revolution as they existed in 1815 were remembered less vividly by most people. The ruling princes began to let down their guard and young people, in particular, once again began to think that political liberty and social reform were possible to obtain. Thus, the popular mood gradually shifted from gloom and doom to one of hope and expectation and young men such as Christopher Reitze, who was

---

[20]Becker, p. 314.

[21]Hajo Holborn, *A History of Modern Germany - 1840 to 1945*, (Princeton, New Jersey: Princeton University Press, 1969), p. 24.

[22]Becker, p. 334.

[23]Becker, p. 318.

sixteen years old at the time, began to looked forward with enthusiasm to better times.[24]

THE DECISION TO LEAVE HOME

Although much of German history was marked by wars of expansion, religious troubles, changes in ruling families, conflicts between emperors and popes, and strife among the states, cities, and the central authority, the years just preceding 1848 were characterized by the growing faith of the people in better times to come.[25] This faith took different forms for different people, but generally included the belief in the possibility of abolishing poverty and social injustice; the belief in popular government; and the belief that war would shortly disappear among civilized nations.[26] Undoubtedly, the inhabitants of Hesse-Cassel must have been influenced in their thinking by these ideas. So, too, must have been Christopher Reitze.

The Revolution of 1848

Christopher Reitze was just shy of twenty-four years old on the eve of the Revolution of 1848. As far as is known, he was still single at that time. Presumably, he still lived somewhere in Hesse-Cassel. Undoubtedly, he spoke a Hessian dialect with a distinct Hessian accent and was probably a member of the Protestant majority.[27,28]

All around him, in each of the states into which Germany was divided, revolutionaries were suddenly demanding the establishment of state constitutions by which the people would be given a representative share in the government.[29] Even the evil Elector of Hesse-Cassel, William Frederick I, had to bow to the revolutionaries.[30] The intensity of the revolutionary movement was so powerful that on March 16, just six days before Christopher Reitze's twenty-fourth

---

[24]Becker, p. 335.

[25]Anthony M. Kronbauer, editor, *The International Standard Atlas of the World*, (New York: Grosset & Dunlap, Inc., 1961), p. 29.

[26]Becker, p. 335.

[27]Romer, Dreikandt and Wullenkord, p. 21.

[28]Charles M. Hall, *The Atlantic Bridge to Germany - Volume 2: Part A - Hessen and Part B - Rhineland/Pfalz (The Palatinate)*, (Logan, Utah: The Everton Publishers, Inc., 1976), p. X, states, in part, that in 1560 Hessen was 80% Protestant. In 1618 at the outbreak of the Thirty Years War, 70% of Hessen's Protestant population was Calvinist and 30% was Lutheran.

[29]Becker, p. 345.

[30]Hajo Holborn, *A History of Modern Germany 1840 to 1945*, (Princeton, New Jersey: Princeton University Press, 1969), p. 48.

birthday, Frederick William IV, the King of Prussia, stepped out on his balcony and promised to call together an assembly to aid in the formation of a constitution for Prussia. But the revolutionaries wanted more than constitutional government in each of the states. They wanted national unity in Germany.[31]

A national assembly was quickly elected to sit in Frankfurt to accomplish this purpose. A year later, on March 28, 1849, after much disagreement, the assembly finally voted to establish a hereditary empire in Germany. It offered the hereditary imperial crown to Frederick William IV, King of Prussia. A substantial part of the military and civilian establishment urged the king to accept. Nevertheless, he declined. Twenty-nine states ultimately accepted the constitution, but it did not include the important ones - Prussia, Austria, Bavaria, Hanover or Saxony.[32]

On May 4, 1849, in one final attempt to save the revolution, the national assembly called on state governments, elected bodies at all levels, and the whole of the German people to recognize the constitution and bring it into effect.[33] Although their spirit remained defiant, nothing substantial happened and the members gradually drifted away or were ordered home by their state governments.

The national assembly was dissolved by Prussian troops in June of 1849, but not before a long and bloody three months of demonstrations, uprisings, and revolts that erupted throughout the leading German states. Revolutionary governments were briefly established in some states. Barricades were erected, armories were stormed, revolutionary committees were formed and soldiers of the reserve went over to the revolution in some parts of Prussia. Regular units did the same in Bavaria and Baden.[34] In the end, the armed forces of the German princes remained intact and easily defeated the revolutionaries. The national assembly was dispersed and the old Confederation of 1815 was restored. The princes withdrew the state constitutions they had granted to the people and the state governments became more repressive than ever before. People became discouraged and their thoughts became increasingly more pessimistic.[35]

The reaction in Hesse-Cassel was no different. Its people had for a very long time suffered more than any other state under the arbitrary despotism of its wretched rulers. Now, as the revolutionary tide was ebbing, the Elector, Frederick William I, wishing to rid himself of the

------

[31]Becker, p. 348.

[32]David Blackbourn, *The Long Nineteenth Century - A History of Germany, 1780 - 1918,* (New York & London: Oxford University Press, 1998), p. 161.

[33]Blackbourn, p. 161.

[34]Blackbourn, p. 162.

[35]Becker, p. 354.

limitations on his sovereignty imposed by the liberal constitution adopted in 1831, dissolved the liberal chamber and demanded the new chamber approve the continuation of all existing taxes while withholding from it the budget estimates.

When the new chamber refused to pass the taxes, it was dissolved by Frederick William I who imposed the taxes by decree. Thereafter, the state judges and officials in Hesse-Cassel refused to support the new constitution and all the officers of the Hessian army resigned their commissions. The Elector, Frederick William I, declared Hesse-Cassel in a state of siege and removed himself to Frankfurt.[36] The ensuing conflict lasted until 1866 - the ending date for the state of Hesse-Cassel - a state whose only claim to fame was that it exploited its people shamelessly for over a century.[37]

So, what part did Christopher Reitze play in all this? The only tangible evidence of his activities or whereabouts immediately preceding his decision to leave home is a tiny leather change purse imprinted with the royal Prussian seal.[38] Although it is uncertain exactly how Christopher Reitze came into its possession, the purse is said to have originally belonged to him, and may be associated somehow with the Prussian army.[39]

Even though nothing is known for certain, family legend has it that Christopher Reitze arrived in America after having gotten into some sort of trouble in his homeland. By one account, he may have been cashiered (i.e., dismissed in dishonor) or deserted from the army.[40] By another account, he may have dodged military conscription altogether in that he was opposed to military service as a matter of conscience.[41] Either way, given the unstable political situation

---

[36]Hajo Holborn, *A History of Modern Germany 1840 to 1945*, (Princeton, New Jersey: Princeton University Press, 1969), p. 96.

[37]Hajo Holborn, *A History of Modern Germany 1840 to 1945*, (Princeton, New Jersey: Princeton University Press, 1969), p. 113.

[38]The tiny leather change purse imprinted with the royal Prussian seal was in the possession of the late Josephine Thompson Marshall, 121 Reillywood Avenue, Haddonfield, New Jersey 08033-2201.

[39]Letter dated October 21, 1999, from the late Josephine Thompson Marshall, 121 Reillywood Avenue, Haddonfield, New Jersey 08033-2201.

[40]Conversation on September 1, 1996, with the late William Scott Chambers, 325 N.W. 95th Avenue, Plantation, Florida 33324-7021.

[41]Conversation on November 29, 1996, with the late Josephine Thompson Marshall, 121 Reillywood Avenue, Haddonfield, New Jersey 08033-2201, and David Harrington Marshall, Jr., 121 Reillywood Avenue, New Jersey, 08033-2201.

in Hesse-Cassel, it is not surprising that Christopher Reitze decided to leave home.

THE JOURNEY TO AMERICA

According to Christopher Reitze's petition for naturalization, he arrived at the Port of New York in 1851.[42] If, at the time of his departure, he was living in a rural farming community or a small village or town near Bottendorf in Hesse-Cassel, he probably left home in the company of others, either family or friends. They may have taken a horse drawn wagon to the nearest large town or city (possibly Kassel) where they would have transferred to a train.[43] From there, they would have traveled north through Gottingen and Hanover to the port city of Bremen - Germany's oldest and second largest port.[44,45] From Bremen they would have traveled an additional 30 miles to the Emigrant House in Bremerhaven.

Construction of the Emigrant House in Bremerhaven was completed in 1850. It was equipped to house 1,500 to 2,000 people in nine sleeping halls. The kitchen could accommodate about 3,500 people and the hospital's capacity was 35 patients. There was also a chapel with both Protestant and Catholic facilities.[46] Christopher Reitze would have been housed at the Emigrant House for anywhere from four days to two weeks waiting to board a ship.[47] Fortunately for Christopher Reitze, Bremen actively sought the emigrant trade and was considered one of the safest ports in Europe.[48]

Perhaps the ultimate disappointment to Christopher Reitze must have been the sight of the ship that was to carry him on his journey to America. While it is true that steamships were

---

[42]Petition for Naturalization of Christopher Reitze, Supreme Court of Pennsylvania, September 28, 1868, Pennsylvania State Archives, Harrisburg, Pennsylvania.

[43]Hajo Holborn, *A History of Modern Germany 1840 to 1945*, (Princeton, New Jersey: Princeton University Press, 1969), p. 12.

[44]Hajo Holborn, *A History of Modern Germany 1840 to 1945*, (Princeton, New Jersey: Princeton University Press, 1969), p. 15 (railroad map).

[45]*Railroad Map of Germany and Neighboring Countries - 1849*, Title in German: *Eisenbahn Karte von Deutschland und Nachbarländern - 1849*, <<https://en.wikipedia.org/wiki/ History_of_rail_transport_in_Germany#/media/File:Bahnkarte_Deutschland_1849.jpg>>, downloaded July 16, 2017.

[46]Maralyn A. Wellauer, *German Immigration to America in the Nineteenth Century: A Genealogists Guide*, (Milwaukee, Wisconsin: Roots International, 1985), p. 48.

[47]Wellauer, p. 44.

[48]Wellauer, p. 47.

rapidly replacing sailing ships by the mid-19th Century, it appears that Christopher Reitze departed Bremen on a 190 ton, two-masted wooden ship with square sails named the Brig Hiram.[49] Based on its registered tonnage, this was a small ship. It was also an old ship having made at least 17 voyages to the Port of New York between 1823 and 1850 from such diverse foreign ports as Marseilles, Gibraltar, Barbados, Vera Cruz, Mexico, and Matanzas, Cuba.[50]

The ship's master was Captain [T.] Grabau. He appears to have been in command of the Brig Hiram since at least 1849.[51] On this particular voyage from Bremen, there were only 94 passengers on board the vessel. Two were cabin class passengers while the remainder, including Christopher Reitze, were in steerage. The ship departed Bremen on May 6, 1851.[52]

The Brig Hiram was a foreign-owned vessel. In 1851, its port of registry was Bremen.[53] In theory, it was required to adhere to all the official regulations set forth for ships departing from the seaports of Bremen and Hamburg. These regulations concerned the safety of the voyage, the condition of the vessel, the sufficiency of room for the passengers, and the quantity and quality of provisions. In actuality, once on board, Christopher Reitze probably discovered that very little room was allocated to steerage class passengers - less than six feet overhead and between fourteen and twenty square feet of floor space to serve as both sleeping quarters and an area for food preparation.

Further, he and the other passengers in steerage likely would have been required to spend the majority of their time below deck. If there were any portholes on the Brig Hiram they would have been small and it is doubtful that they provided much, if any, ventilation. Thus, the conditions in steerage would have been dark, stuffy, and putrid. Nausea and seasickness were not uncommon. So was disease.

Although there is no record of the weather conditions during the voyage, the situation in steerage would have been worse if the weather was stormy as the hatch door would have

---

[49]Entry for Chr. Ritz, Bremen Brig Hiram Passenger Manifest, June 18, 1851, p. 1, line 24, Passenger List of Vessels Arriving in New York, NY, 1820-1897, National Archives Microfilm Publication M237, Roll 100.

[50]Bradley W. Steuart, editor, *Passenger Ships Arriving in New York Harbor, Volume I (1820 - 1850)*, (Bountiful, Utah: Precision Indexing, 1991), p. 256.

[51]Steuart. p. 256.

[52]Arrivals - Port of New York, *The New York Herald*, Wednesday, June 18, 1851, p. 4.

[53]Entries for the Brig Hiram, Register of Vessels Arriving at the Port of New York from Foreign Ports, 1789-1919, National Archives Microfilm Publication M1066, Roll 7 (Targets 3, 5, 6, and 7).

remained closed. Kerosine lanterns, used for lighting, would have added smoke to the air.[54]

As did everyone else, Christopher Reitze would have brought some personal belongings with him (including his tiny leather change purse imprinted with the royal Prussian seal). Most passengers carried their belongings in wicker baskets or tied securely in pillow cases. He would have spent much of his time guarding these meager belongings as there was next to no personal privacy or security in steerage. If he thought ahead about what he was doing, he probably brought a water jug, dried meat, flour and some sugar with him just in case the ship ran out of provisions during the voyage due to delays caused by bad weather or other unforeseen events.[55]

The Brig Hiram arrived at the quarantine station in the Port of New York on June 18, 1851.[56] Notice of its arrival appeared in the New York Herald as follows:

> Brig Hiram (Brem), Grabau, Bremen, 44 days, in ballast *[i.e., no cargo]* and 92
> passengers, to Bechtel & Dreyer. June 2 lat 58, lon 55 21 spoke Holland brig Regina
> from Bremen for Baltimore.[57]

As required by the Immigration Commission of the State of New York, Captain Grabau should have given Christopher Reitze a handbill written in German entitled *Good Advice for Immigrants on Their Arrival in New York.*[58] Port officials were sent on board the Brig Hiram to inspect the ship and question the passengers about any complaints they may have had about the crossing. Any passengers who were sick or injured were sent to the hospital. After an accounting was made of all on board, the passengers, including Christopher Reitze, were sent on their way with their wicker baskets, pillow cases and a copy of the handbill.

THE LIFE AND TIMES OF CHRISTOPHER REITZE IN AMERICA

There is no record of who, if anyone, may have met Christopher Reitze at the Port of New York, or how he made his way to his ultimate destination, or even where he was headed.

---

[54]Wellauer, p. 45.

[55]Wellauer, p. 45.

[56]Entries for the Brig Hiram, Register of Vessels Arriving at the Port of New York from Foreign Ports, 1789-1919, National Archives Microfilm Publication M1066, Roll 7 (Targets 3, 5, 6, and 7).

[57]Arrivals - Port of New York, *The New York Herald*, Wednesday, June 18, 1851, p. 4.

[58]Wellauer, p. 67.

According to family legend Christopher Reitze initially lived in New Jersey after he arrived in America, but exactly where he lived is unknown. There are three possibilities none of which has been corroborated despite extensive research in South Jersey primary and derivative sources. The three possibilities are as follows:

WOODBURY, DEPTFORD TOWNSHIP, GLOUCESTER COUNTY. By one account, Christopher Reitze is said to have had two sisters who lived in Woodbury.[59] To date, no evidence of the existence of these sisters has been found.[60] Thus, it is not known when they arrived in the United States, whether he lived with them, or whether they lived in Woodbury. Interestingly, the only connection found so far between Christopher Reitze and Woodbury involves the Hessian soldiers sold as mercenaries to the British during the Revolutionary War by Frederick II, the ruthless Landgrave of Hesse-Cassel. It seems that many of the Hessians wounded at the Battle of Red Bank (October 21/22, 1777) were cared for in Woodbury and some of those who died were buried in the Strangers Burying Ground.[61] Perhaps one of these Hessian soldiers was an ancestor of Christopher Reitze.

MULLICA HILL, HARRISON TOWNSHIP, GLOUCESTER COUNTY. By another account, Christopher Reitze may have lived and worked in Mullica, New Jersey.[62] This reference may be to Mullica Hill, the principal town in Harrison Township. Other possibilities include Mullica Township in Atlantic County and the Mullica River which runs between Atlantic and Burlington Counties.[63]

If the reference is to Mullica Hill, which is south of Woodbury, it is unclear when Christopher Reitze may have lived there or what may have steered him in that direction. In 1851,

---

[59]Information about Christopher Reitze's sisters (Mrs. Wicks/Weeks and Mrs. Westcott/Wolcott) was provided on October 15, 1996, by the late Josephine Thompson Marshall, 121 Reillywood Avenue, Haddonfield, New Jersey 08033-2201.

[60]Verticle Files (Bible Records, Pedigree Sheets, Family Group Sheets, Wills, Vital Statistics & Other Documents for South Jersey/Delaware Valley Families), Gloucester County Historical Society, Woodbury, New Jersey.

[61]Alfred M. Heston, editor-in-chief, *South Jersey - A History 1664 - 1924*, (New York & Chicago: Lewis Publishing Company, 1924), p. 466.

[62]Conversation on June 16, 1999, with the late Christopher C. Reitze III, 27 Riverside Drive, Florham Park, New Jersey, 07932-2402.

[63]Henry Charlton Beck, *Jersey Genesis - The Story of the Mullica River*, (New Brunswick, New Jersey: Rutgers University Press, 1945).

the town of Mullica Hill was still relatively small. The Quakers were the first religious denomination to settle in Mullica Hill, followed by Methodist Episcopal and Baptist congregations. A grist mill, carding mill, and a cotton cloth mill were built at varying times, but eventually failed due to a lack of adequate transportation. By the mid-19th Century, the economy of the town of Mullica Hill tended to support the needs of its local inhabitants and the needs of the landowners of the farms that thrived in the surrounding community.[64]

One of these landowners was S.C. Allen, a Quaker, who appears to have owned land near Mullica Hill as late as 1850.[65,66,67,68,69] Although no records have emerged to conclusively connect Christopher Reitze to Mullica Hill, the significance of the surname Allen will become clear momentarily.

BLACKWOOD, GLOUCESTER TOWNSHIP, CAMDEN COUNTY. By a third account, Christopher Reitze may have lived and worked on a farm in Blackwood that belonged to a farmer

---

[64]Heston, p. 475.

[65]Alexander C. Stansbie, James Keily, and Samuel M. Rea, *Map of the Counties of Salem and Gloucester, New Jersey*, (Philadelphia, Pennsylvania: Smith and Wistar, 1849), Scale Not Stated, 38 x 58, Library of Congress, Land Ownership Maps, No. 462.

[66]1850 U.S. Census (population), New Jersey, Gloucester County, Harrison Township, page 53B, National Archives Microfilm Publication M432, Roll 451, re: Samuel C. Allen. 59 b. New Jersey, farmer.

[67]Gloucester County, New Jersey, Grantee Index, FHL Microfilm Roll 846539, <<www.familysearch.org>>, downloaded July 19, 2017, re: Samuel P. (sic) Collins to Collins Allen, September 3, 1850 (sic), September 6, 1853 (sic). Samuel C. Allen was the father of both Samuel P. Allen and Collins Allen.

[68]Marriage Record of Samuel C. Allen and Mary Ann Bassett dated 1838-2-8, Woodbury Monthly Meeting, New Jersey, Hinshaw Index to Selected Quaker Records, 1680-1940, Original Data: *William Wade Hinshaw's Index to Unpublished Quaker Records*, (Swarthmore, Pennsylvania: Friends Historical Library, Swarthmore College, n.p.), <<www.ancestry.com>>, downloaded July 23, 2017.

[69]Allen Family Record, Salem Monthly Meeting, New Jersey, Encyclopedia of American Quaker Genealogy, Volumes I-VI, 1607-1943, Original Data: William Wade Hinshaw, et al., compilers. *Encyclopedia of American Quaker Genealogy*, 6 volumes, 1936–1950. Reprint, Baltimore, Maryland: Genealogical Publishing Co., 1991–1994, and William Wade Hinshaw and Thomas Worth Marshall, compilers, *Encyclopedia of American Quaker Genealogy. Supplement to Volume 1*, (Washington, D.C.: n.p. 1948), <<www.ancestry.com>>, downloaded July 23, 2017.

named Allen. Christopher Reitze is said to have met his future wife, Lucy Devlin, on the farm where she was living with her grandmother, a widow, then married to the farmer named Allen.[70,71] The farm is said to have been near the town of Blackwood which is about 12 miles from Mullica Hill. To date, no record has been found of the farm where Christopher Reitze is said to have lived and worked.[72,73,74]

Blackwood is the oldest town in Gloucester Township having been named for John Blackwood who purchased large land holdings there in the middle of the 18th Century. The Presbyterian Church in Blackwood goes back to at least 1750. The Methodists made their appearance in Blackwood in 1800 and the Baptist Church was organized under the Reverend Henry Westcott in 1848.[75,76]

The Marriage of Christopher Reitze and Lucy Devlin

According to the *Reitze Family Bible*, Christopher Reitze and Lucy S. Devlin were

---

[70]Conversation on September 2, 1995, with the late William Scott Chambers, 325 N.W. 95th Avenue, Plantation, Florida 33324-7021 who said the farmer was named "Allen from Blackwood" who was married to a widow named Abigail.

[71]Conversation on March 21, 1995, with the late Josephine Thompson Marshall, 121 Reillywood Avenue, Haddonfield, New Jersey 08033-2201 who said the farmer was named Allen, possibly Collins Allen, who was married to a widow named Elizabeth.

[72]Frederick C. Merry, *Map of Camden County, New Jersey*, (Philadelphia, Pennsylvania: R.L. Barnes and Lloyd Vanderveer, 1857), Scale 1½ Inch to 1 Mile, 33 x 40, Library of Congress, Land Ownership Maps, No. 443.

[73]1850 U.S. Census (agricultural), New Jersey, Camden County, Gloucester Township (4 double pages, dated September-October 1850), Microfilm Publication # 197, Roll 1 (Atlantic - Mercer counties), Camden County Historical Society, 1900 Park Blvd, Camden, NJ 08103.

[74]1855 State Census (population), New Jersey, Camden County, Gloucester Township, FHL Microfilm Roll 0865492, <<www.familysearch.org>>, downloaded July 23, 2017.

[75]Heston, p. 351, 352.

[76]According to Heston, p. 352, "For some years before the Civil War, the brick house built by George Cheeseman in 1845 and kept by him as a temperance hotel, was used as a boarding school, to which the attendance of several young Cubans gave a somewhat international aspect."

married on March 3, 1855, but the location of their marriage was not stated.[77] According to family legend, the couple was married from the Allen family farm in Blackwood in a Quaker (Hicksite) ceremony.[78] In fact, according to Lucy's great-granddaughter, Josephine Thompson Marshall:

> Lucy lived with her maternal Quaker grandmother in New Jersey and was familiar with the Quaker faith. Legend has it her grandmother made her change the hat she planned to wear to the wedding. Afterward, it was proper decorum to wear a bonnet, as a married woman.[79]

No record of the marriage was found in South Jersey records.[80] A review of Philadelphia

---

[77]*The Reitze Family Bible - Latin Vulgate Version.* (New York: D & J Sadlier, 1844) was in the possession of the late Josephine Thompson Marshall, 121 Reillywood Avenue, Haddonfield, New Jersey 08033-2201.

[78]Conversation on March 21, 1995, with the late Josephine Thompson Marshall, 121 Reillywood Avenue, Haddonfield, New Jersey 08033-2201.

[79]Letter dated October 21, 1999, from the late Josephine Thompson Marshall, 121 Reillywood Avenue, Haddonfield, New Jersey 08033-2201.

[80]There is no record of the marriage in any of the following records or publications:

1) Marriage Records 1848 to 1863, Camden County, New Jersey, New Jersey State Archives, Trenton, New Jersey.
2) H. Stanley Craig, compiler, *Records Filed in the Office of the County Clerk - Camden County, New Jersey, Marriages*, (Merchantville, New Jersey, 1932, reprint: Woodbury, New Jersey: Gloucester County Historical Society, 1980).
3) H. Stanley Craig, compiler, *Gloucester County Marriages*, (Merchantville, New Jersey, 1930, reprint: Woodbury, New Jersey: Gloucester County Historical Society, 1976).
4) H. Stanley Craig, compiler, *South Jersey Marriages - Supplementing the Cape May, Cumberland, Gloucester, and Salem County Marriage Records*, (Merchantville, New Jersey, 1935, reprint: Woodbury, New Jersey: Gloucester County Historical Society, 1980).
5) H. Stanley Craig, compiler, *Atlantic County New Jersey Marriage Records*, (Merchantville, New Jersey, 1932, reprint: Woodbury, New Jersey: Gloucester County Historical Society, 1979).
6) Haddonfield Monthly Meeting - Orthodox: Births and Deaths 1758 to 1864; Minutes 1827 to 1855. Friends Historical Library of Swarthmore College. Swarthmore, Pennsylvania 19081-1399.
7) Haddonfield Monthly Meeting - Hicksite: 1804 to 1813; 1814 to 1832; 1832 to 1863. Friends Historical Library at Swarthmore College, Swarthmore, Pennsylvania 19081-1399.
8) Sarah A. Risely, compiler, *Marriage Records of Atlantic County New Jersey (P - Z) (1837 - 1884)*, (Atlantic City, New Jersey: General Lafayette Chapter NSDAR, 1920).
9) Sarah A. Risely, compiler, *Marriage Records of Old Gloucester County New Jersey 1795 - 1837 and Gloucester County New Jersey 1837 - 1878, Volume X, Part I (A - J) and Volume X, Part II (K - Z)*, (Atlantic City, New Jersey: General Lafayette Chapter NSDAR, 1934).
10) Elizabeth Ann Grant, compiler, *Ocean County Marriages c. 1740 - 1960*, (Toms River, New Jersey: Ocean County Historical Society, 1990).
11) Jeanne M. Hammell, compiler and indexer, *South Jersey Church Records - Baptisms, Marriages,*

marriage records revealed that the marriage was recorded in German script in the register of Saint Michael's and Zion Church. It read as follows:

1855	Christoph Reitze v Bottendorf	Lucy Devlin of	Peter Devlin (father of the bride)
Mar 3	Curhessen	Philadelphia	Isabella Devlin
			Margaret Epley
			[??? ??? ???][81]

It is unclear whether the couple was married in Philadelphia or by a Lutheran priest from Saint Michael's and Zion Church who may have been traveling in South Jersey. In addition, it is unclear whether they were also married in a separate Quaker ceremony. In any event, Christopher Reitze was 31 and Lucy Devlin was 19 when they were married. He must have acquired a good command of the English language in the four years he had been in New Jersey because there is no evidence that Lucy Devlin spoke German.

Christopher and Lucy's Life in New Jersey

According to family legend Christopher Reitze continued to work on the Allen family farm in Blackwood, Camden County, New Jersey, after he and Lucy Devlin were married.[82] On June 6, 1855, however, they were living about 15 miles away in Woolwich Township, Gloucester

---

Deaths, 1750 - 1900, 4 volumes, (Woodbury, New Jersey: Gloucester County Historical Society, 1990/92/97/99).

12) James G. Engle, compiler, *Records of the Woodbury Monthly Meeting of the Religious Society of Friends (Hicksite Branch) 1828 - 1936*, (Clarksboro, New Jersey: James G. Engle, no date).

13) Marriage Notices, *The Constitution & Farmers & Mechanics Advertiser*, January 3, 1854 - April 29, 1856, Woodbury, New Jersey.

14) Vital Statistics Index Cards (Marriages Extracted From Area Newspapers Since 1800), Gloucester County Historical Society, Woodbury, New Jersey.

15) Elizabeth Hasbrouck, compiler, *Gloucester County Marriages by Justices of the Peace 1782 - 1894*, (Woodbury, New Jersey: Gloucester County Historical Society, no date).

16) Hinshaw Index to Selected Quaker Records, 1680-1940, Original Data: *William Wade Hinshaw's Index to Unpublished Quaker Records*, (Swarthmore, Pennsylvania: Friends Historical Library, Swarthmore College), <<www.ancestry.com>>, downloaded July 23, 2017.

17) Encyclopedia of American Quaker Genealogy, Volumes I-VI, 1607-1943, Original Data: William Wade Hinshaw, et al., compilers. *Encyclopedia of American Quaker Genealogy*, 6 volumes, 1936–1950. Reprint, Baltimore, Maryland: Genealogical Publishing Co., 1991–1994, and William Wade Hinshaw and Thomas Worth Marshall, compilers, *Encyclopedia of American Quaker Genealogy. Supplement to Volume 1*, (Washington, D.C.: n.p. 1948), <<www.ancestry.com>>, downloaded July 23, 2017.

[81]Marriage Record of Christoph Reitze and Lucy Devlin dated March 3, 1855, Saint Michael's and Zion Church, Historic Pennsylvania Church and Town Records, Historical Society of Pennsylvania, Philadelphia, Pennsylvania, <<www.ancestry.com>>, downloaded March 16, 2016. Note: Margaret Epley nee Douglass, wife of William Epley. The last name is unreadable.

[82]Conversation on August 12, 1995, with the late Josephine Thompson Marshall, 121 Reillywood Avenue, Haddonfield, New Jersey 08033-2201.

County, New Jersey, where they were enumerated in the state census as follows:

Number of Persons:	2
Name:	Christopher Ritesey (sic)
Native White Males:	0
Native White Females:	1
Foreign White Males:	1
Foreign White Females:	0
White Children 5-16:	0[83]

According to the *Reitze Family Bible*, their first child, also named Christopher, was born on September 9, 1855, but the place of birth is not stated.[84] Nevertheless, a review of South Jersey county birth records indicates he was born in Woolwich Township, Gloucester County, New Jersey. His birth record read as follows:

Name:	...
Birthplace:	Woolwich Township, Gloucester County
Birth Date:	09 September 1855
Father's Name:	Christopher ...
Mother's Name:	Lucy ...[85]

Despite the child's first name and the surname of his parents not having been recorded there is little doubt this is a reference to the birth of Christopher Reitze, Jr. It is also consistent with information supplied by Christopher Reitze, Jr., in both the 1870 census and the 1900 census; with information contained in his 1907 death certificate; and with information provided by his great-great-grandson, Christopher C. Reitze, III.[86,87,88,89]

---

[83] 1855 State Census (population), New Jersey, Gloucester County, Woolwich Township, page 8, line 15, Household of Christopher Ritesey (sic), FHL Microfilm Roll 802944, <<www.familysearch.org>>, downloaded July 23, 2017.

[84] *The Reitze Family Bible - Latin Vulgate Version.* (New York: D & J Sadlier, 1844) was in the possession of the late Josephine Thompson Marshall, 121 Reillywood Avenue, Haddonfield, New Jersey 08033-2201.

[85] Birth of Christopher Reitze, New Jersey Births and Christenings, 1660-1980, Original Data: Gloucester County, New Jersey, Birth Records, Volume O, p. 103, line 28, Woolwich Township, FHL Microfilm Roll 584565 <<www.familysearch.org>>, downloaded July 21, 2017.

[86] 1870 U.S. Census (population), First Enumeration,Conversation on June 16 Pennsylvania, Philadelphia County, City of Philadelphia, 10th Ward, page 353, National Archives Microfilm Publication M593, Roll 1395.

[87] 1900 U.S. Census (population), Pennsylvania, Philadelphia County, City of Philadelphia, E.D. 736, sheet 1, line 29, National Archives Microfilm Publication T623, Roll

Sometime prior to 1859, Christopher Reitze and his family are believed to have left their home in Woolwich Township, Gloucester County, New Jersey, and headed to Holmesburg in the northeast section of the city of Philadelphia near Pennypack Creek. They may have traveled by wagon to Woodbury where they would have boarded the 10 A.M. train to Philadelphia.[90] From downtown Philadelphia, they would have traveled north to their new home in Holmesburg.

Before the city and county of Philadelphia were consolidated, Holmesburg was a post-town and village in Lower Dublin Township. In 1832, there were about seventy houses, four taverns, and four stores in Holmesburg. Its dwelling houses and stores were reported to be finished neatly and its streets and footways kept in good order. In the northern part of the town, there were reported to be several manufacturing establishments including a cotton factory and two saw mills.[91] Perhaps Christopher Reitze gave up working on the farm in New Jersey to try his hand as a laborer in one of the factories in Holmesburg.

It is in Holmesburg that Christopher and Lucy's second child, a daughter named Susan, may have been born on December 1, 1858.[92] It is also where she died on August 8, 1859.[93]

1471.

[88]Death Certificate for Christopher Reitze, March 7, 1907, # 6778 & # 29110, Pennsylvania Division of Vital Statistics, New Castle, Pennsylvania 16103.

[89]Conversation on June 16, 1999, with the late Christopher C. Reitze III, 27 Riverside Drive, Florham Park, New Jersey 07932-2402.

[90]Charles Boyer, President, Camden County Historical Society, *Camden History*, (Camden, New Jersey: Camden Press, 1935), Volume I, Nos. 10, 11, 12, p. 9.

[91]Thomas F. Gordon, *A Gazetteer of the State of Pennsylvania.* (Philadelphia, Pennsylvania: 1832, reprint: New Orleans, Louisiana, Polyanthos Press, 1975), p. 203.

[92]*The Reitze Family Bible - Latin Vulgate Version.* (New York: D & J Sadlier, 1844) was in the possession of the late Josephine Thompson Marshall, 121 Reillywood Avenue, Haddonfield, New Jersey 08033-2201. The Bible contains a birth entry for Susan Reitze of "December the 1 1859" which is believed to be incorrect with respect to the year.

[93]*The Reitze Family Bible - Latin Vulgate Version.* (New York: D & J Sadlier, 1844) was in the possession of the late Josephine Thompson Marshall, 121 Reillywood Avenue, Haddonfield, New Jersey 08033-2201. The Bible contains a death entry for Susan Reitze of "8 day of August 1859" which is believed to be correct given the Emmanuel Church burial record of "August 10th 1859."

Although there is no record of her death in the Philadelphia cemetery returns and no obituary appeared in the *Philadelphia Public Ledger* to commemorate her passing, the burial records of the Emmanuel Church in Holmesburg contain the following entry:

Reitze   Buried in Emmanuel Churchyard, Susan R. Reitze, infant of
Mrs. Reitze, a nurse at Mr. W. Stuart's, August 10th 1859[94]

The Reverend John P. Lundy, D.D., officiated at her funeral.

Christopher and Lucy's Life in Brewerytown

Having lost their infant daughter, Susan, in Holmesburg, Christopher Reitze next moved his wife, Lucy, and young son, Christopher, Jr., to north Philadelphia. As best can be ascertained, the family lived in Brewerytown, or the immediate vicinity.[95] And, it was in that location that they were duly recorded in the 1860 census schedule. The enumeration was as follows:

Christian Ritchey (sic)   35 M   Day Laborer   born in Hesse-Cassel
Lucy   24 F   born in Pennsylvania
Christopher   4 M   born in Pennsylvania (sic)[96]

EARNING A LIVING. Based on information contained in the 1860 census, Christopher Reitze initially took a job as a day laborer when he arrived in Brewerytown. According to family legend, his day laborer job consisted of driving a beer wagon for the Bergdoll and Psotta Brewing Company located at 29th and Parrish Streets. In this capacity, he is said to have been responsible for dropping off barrels of beer at the saloons in Philadelphia.[97] This family legend concerning Christopher Reitze's occupation appears to be corroborated by the following entry in the 1863

---

[94]Emmanuel Church (Protestant Episcopal) Burial Register 1844-1863, p. 134, (XCh/676) Historical Society of Pennsylvania, Philadelphia, Pennsylvania.

[95]Brewerytown is a neighborhood in North Philadelphia loosely bound by 21st Street on the east, the Schuylkill River on the west, Columbia Avenue (now Cecil B. Moore) on the north, and Brown Street on the south. It included parts of both the 15th Ward and the 29th Ward of the City of Philadelphia prior to 1870 and the 15th Ward and the 29th Ward thereafter.

[96]1860 U.S. Census (population), Pennsylvania, Philadelphia County, City of Philadelphia, 20th Ward, page 484, line 30, National Archives Microfilm Publication M653, Roll 1171.

[97]Conversation of July 7, 1996, with the late William Scott Chambers, 325 N.W. 95th Avenue, Plantation, Florida 33324-7021, in which he remembered being told by his father that Christopher Reitze worked for the Bergdoll Brewing Company and that the son of the owner of the brewery was arrested, prosecuted, and jailed for evading military service during World War I.

Philadelphia city directory:

Reitzer (sic), Christopher, driver, 2519 Penna Ave[98]

The importance of the beer wagon to the brewing industry in Philadelphia cannot be overemphasized. At that time, wagons were the only means by which the breweries could transport their product to their customers and it took a strong man to drive a two-horse wagon loaded with beer barrels. The barrels were heavy and unwieldy. In those days, they were all made of wooden staves bound together with hoops. The staves were bowed to make the barrels wider in the middle than at the ends. This shape may have helped the barrels to better withstand the pressure from within, but it certainly didn't make them any easier to handle in loading and unloading the beer wagons.

Much like the other drivers of his time, Christopher Reitze probably walked to the brewery stables every morning where he hitched up the two-horse team to the wagon. After that, he would have pulled the wagon around to the loading dock to pick up the day's delivery of beer. Every work day, rain or shine, Christopher Reitze would have navigated the streets of Philadelphia delivering beer to the many saloons along his route. Even in the summer time, when temperatures soared into the 90s, he would have been out on his route with nothing more than a cap to protect him from the sun. He must have gotten awfully hot by the end of the day dressed as he was in his long-sleeved shirt and pants, covered by a huge heavy apron, and wearing heavy, ankle high work shoes.

How long Christopher Reitze drove the beer wagon is unclear, but he was documented as a brewer in June 1863 when he registered for the draft in Philadelphia. The entry read as follows:

Ward:	15
Residence:	2519 Pennsylvania Avenue
Name:	Ritze (sic) Christopher
Age 1st July 1863:	34 (sic)
Race:	White
Occupation:	Brewer
Marital Status:	Married
Remarks:	Claims Alien[99]

---

[98]This is the only entry that has been found for Christopher Reitze in a Philadelphia City directory from 1860 to 1879.

[99]Christopher Ritze (sic), No. 524, Civil War Union Draft Registration Records, 1863-1865, RG 110: Records of the Provost Marshall General's Bureau, Pennsylvania: 4th Congressional District, Class I, Contents R-Z, Volume 4, <<www.ancestry.com>>, downloaded April 20, 2017. Note: Class I comprised all persons subject to do military duty between the ages of 20 and 35 years and all unmarried persons subject to do military duty above the age of 35 years and under the age of 45. Class II comprised all other persons subject to do military duty.

Then, in 1865, Christopher Reitze appeared once again in South Jersey where he was enumerated in Deptford Township, Gloucester County, New Jersey, with his family, but without any information about his occupation. The record reads as follows:

2614	Christopher Rietze (sic)	Foreign Male White
2615	Lucy Rietze (sic)	Native Female White
2616	Christopher Rietze Jr. (sic)	White Male Child Aged 5-16
2617	Elizabeth Rietze (sic)	Native Female White[100]

Five years later, in the 1870 census, he was once again enumerated as a brewer, living in Brewerytown with his family, as follows:

Reitz (sic), Christian	40 M	Brewer	born in Prussia
- , Lucy	34 F	Keeping House	born in Penna
- , Christopher	16 M		born in Penna (sic)
- , Charles	3 M		born in Penna
- , John	1 M		born in Penna
- , Lizzie	6 F		born in Penna[101,102]

There is no doubt that brewing was an important industry in Philadelphia. The brewing of ale and porter began in Philadelphia in 1831. Philadelphia was also the first place in America where lager beer was brewed beginning in 1846.[103] Thus, it is believed that Christopher Reitze was employed primarily as a brewer of lager beer from about 1863 until he died in 1879.[104,105]

----

[100]1865 State Census (population), New Jersey, Gloucester County, Deptford Township, page 56, line 2614-2617, Household of Christopher Rietze (sic), FHL Microfilm Roll 802948, <<www.familysearch.org>>, downloaded July 22, 2017.

[101]1870 U.S. Census (population), First Enumeration. Pennsylvania, Philadelphia County, City of Philadelphia, 20th Ward, page 195, line 17, National Archives Microfilm Publication M593, Roll 1406.

[102]1870 U.S. Census (population), Second Enumeration, Pennsylvania, Philadelphia County, City of Philadelphia, 20th Ward, page 590, National Archives Microfilm Publication M593, Roll 1435.

[103]Scharf and Westcott, *History of Philadelphia: 1609-1884*, 3 volumes (Philadelphia, Pennsylvania: Everts and Company, 1884), p. 2280.

[104]1872 Birth Register, City of Philadelphia, p. 267, William and Lucy KEITZE (sic) March 16, 1872, Philadelphia City Archives, Philadelphia, Pennsylvania, states that Christopher Reitze was a driver.

[105]1879 Death Register, City of Philadelphia, p. 123, Christopher REITZ (sic), April 16, 1879, Philadelphia City Archives, Philadelphia, Pennsylvania, states he was a brewer.

The reason he decided to become a brewer was probably financial. By 1870, there were sixty-nine breweries in Philadelphia equipped with 140 steam-powered machines. These breweries employed 620 men and twelve women in various capacities to whom wages were paid during the year in the amount of $500,000. Also, by 1875, these breweries produced 970,000 barrels of beer a year valued at $10.00 a barrel.[106] In addition to the profits produced for the owners of the breweries and the taxes generated for the City of Philadelphia, beer brewing was an important source of income for working class people in Philadelphia. It also provided a safe source of nourishment that was not too strong even for young children to drink. Thus, in many households in Philadelphia, where water borne illnesses and problems preserving food were still common, beer was served with almost every meal.

Apart from the increase in his wages, it is debatable whether Christopher Reitze's job as a brewer brought about an improvement in his overall working conditions. The breweries operated pretty much continuously. As a brewer of lager beer, Christopher Reitze would have been expected to participate in any part of a physically strenuous, repetitive process that consisted of four basic steps performed in a hot, humid, and smelly environment.

In the first step, known as mashing, he would have mixed crushed or ground malt (usually barley) in hot water from which a liquid was produced known as wort. In the second step, he would have boiled the wort and added hops for flavoring. In the third step, he would have fermented the liquid which involved adding yeast to the wort, resulting in the production of alcohol and carbon dioxide gas, the byproducts of the action of yeast on sugar. In the last step, known as aging, he would have tended the brew for two to twenty-four weeks while the proteins settled out of the beer or were digested by enzymatic action. Only at the conclusion of this arduous process was the beer ready for distribution to customers.

A HOUSE IS NOT A HOME. On the home front, life did not always proceed smoothly. The Reitze family moved around quite a bit during the nineteen years they lived in and around Brewerytown. Precisely why they moved around so often is unknown.

They also appear to have lived within easy walking distance of the breweries in Brewerytown with the exception of their sojourn in Deptford Township, Gloucester County, New Jersey in 1865.[107] The locations where they lived were:

---

[106]Scharf and Westcott, p. 2281.

[107]1865 State Census (population), New Jersey, Gloucester County, Deptford Township, page 56, line 2614-2617, Household of Christopher Rietze (sic), FHL Microfilm Roll 802948, <<www.familysearch.org>>, downloaded July 22, 2017.

June 1860	- (15th Ward)	(1860 Census)
August 1862	2519 Pennsylvania Avenue (15th Ward)	(Death of Harry)
January 1863	2519 Pennsylvania Avenue (15th Ward)	(1863 City Directory)
July 1863	2519 Pennsylvania Avenue (15th Ward)	(Civil War Registration)
December 1863	2819 Coates Street (15th Ward)	(Birth of Elizabeth)
June 1865	*Deptford Township, Gloucester County, NJ*	*(1865 NJ State Census)*
July & November 1870	- (20th Ward)	(1870 Census- 1st & 2nd)
March 1872	1226 Taney Street (29th Ward)	(Birth of William & Lucy)
May 1875	907 N. 28th Street (29th Ward)	(Death of Maggie)
March 1876	2721 N. 28th Street (sic) (29th Ward)	(Birth of Conrad)
July 1877	2721 Scott Street (29th Ward)	(Birth of Josephine)
August 1877	905 N. 25th Street (29th Ward)	(Death of Conrad)
April 1879	2721 Scott/Poplar Street (29th Ward)	(Death of Christopher)

There are a variety of reasons why they may have moved so often. For one, they were sharing rented housing with other families in the neighborhood so they may have needed more space as their children were born. Also, times were hard and work was scarce. At times, they may have fallen behind in their rent payments and been evicted or simply moved whenever the landlord raised the rent. Or, they may have been asked to leave by the property owner because Christopher Reitze's bad temper and unpredictable behavior was probably intolerable to other people living or boarding in the house.

According to family legend, he was very hard to get along with and frequently carried home with him the long black whip that he used to drive the two horses that pulled the beer wagon. Reportedly, he would crack the whip - a five foot hickory stick with a twelve foot lash - menacingly in the air while he walked home from the brewery stables each night after work. His temper was so bad that his wife, Lucy, would send the children out to watch for him on the way home so that they could warn her that he was coming.[108]

His disposition was so nasty that he is reported to have thrown his young son, John, a sickly child, into the Schuylkill River when he was only three years old with the admonition that he "sink or swim." To make matters worse, he was stingy with his money. He sent the children out to work at an early age making segars *[i.e., cigars]* and tending bar, and he did not give his wife, Lucy, much to live on. To make ends meet, the family ate a lot of fried mush, scrapple with molasses, and, on occasion, mutton.[109]

Christopher Reitze trusted no one. In fact, he is said to have hidden his money in the outhouse to keep it safe, but his wife found his stash of bills and took it. Suspicious that she was to blame for the disappearance of his money, he kept demanding to know whether she knew

---

[108]Conversation on November 29, 1996, with the late William Scott Chambers, 325 N.W. 95th Avenue, Plantation, Florida 33324-7021.

[109]Conversation on February 23, 1998, with John J. Page, 2524 Lombard Street, Philadelphia, Pennsylvania 19146-1025.

where it was. Fortunately for her, she held her ground insisting that she knew nothing about it. Consequently, she was never able to spend any of the money to meet her family's needs because he would have known that she had taken it. Rather than face his wrath for having taken his money, it remained for a long time where she had hidden it between the pages of the *Reitze Family Bible*. Apparently that was the last place he would have thought to look for it.[110]

    THE REITZE FAMILY BIBLE. Lucy treasured the *Reitze Family Bible*. She probably acquired it from someone on her side of the family, possibly her brother, John, or her brother, James, as there is a stamp inside the Bible indicating that it was once the property of someone named J. Devlin. The *Reitze Family Bible* is the Catholic version of the Holy scriptures. It was printed in New York by D & J Sadlier then located at 35 Gold Street. And, it was copyrighted in 1844 which closely coincides with the time frame of the anti-Catholic riots in Philadelphia.[111]

    After receiving the gift of the Bible, Lucy inscribed it with her name as her property and began making entries. First, she documented the marriage of her parents, Peter Devlin and Susan Kennady (sic), at St. Augustine's Church on March (sic) 19, 1835.[112] Then, she documented her own marriage to Christopher Reitze on March 3, 1855. After that she entered all the information she could recall about the births and deaths of her thirteen children.

    Her entries are remarkably accurate for having been entered after the fact and reflect the sadness of a parent who has lost eight of her children at an early age and her desire that they not be forgotten.

    One after the other, she entered all their births and then, all the deaths of the little ones who did not survive their infancy. Birth and death certificates were not issued in those years, and no obituaries appeared in the *Philadelphia Public Ledger* for any of the children, so her Bible entries were probably made from her memory about 1879. She did not forget any of them. Her deceased children's birth and death days must have been lonely and sad for her and her grief at having lost so many of her children at such a tender age must have been with her each and every day of her life.

---

[110]Conversation on November 29, 1996, with the late Josephine Thompson Marshall, 121 Reillywood Avenue, Haddonfield, New Jersey 08033-2201.

[111]Michael Feldberg, *The Philadelphia Riots of 1844: A Study of Ethnic Conflict*, (Westport, Connecticut: Greenwood Press, 1975).

[112]This marriage actually took place May 19, 1835, at St. Augustine's Church.

Her entries, in her own handwriting, in the *Reitze Family Bible* are as follows:

BIRTHS[113]

Christoffer	September 9 1855
Susan	December the 1 1859 (sic) (Correction: 1858)
Henry	January the 9 1861
Lizzie	1 December 1863
Charley	February the 7 1866
John	30 October 1869
Maggie	15 July 1875 (sic) (Correction: 1874)
Coney	12 of Mar 1876
Josey	July 4 1877
Willey & Lucy	1872 (sic) (Correction: March 16, 1872)
July & Elley	1873

DEATHS[114]

Susan	8 day of August 1859
Henry	28 September (sic) 1862 (Correction: August 28, 1862)
Willey & Lucy	18 (sic) January (sic) 1872 (Correction: Lucy: March 16, 1872 & William: March 17, 1872)
July & Elley	September 18 1873
Maggie	May the 24 (sic) 1875 (Correction: May 20, 1875)
Coney	27 (sic) Aug 1877 (Correction: August 23, 1877)

GLENWOOD CEMETERY. Glenwood Cemetery was incorporated on February 19, 1850, and was largely made up of Odd Fellows.[115] It was located on the corner of Ridge Avenue and Islington Lane immediately north of Brewerytown in a section of Philadelphia known as Strawberry Mansion.

According to the Philadelphia Death Registers, five of the Reitze children - Harry, Lucy,

---

[113]To date, only the following five births have been located in the Philadelphia birth registers:

> 1863 Birth Register, Vol 6, p. 130: Eliza REES (sic), December 1, 1863
> 1872 Birth Register, p. 267: William & Lucy KEITZE (sic), March 16, 1872
> 1876 Birth Register, p. 90: Conrad REITZ (sic), March 12, 1876
> 1877 Birth Register, p. 181: Josephine REIZ (sic), July 4, 1877

[114]To date, only the following five deaths have been located in the Philadelphia death registers:

> 1862 Death Register, Vol 3, p. 182: Henry REITZE, August 28, 1862 (hydrocephalic)
> 1872 Death Register, p. 131: Lucy REITZE, March 16, 1872 (stillborn)
> 1872 Death Register, p. 131: William REITZE, March 17, 1872 (debility)
> 1875 Death Register, p. 188: Maggie REITZE, May 20, 1875 (catarrhal pneumonia)
> 1877 Death Register, Vol 2, p. 32: Conrad RETZE (sic), August 23, 1977 (meningitis)

[115]Scharf and Westcott, p. 2360.

William, Maggie, and Conrad - were buried at Glenwood Cemetery.[116,117]

According to Glenwood Memorial Gardens, the plot where the Reitze children were buried was owned by E.S. Early (sic), possibly Edward Earley, an undertaker in Philadelphia.[118,119] All that is known about Edward Earley, the undertaker, is that he was born in New Jersey about 1822. Further attempts to trace him have been unsuccessful. Suffice it that he may have been a friend or a relative or he may have sold the plot to Christopher Reitze in a business transaction and then neglected to have the name on the deed changed to reflect the new ownership.

Glenwood Cemetery was relatively close to Brewerytown where the Reitze family lived so Lucy could walk to the cemetery whenever she pleased to tend to her children's graves.

BECOMING A CITIZEN. The record indicates that Christopher Reitze, a native of Germany, appeared before the Prothonotary of the Supreme Court of Pennsylvania on September 28, 1868, to renounce his allegiance to the Grand Duke of Hesse-Cassel and take the oath prescribed by law to admit him as a citizen of the United States of America.[120]

His petition included the following sworn statement:

---

[116]The Philadelphia Death Registers indicate that the following five children of Christopher and Lucy (Devlin) Reitze were buried at Glenwood Cemetery: Henry Reitze, August 28, 1862 (hydrocephalic); Lucy Reitze, March 16, 1872 (stillborn); William Reitze, March 17, 1872 (debility); Maggie Reitze, May 20, 1875 (catarrhal pneumonia); and Conrad Retze (sic), August 23, 1977 (meningitis).

[117]Letter dated August 3, 1995, from Glenwood Memorial Gardens, 2321 West Chester Pike, Broomall, Pennsylvania 19008 regarding the plot belonging to E.S. Early (sic) (Section R, Lot 430) states that only four of the children of Christopher and Lucy (Devlin) Reitze, i.e., Henry Reitze (20 mos.), Maggie Reitze (10 mos.), Conrad Reitze (17 mos.), and Lucy Reitze (stillborn), were buried in that plot. This record is believed to be in error with respect to the omission of the burial of William Reitze (1 day).

[118]Letter dated August 3, 1995, from Glenwood Memorial Gardens, 2321 West Chester Pike, Broomall, Pennsylvania 19008 regarding the plot belonging to E.S. Eartly (Section R, Lot 430).

[119]1870 U.S. census (population), First Enumeration, Pennsylvania, Philadelphia County, City of Philadelphia, 13th Ward, page 381A, National Archives Microfilm Publication M593, Roll 1397, re: Edward Early.

[120]Petition for Naturalization of Christopher Reitze, Supreme Court of Pennsylvania, September 28, 1868, Pennsylvania Archives, Harrisburg, Pennsylvania.

I Christopher Reitze do swear that the contents of my petition are true;
that I will support the Constitution of the United States, and I now renounce and
relinquish any title or order of nobility to which I am now or hereafter may be
entitled; and I do absolutely and entirely renounce and abjure all allegiance and
fidelity to any foreign Prince, Potentate, State or Sovereignty whatever, and
particularly to the Grand Duke of Hesse-Cassel of whom I was before a subject.

(signed) Christofer (sic) Reitze[121]

After signing the petition, he took the oath prescribed by law, and departed the courthouse with his Certificate of Naturalization in hand.[122]

In his petition for naturalization, Christopher Reitze claimed to have arrived at the Port of New York in 1851 and that he was *under eighteen years of age* at the time of his arrival. Since he was not a minor at the time of his arrival, what could have motivated Christopher Reitze to commit this fraud upon the court?

The answer lies in the laws of the State of Pennsylvania with respect to voting rights. In 1868, a law was passed by the State legislature that, henceforth, any man of foreign birth desiring to vote in any election in the State of Pennsylvania would be required to present his Certificate of Naturalization to prove he was a citizen eligible to vote. Naturalization was a two-step process requiring, first, the submission of a Declaration of Intent and second, the submission of a Petition for Naturalization. This process took more than one year to complete unless the petitioner was a minor at the time of his arrival. Minors, having attained their majority, were eligible to naturalize immediately in a one-step process.

The Presidential election of 1868 being just around the corner, the only way Christopher Reitze could be naturalized in time to vote was to claim he was under eighteen at the time he arrived in the United States. He was obviously in a hurry to become a citizen and had no time to waste on technicalities such as his age at the time of arrival. One can only speculate about how much he must have been paid and by which party to cast his vote their way.

THE DEATH OF CHRISTOPHER REITZE. Lucy recorded her husband's death in the *Reitze Family Bible* as having occurred on 16 April 1879. This is confirmed by the 1879 Philadelphia Death Register and the Philadelphia Cemetery Returns both of which state that Christopher Reitz

---

[121]This document contains the only known exemplar of Christopher Reitze's signature.

[122]The original Naturalization Certificate of Christopher Reitze dated September 28, 1868, was in the possession of the late Jeanne H. Reitze (widow of Harry E. Reitze, Sr.), 6 Pinewood Trail, Concord, New Hampshire 03301-5247.

(sic) died on April 16 at his residence, 2721 Poplar Street.[123,124] Oddly, his obituary, which appeared in the *Philadelphia Public Ledger* on Friday, April 18, 1879, lists a different home address as follows:

> REITZE - On the 16th inst., Christopher Reitze, aged 54, the relatives and friends
> of the family are respectfully invited to attend the funeral, Friday, April 18th at
> 3 o'clock from his late residence 2721 Scott Street to proceed to Glenwood
> Cemetery.[125]

The death register and the cemetery return both state that Christopher Reitze died of Lympanites (sic).[126] This is consistent with family legend that he died from blood poisoning after having stepped on a nail or cut his leg. Reportedly, he stubbornly refused treatment. Thus, the bacteria entered his lymphatic system and multiplied rapidly. The infected lymphatic vessel in his leg and foot probably became deeply inflamed, causing red streaks to appear just below the surface of his skin indicating that he had contracted septicemia, then known as blood poisoning. Rather than consult a doctor, Christopher Reitze is said to have insisted on putting on his boots so he could go out. Left untreated, the infection probably spread rapidly causing tissue destruction and a pus-filled, painful lump to appear at the site of the injury. Undoubtedly, his immune system was overwhelmed and could not respond fast enough to stop the inevitable. In the end, his foot swelled so badly that his boot had to be cut off his foot. By then it was too late and he died.[127,128]

Inflexible, unyielding, obdurate, and intractable to the end, Christopher Reitze was buried in the family plot at Glenwood Cemetery alongside Harry, Lucy, William, Maggie and Conrad, the five little ones who had not survived their infancy.

---

[123]1879 Death Register, City of Philadelphia, page 123, Christopher REITZ (sic), April 16, 1879, Philadelphia City Archives, Philadelphia, Pennsylvania.

[124]Philadelphia Cemetery Returns, 1879, Week Ending 29 March (N-Z) thru 19 April (A-L), FHL Microfilm Roll 2031099.

[125]Obituary of Christopher Reitz (sic), *Philadelphia Public Ledger*, Friday, April 18, 1879, p. 2.

[126]Now known as acute lymphangitis, a bacterial infection in the lymphatic vessels characterized by painful, red streaks below the skin surface. Even today, it is a potentially serious infection that can spread rapidly to the bloodstream and be fatal.

[127]Conversation on November 29, 1996, with the late Josephine Thompson Marshall, 121 Reillywood Avenue, Haddonfield, New Jersey 08033-2201.

[128]Conversation on August 1, 1999, with the late William Scott Chambers, 325 N.W. 95th Avenue, Plantation, Florida 33324-7021.

There they all lay, undisturbed, but not forgotten, for the next fifty-nine years. Then, on June 22, 1938, as storm clouds once again gathered over his native homeland in Germany, Christopher Reitze and the five children made their final journey from Glenwood Cemetery to Glenwood Memorial Gardens in Broomall, Delaware County, Pennsylvania.[129] The victims of urban development, they were reinterred in an unmarked grave on a gentle slope at the rear of the cemetery.

THE LIFE OF LUCY (DEVLIN) REITZE, WIDOW OF CHRISTOPHER

Shortly after the death of her first husband, Lucy and four of her surviving children - Elizabeth, Charles, John, and Josephine - moved away from Brewerytown and took up residence at the rear of 2313 Vine Street.[130] Then, Lucy remarried.

The Marriage of Lucy (Devlin) Reitze and Peter Benner

Lucy's second husband was Peter Benner. According to family legend, he was her childhood sweetheart, but there is no evidence that they knew each other when they were young.[131,132] He was 12 years her senior. He had been married several times previously and was the father of at least six children, only two of whom appear to have survived childhood. As best can be determined, he was a loving and caring husband and father to his children.

By occupation, Peter Benner appears to have been a teamster in his early years. In those days, teamsters were responsible for moving merchandise by wagon, long haul, over the highways from city to city. In his later years, as the railroads supplanted the wagon as the preferred method of moving merchandise long distance, Peter Benner worked as a driver delivering goods locally within the city of Philadelphia.

During the Civil War, Peter Benner served as a Private and as a Master Wagoner in Company F of the 8th Pennsylvania Cavalry. He was 37 years old when he enlisted on August 19, 1861 and was honorably discharged from the regiment on August 27, 1864, at the expiration of

---

[129]Glenwood Cemetery Removals, (Section A, Lot 606), Genealogical Society of Pennsylvania, Philadelphia, Pennsylvania.

[130]1880 Philadelphia city directory.

[131]Conversation on August 12, 1995, with the late Josephine Thompson Marshall, 121 Reillywood Avenue, Haddonfield, New Jersey 08033-2201.

[132]See Appendix D, *The Benner Family*.

his term.[133,134]

His military service record indicates that he was present with his company during the Battle of Gettysburg. His regiment's activities are inscribed as follows on the reverse side of the monument at Gettysburg to the 8th Pennsylvania Cavalry:

> This regiment detached with the 2nd Corps, covered the rear of the Army on the march from Virginia. At Frederick rejoined the Cavalry Corp and with Gregg's Division moved in the advance to Gettysburg. July 1 moved hastily to Manchester to protect trains. July 4 joined in pursuit of the enemy participating in the night attack at Monteray Pass and the many other cavalry engagements until the enemy retreated into Virginia.

On July 29, 1879, at the age of 53 (sic), Peter Benner joined the Grand Army of the Republic, Post # 18.[135] Later, his name was inscribed on the wall of the Pennsylvania Memorial at Gettysburg. This memorial, which stands on Cemetery Ridge, is a Beaux-Arts colossus, 70 feet tall, made of Pennsylvania Mount Airy granite and bronze from battlefield cannons. It was dedicated on September 27, 1910, to commemorate the sacrifice of those men from Pennsylvania who participated in the Battle of Gettysburg.

As best can be determined, Peter Benner never applied for a pension based on his service in the Civil War.

Such was the life, character, and disposition of Peter Benner, Lucy's second husband.

THE WEDDING. According to the *Reitze Family Bible*, Mr. Peter Benner and Mrs. Lucy Reitze were married November 25, 1879, just seven months after the death of Christopher Reitze.[136] Unfortunately, the entry in the *Reitze Family Bible* does not appear to be in Lucy's

---

[133]Union Compiled Military Service Record of Peter Benner, Co. F, 8th Pennsylvania Cavalry, Records of the Adjutant General's Office, Record Group 94, National Archives, Washington, D.C.

[134]Samuel P. Bates, *History of Pennsylvania Volunteers, 1861-1865*, 5 Volumes, (Harrisburg, Pennsylvania: State Printer, 1870), 3:133.

[135]Entry for Peter Benner, # 204, Grand Army of the Republic Post # 18, Pennsylvania State Archives, Harrisburg, Pennsylvania.

[136]*The Reitze Family Bible- Latin Vulgate Version*. (New York: D & J Sadlier, 1844) was in the possession of the late Josephine Thompson Marshall, 121 Reillywood Avenue, Haddonfield, New Jersey 08033-2201.

handwriting nor does it state where the wedding took place.[137]

Peter Benner was 55 and Lucy was 43 at the time of their marriage.

MARRIED LIFE TOGETHER. After their marriage, Lucy and Peter moved to 3234 St. James Place where they were enumerated in the 1880 census schedule as follows:

Benner, Peter		W M 54 (sic) Driver [----]	born in Penna
-, Lucia	wife	W F 42 (sic) Keeping House	born in Penna
-, Elizabeth	dau	W F 16 Works in chemical works	born in Penna
-, Charles	son	W M 13 Works in wine works	born in Penna
-, John	son	W M 10 At school	born in Penna
-, Josephine	dau	W F 4 (sic)	born in Penna[138]

Sadly, they were only married fourteen months when Peter Benner was killed in a tragic accident.

THE DEATH OF PETER BENNER. Peter Benner's death was recorded in the *Reitze Family Bible* by someone other than Lucy as having occurred on January 21, 1881.[139]

The following account of his death was printed on the front page of the *Philadelphia Public Ledger* on Saturday, January 22, 1881:

> Killed by a Car - Peter Benner, aged 57, of No. 3214 St. James Place, was last evening run over and killed by a freight car, at the west end of the Market street bridge.[140]

More details about his death emerge from a review of the 1881 Philadelphia Death

---

[137]A record of the marriage of Peter Benner and Lucy Reitze could not be located in either of the following sources:

1) 1878, 1879, 1880 Marriage Registers, City of Philadelphia, Philadelphia City Archives, Philadelphia, Pennsylvania. (See **No Record of Registration** # 951628, August 1997, Benner/Reitze Marriage.)
2) New Jersey State Marriage Index (1878-1900), New Jersey State Archives, Trenton, New Jersey.

[138]1880 U.S. Census (population), Pennsylvania, Philadelphia County, City of Philadelphia, E.D. 582, sheet 31, line 34, National Archives Microfilm Publication T9, Roll 1186.

[139]*The Reitze Family Bible - Latin Vulgate Version.* (New York: D & J Sadlier, 1844) was in the possession of the late Josephine Thompson Marshall, 121 Reillywood Avenue, Haddonfield, New Jersey 08033-2201.

[140]News Story, *Philadelphia Public Ledger*, Saturday, January 22, 1881, p. 1.

Register which states that Peter Benner died because he was "injured on the Pa. R.R." perhaps a reference to the Pennsylvania Railroad which operated the tracks over the Market Street bridge.[141]

His obituary, which appeared in the *Philadelphia Public Ledger* on Monday, January 24, 1881, read as follows:

> BENNER - Suddenly, on the 21st inst., PETER BENNER, aged 57 years.
>
> The relatives and friends of the family, also members Company F, Eighth Regiment, Penna Cavalry, and Post No. 18, G.A.R., are respectfully invited to attend the funeral, on Tuesday afternoon at 2 o'clock, from his late residence, 3214 St. James street, west of Thirty-second, below Walnut, West Phila. To proceed to Ronaldson's Cemetery.[142]

Peter Benner was buried on January 25, 1881 in the Vault of Peter Benner (his grandfather) at Ronaldson's Cemetery.[143] This cemetery was also known as Philadelphia Cemetery. Ronaldson's Cemetery stood at 10th and Wharton Streets until some time after 1930 when 13,500 bodies including those of the Benner family were removed to Forest Hills Cemetery. The former site of the cemetery is today occupied by a public playground.[144]

The Vault of Peter Benner is thought to have been an underground family burial vault. Those interred in the vault include both of Peter Benner's parents, Henry and Mary (Buser) Benner; both his grandparents, Peter and Sarah Benner; his young sons, Henry and Peter, who died in childhood; as well as several other family members including two of his sisters, Maria (Benner) Shultz and Sarah (Benner) Shields.[145] No inscriptions or epitaphs were recorded for the Vault of Peter Benner when the cemetery was surveyed in 1929.[146]

---

[141]1881 Death Register, City of Philadelphia, page 37, Peter BENNER, January 21, 1881, Philadelphia City Archives, Philadelphia, Pennsylvania.

[142]Obituary of Peter Benner, *Philadelphia Public Ledger*, Monday, January 24, 1881, p. 2.

[143]Ronaldson's Cemetery Lot Holders Books, Lot # 4E3S, Historical Society of Pennsylvania, Philadelphia, Pennsylvania.

[144]Helen Hutchinson Woodroofe, *A Genealogists Guide to Pennsylvania Records*, (Philadelphia, Pennsylvania: Genealogical Society of Pennsylvania, 1995), p. 347.

[145]Ronaldson's Cemetery Lot Holders Books, Lot # 4E3S, Historical Society of Pennsylvania, Philadelphia, Pennsylvania.

[146]Gravestone Inscriptions - Ronaldson's Cemetery, Philadelphia, Pennsylvania, FHL Microfilm Roll 1033988, item 26.

In 1881, Lucy would have needed about $650 a year to support her family of five. Even a man had trouble making that kind of money in those days and many of those men made up the difference through the earnings of working wives and children, by taking in boarders, or through systemic self-privation.[147]

What little is known about Lucy's whereabouts and her occupation in the years immediately following the death of Peter Benner is contained in the following Philadelphia city directories:

1882	Benner, Lucy	grocer	3214 St. James
1883	Benner, Lucy	widow	3214 St. James
1884	Benner, Lucy S.	widow, Peter	3214 St. James

Assuming Lucy owned and operated a grocery business, it is unclear where she got the money to set up her business and how long she pursued her occupation.

Other than the Grand Army of the Republic, there is no indication that Peter Benner belonged to any fraternal organization that would have paid Lucy a death benefit nor is there any record that she received any form of payment from the railroad to compensate her for her husband's accidental death. Thus, she was left with the burden of how to support her family. One theory is that she may have had financial help from the Benner family.[148] A second possibility, albeit unlikely, was financial help from the Reitze family.[149]

In any case, Lucy disappears from the Philadelphia city directories in 1885 for a period of three years. In a deposition contained in her daughter, Elizabeth's divorce file, Lucy says that she moved away from St. James Place because she could not bear to see how poorly her daughter

---

[147]Kerby A. Miller, *Emigrants and Exiles - Ireland and the Irish Exodus to North America*, (New York: Oxford University Press, 1985), p. 504.

[148]As early as 1837, entries appear in the Philadelphia city directory for a grocer named Henry Benner living at 13th north of Locust. This is the same area of the city where Peter Benner's parents, grandparents, siblings and cousins lived. The family of a grocer named Charles Benner was also in business after 1850 in West Philadelphia.

[149]From 1861 to 1893 various entries appear in the Philadelphia city directories for butchers named Henry, Christopher, and John Reitze. In 1862, Henry Reitze lived on Cuba below Morris. For several years after 1870, he lived at 610 Moore. Christopher and John Reitze lived at 411 Moore (1st Ward). They worked at 84 Washington Market.

was being treated by her errant husband, Edward J. Collins.[150,151]

Then, she and her son, Charles, both reappear in the 1888 Philadelphia city directory living at 522 S. 21st Street in South Philadelphia. Presumably, her two youngest children -John and Josephine - were there, too. From an analysis of subsequent city directories, marriage license applications, and other documents, it appears that Lucy, and her children - Charles, John, and Josephine - lived together (or next door to each other) until early 1893 when her son, Charles, got married. Thereafter, Lucy, and the two youngest children - John and Josephine - lived in West Philadelphia with Lucy's oldest daughter, Elizabeth, who was by then married to her second husband, Henry G. Douglass.

A compilation of the addresses where Lucy is known to have lived in Philadelphia from 1888 forward is as follows:

1888	522 South 21st (City Directory - Lucy Reitz (sic), widow Christoph)
1891	500 South 19th (City Directory - Lucy Reitze, wid Christopher)
1891	2403 South Street (Collins v Collins Divorce Case File)
1892	2403 South Street *(Marriage of Elizabeth Reitze)*
1892	2403 South Street (City Directory - Lucy Reitze, boarding)
1893	2403 South Street *(Marriage of Charles Reitze)*
1894	886 North 43-1/2 WP (City Directory - Lucy Reitze wid Christopher)
1895	886 North 43-1/2 WP *(Marriage of John Reitze)*
1896	4230 Lancaster Avenue WP *(Marriage of Josephine Reitze)*
1900	4242 Lancaster Avenue WP (City Directory - Lucy Reitze, stationer)
1906	4242 Lancaster Avenue WP (City Directory - Lucy Reitze, stationer)
1907	4242 Lancaster Avenue WP (City Directory - Lucy Reitze, stationer)
1908	4242 Lancaster Avenue WP (City Directory - Lucy Reitze, variety)

Taking Care of the Children

By the time Lucy was twice widowed her oldest son - Christopher, Jr. - was married and out on his own. The next two oldest children - Elizabeth and Charles - were still living at home, but working full-time. Nevertheless, Lucy still had two younger children at home most of the day who needed her care. Her son, John, was only eleven years old when his step-father died.

---

[150]Elizabeth M. Collins v Edward J. Collins, CP # 3, January Term 1891, Case # 31, Court of Common Pleas of Philadelphia County, Certifications Unit, Room 266, City Hall, Philadelphia, Pennsylvania 19107.

[151]In a conversation on February 6, 1998, with John J. Page, 2524 Lombard Street, Philadelphia, Pennsylvania 19146-1025, he said that family legend on his side of the family has it that Lucy remarried and moved to Lancaster. He said that her husband was thought to have been a judge named Boyer or Breyer, that he did not like her children, and mistreated them. To date, no documentary evidence of this marriage has been located.

He is said to have been sick frequently and missed a lot of school.[152] Her daughter, Josephine, the youngest, was not yet four years old, so she was not old enough to attend school.

Although nothing is known for certain about how Lucy solved her child care problems, there are some clues based on family legend. Lucy's youngest son, John, is said to have told his children and his grandchildren that he lived with relatives in Lancaster when he was young. Although the identity of these relatives in Lancaster is unknown, two of John's grandsons say that the relatives in Lancaster were Quakers and that John, himself, was raised a Quaker by these relatives. John's grandsons were also told that while their grandfather was raised a Quaker, John's sisters were raised as Catholics.[153]

Interestingly, Lucy's youngest daughter, Josephine, often told her granddaughter that she was sent to a private Catholic school (or convent school) when she was a little girl and that her tuition was paid by her mother's family - the Devlins - who had money. Josephine also told her granddaughter that she didn't like the Catholic school and was constantly getting into trouble. To avoid being punished for her bad behavior, she would hide in the toilet stall (sometimes known as the water closet) where she would stand on the rim of the commode so that the nuns couldn't see her feet under the door. Eventually, she claims to have been expelled from the school as a result of her escapades.[154]

Christopher, Jr., tried to help his mother manage the antics of his boisterous little sister. He often visited his mother and acted as a surrogate father to Josephine.[155] He was frequently accompanied on his visits by his own daughters - Elizabeth and Margaret - who were about the same age as his little sister. Reportedly, the three young girls were very close and enjoyed playing with Josephine's ivory-colored porcelain tea set.[156] Despite everyone's best efforts,

---

[152]Conversation on November 29, 1996, with the late Josephine Thompson Marshall, 121 Reillywood Avenue, Haddonfield, New Jersey 08033-2201.

[153]Conversation of February 23, 1998, with John J. Page, 2524 Lombard Street, Philadelphia, Pennsylvania 19146-1025.

[154]Conversation on April 14, 1997, with the late Josephine Thompson Marshall, 121 Reillywood Avenue, Haddonfield, New Jersey 08033-2201.

[155]Conversation on July 14, 1996, with the late William Scott Chambers, 325 N.W. 95th Avenue, Plantation, Florida 33324-7021.

[156]The porcelain tea set is in the possession of Kathryn C. Torpey, 5035 Domain Place, Alexandria, Virginia 22311.

however, Josephine refused to return to school so she never went beyond the third grade.[157]

The Character of Lucy (Devlin) Reitze

The following stories, recalled by Lucy's great-granddaughter, Josephine Thompson Marshall, as told to her by her grandmother, Josephine (Reitze) Chambers, illustrate Lucy's wonderful character:

> Christopher, Jr., Lucy's oldest son, along with a young friend, furtively appeared at his mother's door one day. Lucy immediately recognized the deadly disease smallpox. The city was in quarantine and anyone with smallpox was to be reported and isolated. Lucy quickly took them both to her attic, hung a sheet dipped in a solution of her own making over the door, and treated them with her self-known skills. They both recovered completely and without a scar. No one was ever the wiser nor did anyone else in the household get the dreaded disease.[158]

> A young girl in the neighborhood was evicted by her parents because she was pregnant. She had nowhere to go. Lucy, who had a hard time raising her own children, took the girl in and let her sleep on the kitchen settee. The girl stayed until Lucy delivered her baby and she regained her strength and was able to make her own way.[159]

> The poor neighbor woman who lived next door to Lucy had twins and died in childbirth. The woman's husband was helpless and someone again turned to Lucy. Lucy raised the twins until they were three years old and the father could take care of them on his own.[160]

> One day Lucy's son, Charles, found a child wandering around on the wharfs. The little boy claimed to have disembarked from a ship that arrived from England. He said he was supposed to have been met on arrival by an uncle who never materialized to claim the child. Charles brought the boy home and turned him over to his mother. No one ever came looking for the child so Lucy raised him. She called him English Charlie and he is said to have lived with Lucy until

---

[157]Conversation on July 14, 1996, with the late William Scott Chambers, 325 N.W. 95th Avenue, Plantation, Florida 33324-7021.

[158]Letter dated October 21, 1999, from the late Josephine Thompson Marshall, 121 Reillywood Avenue, Haddonfield, New Jersey 08033-2201.

[159]Letter dated October 21, 1999, from the late Josephine Thompson Marshall, 121 Reillywood Avenue, Haddonfield, New Jersey 08033-2201.

[160]Letter dated October 21, 1999, from the late Josephine Thompson Marshall, 121 Reillywood Avenue, Haddonfield, New Jersey 08033-2201.

he grew up, married, and set out on his own.[161]

The Later Years in Philadelphia

In 1890, Congress passed a law, known as the Dependent Pension Act, which pensioned all soldiers of the Union who had served ninety days or more in the Civil War, and who were unable to do manual labor. It also pensioned the widows and children and the dependent parents of these soldiers. The result of the Act was to increase the Federal pension rolls in seven years by nearly half a million names.[162] Oddly, Lucy's name was not on the pension rolls and there is no evidence that she ever applied for a widow's pension based on the Civil War military service of her second husband, Peter Benner.

Although she never applied for a pension, she continued to work. Evidently, her energy was boundless as she took in boarders to supplement any income she may have had from other sources.[163] She also operated a stationery store.[164] And later a variety shop stocked with many beautiful toys including a selection of large hobby horses.[165,166] When she was enumerated in the 1900 census at the age of 64 (under the name Lucy Ritz) she was reported not to have been out of work at any time during the preceding twelve months.[167] In addition to all her documented occupations, she is also said to have worked for Andrew Bair and Oliver Bair, funeral directors in Philadelphia. According to the recollection of Lucy's great-granddaughter, Josephine Thompson Marshall, Lucy dressed the dead for them. In fact, she was their only employee when they started out and their personal relationship lasted until she died.[168]

---

[161]Conversation on November 29, 1997, with the late Josephine Thompson Marshall, 121 Reillywood Avenue, Haddonfield, New Jersey 08033-2201.

[162]Waddy Thompson, *A History of the United States*, (Boston, Massachusetts: D.C. Heath & Co., Publishers, 1909), p. 458.

[163]1892 Philadelphia city directory.

[164]1900, 1906, 1907 Philadelphia city directories.

[165]1908 Philadelphia city directory.

[166]Conversation on September 14, 1999, with the late Josephine Thompson Marshall, 121 Reillywood Avenue, Haddonfield, New Jersey 08033-2201.

[167]1900 U.S. Census (population), Pennsylvania, Philadelphia County, City of Philadelphia, E.D. 568, sheet 1, line 88, National Archives Microfilm Publication T623, Roll 1466.

[168]Letter dated October 21, 1999, from the late Josephine Thompson Marshall, 121 Reillywood Avenue, Haddonfield, New Jersey 08033-2201.

Apparently, the specter of hard times always loomed large on the horizon for Lucy. She continued to work until 1908 when she was 72 years old even though it probably wasn't necessary after 1893 when she went to live with her oldest daughter, Elizabeth, and her son-in-law, Henry G. Douglass. Reportedly, Lucy also insisted that everyone in the family buy funeral insurance through the Oliver Bair Funeral Home, after her son, Charles, died unexpectedly in 1893.[169]

The Death of Lucy (Devlin) Reitze

Sometime during 1908, Lucy packed her belongings and accompanied her daughter, Elizabeth, and her son-in-law, Henry G. Douglass, when they moved from West Philadelphia to Gloucester City, Camden County, New Jersey. There, they took up residence at 15 Thompson Avenue. And, it was there that Lucy became seriously ill, probably for the first time in her life.

Her illness lingered for about a year. As it became clear that Lucy was nearing the end of her life, her oldest daughter, Elizabeth, notified the Devlins in North Philadelphia that she was not expected to live. Reportedly, Lucy's sisters promptly arrived in Gloucester City with a Catholic priest to administer the last rites to their sister. Despite the seriousness of her illness, Lucy is said to have sat up in her bed and declined the sacrament as she was a Protestant.[170]

Lucy died of Chronic Intestinal Catarrh on Friday, May 7, 1909.[171,172] She would have been 73 years old on June 12, 1909. She was predeceased by two husbands and ten children.[173]

---

[169]Conversation of February 23, 1998, with John J. Page, 2524 Lombard Street, Philadelphia, Pennsylvania 19146-1025.

[170]Conversation on November 29, 1997, with the late Josephine Thompson Marshall, 121 Reillywood Avenue, Haddonfield, New Jersey 08033-2201.

[171]Letter dated May 6, 1996, from Edward L. Clapper, President and General Manager, Fernwood Cemetery and Mausoleum, 6501 Baltimore Avenue, Fernwood, Pennsylvania 19050 regarding the exact date of death of Lucy Reitze buried in Lot 369, Section 18, owned by Henry G. Douglass.

[172]Death Certificate for Lucy Reitze, May 7, 1909, State of New Jersey - Bureau of Vital Statistics, Certificate and Record of Death, New Jersey Archives, Trenton, New Jersey.

[173]There is a discrepancy in the number of children born to Lucy (Devlin) Reitze. In the *Reitze Family Bible* she recorded, in her own handwriting, the birth of 13 children. In the 1900 census she reported that she was the mother of 14 children four of whom were still living at the time of the census. It is believed that the *Reitze Family Bible* probably contains more accurate information than the 1900 census schedule with respect to the number of children born to Lucy (Devlin) Reitze.

38

At the time of her death, she was described as being 5 foot 7 inches tall and weighing 130 pounds. Although her hair had turned white, she still had the same imperturbable brown eyes.[174]

Burial at Fernwood Cemetery

According to Lucy's great-granddaughter, Josephine Thompson Marshall, Oliver Bair personally came to 15 Thompson Avenue and directed her funeral. At that time, the Oliver Bair Funeral Home was one of the most respected establishments of its kind in Philadelphia and it was an honor that Oliver Bair himself took charge of the funeral arrangements.[175]

The following obituary appeared in the *Philadelphia Public Ledger* on Saturday, May 8, 1909 to announce Lucy's death:

> REITZE - On May 7, 1909, LUCY, wife of the late Christopher Reitze, aged 72
> years. Relatives and friends are invited to attend the funeral services on Monday
> at 2 p.m. at the residence of her son-in-law, Henry G. Douglass, 15 Thompson
> Ave., River View Heights, South Gloucester, N.J. Interment private.[176]

Lucy was laid out in the front parlor of her daughter's home in South Gloucester. She was dressed in one of her own dresses and a brand new pair a slippers . Perhaps because the funeral services were held in New Jersey, her clergyman, Mr. Gerhart, was not asked to officiate.[177]

After the viewing was concluded and the casket was closed, Lucy most likely would have been transported by train to Philadelphia. According to the records of the Oliver Bair Funeral Home, she made the trip from Philadelphia to Fernwood Cemetery in a black hearse followed by six rented coaches.

It was a long trip to Fernwood Cemetery which is located in Delaware County, Pennsylvania, just across the city limits from West Philadelphia. She was buried on Monday,

---

[174]Oliver Bair Funeral Home Record for Lucy Reitze, May 10, 1909, Pennsylvania Historical Society, Philadelphia, Pennsylvania.

[175]Letter dated October 21, 1999, from the late Josephine Thompson Marshall, 121 Reillywood Avenue, Haddonfield, New Jersey 08033-2201.

[176]Obituary of Lucy Reitze, *Philadelphia Public Ledger*, Saturday, May 8, 1909, p. 9.

[177]A minister named the Rev. Elias Henry Gerhart appears in the 1889 Philadelphia city directory at 165 Venango and, later, in the 1890 to 1892 Philadelphia city directories at 3513 N. 17th Street. He is also listed as the minister of the Church of the Nativity, a Lutheran Church, located at N. 20th and Tioga. It is unclear whether the Rev. Elias Henry Gerhart is the minister being referred to in the Oliver Bair Funeral Home Record for Lucy Reitze.

39

May 10, 1909, in the center grave of an 80 square foot plot purchased by her son-in-law, Henry G. Douglass. The plate inscription on her oak casket read:

Lucy Reitze
June 12, 1836 - May 7, 1909

Her pall bearers were all family members. They didn't have far to carry her casket as her burial plot was located just inside the main gate of the cemetery immediately beside the cemetery office. For some reason, no headstone was placed on her grave. A bill for $82.75 was sent to her daughter, Elizabeth, to be paid after receipt of the funeral insurance money.[178]

There Lucy lay, alone, in her unmarked grave at Fernwood Cemetery until December 29, 1937, when Charles Wilkins (aged 63 years) was buried in the family plot. Later, on August 27, 1945, Ella Marie Wilkins (aged 72 years), was buried there, too.[179,180]

In Memoriam

The following memoriam appeared in the *Philadelphia Inquirer* a year after the death of Lucy (Devlin) Reitze:

REITZE - In fond remembrance of my dear mother, LUCY REITZE, who departed this life May 7, 1909.

DAUGHTER[181]

---

[178]Oliver Bair Funeral Home Record for Lucy Reitze, May 10, 1909, Pennsylvania Historical Society, Philadelphia, Pennsylvania.

[179]Letter dated August 4, 1995, from Edward L. Clapper, President and General Manager, Fernwood Cemetery and Mausoleum, 6501 Baltimore Avenue, Fernwood, Pennsylvania 19050 regarding burials in Lot 369, Section 18, owned by Henry G. Douglass.

[180]In a conversation on November 29, 1997, with the late Josephine Thompson Marshall, 121 Reillywood Avenue, Haddonfield, New Jersey 08033-2201 she said that she was once told by her grandmother that Elizabeth (Reitze) Douglass talked about selling the burial rights to the empty graves in the family plot at Fernwood Cemetery. If the family plot was partitioned and the empty graves were sold, it may have been a private transaction between Elizabeth (Reitze) Douglass and the Wilkins family because the name of the owner that appears in the plot burial book at Fernwood Cemetery is Henry G. Douglass. Charles Wilkins' obituary, which appeared in the *Philadelphia Inquirer* on December 28, 1937, indicates that he and his wife, Ella (Riley) Wilkins, lived at 720 Division Street, Gloucester, Camden County, New Jersey.

[181]Memoriam, *Philadelphia Inquirer*, Saturday, May 7, 1910, p. 12, <<www.newspapers.com>>, downloaded August 11, 2017.

THE CHILDREN OF CHRISTOPHER REITZE AND LUCY (DEVLIN) REITZE

Charles Archibald Reitze

According to the *Reitze Family Bible*, Charlie Reitze was born on February 7, 1866.[182] He can best be described as an unfailing and faithful son to his mother, Lucy, in every respect. He was her Rock of Gibraltar. He had very little formal education because he was out working, full-time, at a wine factory, by the time he was thirteen years old.[183] Later, after he was old enough to become a driver, he was probably the main source of support for his mother and his younger brother and sister, John and Josephine. Thus, the four of them lived together until Charlie married in January 1893.

THE DEATH OF CHARLIE REITZE. Sadly, Charlie Reitze died unexpectedly from a deadly case of typhoid fever about eight-and-a-half months after he married .[184]

When Charlie died, it broke his mother's heart. He was the first of her adult children to die and they had always been especially close. Josephine Thompson Marshall, Lucy's great-granddaughter, recalls that:

> I always had the impression that he was the special son and always mentioned as "Our Charlie." He had a happy disposition and brought laughter and lightheartedness into the household. When he left, some of the joy went with him.[185]

Lucy ran his obituary in the *Philadelphia Public Ledger* for three days straight beginning on the morning of September 26, 1893. It read as follows:

---

[182]*The Reitze Family Bible - Latin Vulgate Version.* (New York: D & J Sadlier, 1844) was in the possession of Josephine Thompson Marshall, 121 Reillywood Avenue, Haddonfield, New Jersey 08033-2201.

[183]1880 U.S. Census (population), Pennsylvania, Philadelphia County, City of Philadelphia, E.D. 582, sheet 31, line 34, National Archives Microfilm Publication T9, Roll 1186.

[184]Death Certificate for Charles Reitz (sic), September 25, 1893, # 9380, issued November 3, 1899, Health Office - Registration Department, Room 517, City Hall, is contained in the Application for Admission of Charles A. Reitze, [Jr.], Girard College, 2101 S. College Avenue, Philadelphia, Pennsylvania, 19121-4897.

[185]Letter dated October 21, 1999, from the late Josephine Thompson Marshall, 121 Reillywood Avenue, Haddonfield, New Jersey 08033-2201.

REITZE - On the 25th inst., CHARLES A., son of Lucy and the late Christopher
Reitze.

The relatives and friends of the family are respectfully invited to attend the
funeral on Thusday (sic) morning at 8-1/2 o'clock from his late residence 2507
Pine street.[186] High Mass at St. Patrick's Church.[187]

With great pain, Lucy entered Charlie's death into the *Reitze Family Bible.* It was the last
entry she ever made in her cherished Bible. It read as follows:

Charlie Reitze Died Sep 25th 1893[188]

THE BURIAL OF CHARLIE REITZE. Apparently, Lucy had very little money at the time
Charlie died and his wife, Rachel Kelly, to whom he had been married only eight-and-a-half
months, had none, so the family had to appeal for help in finding a suitable location for Charlie
to be buried. Under these miserable circumstances, Charlie came to be buried in New Cathedral
Cemetery in North Philadelphia in a plot belonging to a woman named Ellen Creedon.

NEW CATHEDRAL CEMETERY. Ellen Creedon appears to have purchased her plot at
New Cathedral Cemetery in 1872. According to the official records of the cemetery, eight people
were laid to rest in this plot. Although none of them presently has a headstone, their names,
ages, and dates of burial are said to be the following:

Name of Deceased	**Age**	**Date of Burial**
(East)		
Irene Martin	7 months	August 16, 1886
Ethel Martin	1 month	April 6, 1889
Margaret Smith	21 years	January 3, 1875
(2/E)		
Josephine Hayes	27 years (sic)	November 22, 1887

---

[186]Kathryn Chambers Torpey, *The Edwards/Scott Family History*, (Alexandria, Virginia:
Torpey Books, 2016), p. 29, states that William Scott Edwards lived at 2502 Pine Street. His
nephew, William Scott Chambers, married Charlie Reitze's youngest sister, Josephine Reitze, on
March 30, 1896.

[187]Obituary of Charles A. Reitze, *Philadelphia Public Ledger*, Tuesday, September 26,
1893, p. 8; Wednesday, September 27, 1893, p. 8; and Thursday, September 28, 1893, p. 8.

[188]*The Reitze Family Bible - Latin Vulgate Version.* (New York: D & J Sadlier, 1844)
was in the possession of Josephine Thompson Marshall, 121 Reillywood Avenue, Haddonfield,
New Jersey 08033-2201. It is possible that Lucy (Devlin) Reitze did not enter the information
into the Bible herself as the handwriting is slightly different from that of the earlier entries.

(2/W)
James Devlin   72 years   April 24, 1872
Ellen Creedon   72 years   January 30, 1909 (sic)[189]

(West)
Charles Reitz (sic)   25 years (sic)   September 30, 1893
Dennis Creedon   68 years   December 24, 1898[190]

Despite a great deal of research, no relationship can be established between Charlie Reitze or his mother, Lucy, and any of the people buried in Ellen Creedon's plot. The Creedon family lived at 2809 Girard Avenue for some years after 1880. As best can be determined, Ellen Creedon was a housewife. Her husband, Dennis Creedon, was a carter who later operated a furniture store and a china shop at 2134 Callowhill Street. Both Dennis and Ellen Creedon are buried in this plot.

Dennis and Ellen Creedon were the parents of three children: Marion L., Josephine, and John. The woman named Josephine Hayes buried in this plot appears to be their daughter, Josephine Creedon, who married Frank M. Hayes, a beef butcher and caulker. The infants named Irene Martin and Ethel Martin are believed to be two of the many children born to their daughter, Marion L. Creedon who married Luther Martin, an insurance broker.[191] The Creedons also had a servant named Catharine Smith.[192] Catharine Smith had a daughter named Margaret Smith who appears to be buried in this plot.[193]

The identity of the man named James Devlin is unknown. No obituary appeared for him in the Philadelphia newspapers. His death was not recorded in the 1872 Philadelphia Death

---

[189]Death Certificate for Ellen Creedon, December 30, 1908, # 121237, Pennsylvania Division of Vital Statistics, New Castle, Pennsylvania 16103 states that Ellen Creedon's parents were James De Odellannde born in Spain and Isabelle Starette born in Philadelphia.

[190]Letter dated May 12, 1997, from Veronica T. Johnson, Assistant Director, Catholic Cemeteries Office, 111 South 38th Street, Philadelphia, Pennsylvania 19104-3179, regarding the burial of Charles Reitze at New Cathedral Cemetery in Section H, Range 6, Lot 19 owned by Ellen Creedon.

[191]1880 U.S. Census (population), Pennsylvania, Philadelphia County, City of Philadelphia, E.D. 286, sheet 19, line 11, National Archives Microfilm Publication T9, Roll 1175.

[192]1880 U.S. Census (population), Pennsylvania, Philadelphia County, City of Philadelphia, E.D. 286, sheet 18, line 16, National Archives Microfilm Publication T9, Roll 1175.

[193]Obituary of Maggie L. Smith, *Philadelphia Public Ledger*, Saturday, January 2, 1875, p 2, states that Maggie L. Smith's parents were William and Catharine Smith.

Register nor was it recorded in the New Cathedral Cemetery Return for the week ending Saturday, April 27, 1872.[194] Interestingly, according to the official records of Old Cathedral Cemetery in West Philadelphia, this same James Devlin is buried at that cemetery in the plot where Lucy's mother, Susan (Kennedy) Devlin, is buried, but his name does not appear in the Old Cathedral Cemetery Return for the week ending Saturday, April 27, 1872, either.[195,196] It seems, therefore, that there is some connection between those buried in the plot at New Cathedral Cemetery and those buried in the plot at Old Cathedral Cemetery, but at this time that connection remains an unsolved mystery.

THE MARRIAGE OF CHARLIE REITZE AND RACHEL KELLY. According to the *Reitze Family Bible*, Charlie Reitze and Rachel Kelly were married on January 4, 1893.[197] The couple was married by the Reverend J.P. Turner in the rectory of St. Patrick's Roman Catholic Church located at 19th and Spruce Streets.[198,199] The witnesses were Henry J. Keenan and Mary McNamara.

On the very day they were to be married, Charlie went down to the courthouse and provided the following information to the Assistant Clerk of the Orphans' Court in support of his application for a marriage license:

> State of Pennsylvania
> Philadelphia County

---

[194]Philadelphia Cemetery Returns, 1872, Week Ending 20 April (Mt. Peace - Z) thru 11 May (A - Cedar), FHL Microfilm Roll 2021140.

[195]Kathryn C. Torpey, *William Kennedy of Chester County Pennsylvania, and His Descendants - A Compiled Genealogy (Including Davis, Smith, Wallace, Russell, and McClure)*, (Alexandria, Virginia: Torpey Books, 2014), p. 209, regarding the plot owned by Ann Coleman.

[196]Philadelphia Cemetery Returns, 1872, Week Ending 20 April (Mt. Peace - Z) thru 11 May (A - Cedar), FHL Microfilm Roll 2021140.

[197]*The Reitze Family Bible - Latin Vulgate Version.* (New York: D & J Sadlier, 1844) was in the possession of Josephine Thompson Marshall, 121 Reillywood Avenue, Haddonfield, New Jersey 08033-2201.

[198]Affidavit of Applicant for Marriage License # 57072, January 4, 1893, (Charles Archibald Reitze & Rachel M. Kelly), City of Philadelphia, Philadelphia City Archives, Philadelphia, Pennsylvania.

[199]Letter dated March 14, 2000, from Christine Friend, Assistant Archivist, Philadelphia Archdiocesan Historical Research Center, 100 East Wynnewood Road, Wynnewood, Pennsylvania 19096-3001.

Personally appeared Charles Archibald Reitze who hereby requests the Clerk of the Orphans' Court for the said County, to issue a License for the Marriage of himself to Rachel M. Kelly and who, being duly sworn according to law, doth depose and say; that he was born in Philadelphia on the 7th day of January (sic) A.D. 1866; that he resides at No. 2403 South Street, Philadelphia; that he is by occupation a team driver; that he is not related by blood or marriage to the person whom he desires to marry; that he has not been married before; that Rachel M. Kelly whom he is about to marry, was born in Scotland on the --- day of (age 23 years) A.D. 1869; that she resides at No. 210[8] Spruce Street, Philadelphia; is by occupation a domestic; that she has not been married before; that he knows no reason why the said marriage may not be lawfully made.

Sworn and subscribed before me (the Assistant Clerk of the Orphans' Court), this 4th day of January A.D. 1893.

(signed) C.A. Reitze

The wedding having taken place as scheduled, the newlyweds set forth to begin their married life together. Unfortunately, from the very beginning, things do not appear to have gone smoothly between Charlie's new wife and his sisters - Elizabeth and Josephine.[200] Sadly, the rocky relationship between the women is reported to have persisted for some time following Charlie's untimely demise. Nonetheless, his only child, Charlie Reitze, Jr., is said to have been much loved by everyone in the Reitze family. He is remembered fondly by his cousin, Josephine Thompson Marshall, as a very pleasant and likable man.[201]

THE PRESTON RETREAT. When Charlie died, his wife, Rachel, was almost eight months pregnant. Apparently, she was left destitute by his death. She had no income and no place to live. Thus, she delivered their son at the Preston Retreat located at 20th and Hamilton Streets.[202]

The Preston Retreat was a lying-in hospital for married women (and widows) of good character, but in indigent circumstances. It was financed by income from an estate left by Dr. Jonas Preston who died in 1836. For many years after Dr. Preston's death the use of the building was given over to the managers of the Foster Home Association so it was not actually opened as a lying-in hospital until 1866 during which year it received forty patients. Apparently, it was still in operation on November 6, 1893, when Rachel gave birth to her only child, Charles Archibald Reitze, Jr.

---

[200]Conversation on November 29, 1996, with the late Josephine Thompson Marshall, 121 Reillywood Avenue, Haddonfield, New Jersey 08033-2201.

[201]Letter dated October 21, 1999, from the late Josephine Thompson Marshall, 121 Reillywood Avenue, Haddonfield, New Jersey 08033-2201.

[202]Birth Certificate for Charles A. Reitz (sic), November 6, 1893, # 2624, Health Office - Registration Department, Room 517, City Hall, issued November 3, 1899, is contained in the Application for Admission of Charles A. Reitze [Jr.], Girard College, 2101 S. College Avenue, Philadelphia, Pennsylvania, 19121-4897.

THE BETHESDA HOME. Very shortly after Charlie, Jr., was born, his mother, Rachel, had to determine how best to support them both. Although putting her child up for adoption was out of the question, the hardships of raising him on her own in the 1890s were enormous. It is believed, therefore, that Rachel soon sought refuge at the Bethesda Home for Orphan Children.[203]

The Bethesda Home was founded around 1855 in Philadelphia through the work of Miss Anna M. Clements. Miss Clements was a lady of Quaker parentage who had departed from the simplicity and plainness of her ancestors. Eventually, she united herself with the Methodist Episcopal Church to found a Christian charity at 11th and Ellsworth Streets that served as a peaceful retreat for the aged and a shelter for destitute and friendless orphans.[204]

In support of her work, a large and commodious house in Chestnut Hill was offered for rent to Miss Clements in 1859. As the location and the premises were exceedingly attractive, the offer was immediately accepted and the "inmates" of the home prepared to move on the 1st of June. Given the healthfulness of the surrounding area, the garden already planted with Spring vegetables, the orchard, and the several acres of ground surrounding the house, even Miss Clements took up residence at the home.

In 1872, the Bethesda Home was moved a short distance away to Springfield Township in Montgomery County where it was situated on the main road dividing the county from the northwestern limits of the city. The new home was built on about eight acres of land owned by Henry J. Williams, a philanthropist and distinguished lawyer from Philadelphia.[205] It was at this location in Montgomery County that Rachel is believed to have enrolled Charlie, Jr., and where she herself worked "at service" in exchange for room and board. As best can be determined, Rachel was still working at the Bethesda Home as late as November 9, 1899 and Charlie, Jr., was enumerated there as an "inmate" at the time of the 1900 census.[206,207]

---

[203]Application for Admission of Charles A. Reitze, November 8, 1899, Girard College, 2101 S. College Avenue, Philadelphia, Pennsylvania, 19121-4897.

[204]Theodore W. Bean, editor, *History of Montgomery County, Pennsylvania - Volume II.* (Philadelphia, Pennsylvania: Everts & Peck, 1884), p. 1075.

[205]Jean Barth Toll and Michael J. Schwager, editors, *Montgomery County - The Second Hundred Years - Volume 1*, (Norristown, Pennsylvania: Montgomery County Federation of Historical Societies, 1983), p. 625.

[206]Application for Admission of Charles A. Reitze, November 8, 1899, Girard College, 2101 S. College Avenue, Philadelphia, Pennsylvania, 19121-4897.

[207]1900 U.S. Census (population), Pennsylvania, Montgomery County, Springfield Township, E.D. 252, sheet 23, line 5, National Archives Microfilm Publication T623, Roll 1444.

It was the very best that Rachel could do for her only child under extremely difficult circumstances. In 1893, the year Charlie, Jr., was born, a severe panic fell upon the country. Although business had been prosperous, severe doubt arose in the great commercial centers concerning the value of money. While the Sherman Silver Act had increased the quantity of paper money, many people feared that the government would not be able to redeem it all in gold. When the value of silver dropped to sixty-seven cents on the dollar, people hastened to exchange their paper money for gold before the treasury was exhausted. They withdrew their deposits from the banks and they hoarded the gold. Money became so scarce that many banks failed and factories closed. A great deal of suffering followed among the thousands that were thrown out of work.[208]

By contrast, the peaceful surroundings of the Bethesda Home were healthful, abounding in highly improved farms and elegant residences. It was located near Wyndmoor Station on the Pennsylvania and Chestnut Hill Railroad and was conveniently accessible by well-kept public highways in all directions. The mission of the home was characterized as so universal in its efforts to benefit those most in need, and so tender in its offices of mercy and philanthropy that no one was more appreciative and responsive to its financial needs than those living in the humble dwellings and homes of affluence within the circle of its influence.[209]

The home itself was described as a large, comfortable-looking stone house, with a fine portico in front and a carriage drive to the door. The parlor was a beautiful room, neatly and appropriately furnished. The schoolroom, on the other side of the hall, was also pleasant, light and cheerful in all appointments. The whole second floor was so nicely heated by the furnace that the children were not confined to one room, but had a range of bedrooms, hall, and play-room, which was conducive to their health. The floors were laid in hard wood, and the chambers were all furnished with single iron bedsteads. The third floor was furnished much like the second. Two communicating rooms were set apart on that floor as sick nurseries so that in case of contagious diseases the patients could immediately be separated from the rest of the family. The beautiful views of the surrounding landscape, which were visible from the large and airy windows of this lovely home, made the neat lodging rooms doubly attractive.[210]

Would that Rachel and Charlie, Jr., could have stayed there indefinitely, but it is believed that the Bethesda Home was not equipped to meet the needs of older children. Thus, Rachel was forced to make other arrangements for her son's future. Unfortunately, it has not been possible to verify these suppositions as the present whereabouts of the home's admission records is

---

[208]Thompson, p. 464.

[209]Bean, p. 1076.

[210]Bean, p. 1076.

unknown.[211] All that is known for certain is that when the Bethesda Home finally closed its doors in 1954, the buildings were demolished and the property was developed with single family homes.[212]

GIRARD COLLEGE. According to the records of Girard College, Rachel Reitze, applied for the admission of her son, Charlie, Jr., on November 9, 1899, just three days after his sixth birthday.[213]

Girard College was built on forty-five acres of land in North Philadelphia. It opened on January 1, 1848, under the terms of the will of Stephen Girard, a French-born financier and philanthropist who was the richest man in America at the time of his death in 1831. Girard's will had been carefully and painstakingly written and rewritten, especially in the final year of his life. In his will, Stephen Girard allocated millions of dollars to build and operate a boarding school for poor, white, male orphans. Although many other charitable groups benefitted substantially from Stephen Girard's generosity, the gift of Girard College was a gesture that stands alone in the educational history of America as perhaps the single, most extraordinary portion of a legacy that speaks to the generosity of Stephen Girard. In accordance with his wishes, the students at Girard College were to be taught the basics of reading, writing, arithmetic and other more advanced subjects including astronomy, philosophy, and the French and Spanish languages. That legacy was carried out as he willed it for one hundred and twenty years. In 1968, the will was amended to strike the "poor, white, male orphan" provision and, later, the will was amended a second time to allow for the admission of females. The school remains today as a leader in providing quality education to hundreds of children from poor families everywhere.[214]

Apparently, Rachel was intent on securing a small piece of that legacy for her son. In her application, she said that her son was of sound mind and body despite having had whooping cough and the measles and not having been vaccinated against small pox. Further, she said that her son's general moral condition was good, but that he had very little education. Finally, Rachel said that she had no means at her disposal to care for her child as she was living at the Bethesda Home and even though his paternal grandmother was living, she had no income. Both the witnesses to her application, including her brother-in-law, Henry G. Douglass, supported her

---

[211]Letter dated December 10, 1996, from Vivian F. Taylor, Assistant Librarian, The Historical Society of Montgomery County, 1854 DeKalb Street, Norristown, Pennsylvania, 19401-5415.

[212]Toll and Schwager, p. 625.

[213]Application for Admission of Charles A. Reitze, November 8, 1899, Girard College, 2101 S. College Avenue, Philadelphia, Pennsylvania, 19121-4897.

[214]The Independence Hall Association, Steven Girard, Part 3, Girard's Remarkable Will, <<www.ushistory.org/people/girard3.htm>>, downloaded August 10, 2017.

application and swore that Rachel had no money of which they were aware.

Having satisfied the condition of the will of Stephen Girard that Charlie Reitze, Jr., was indeed a poor, white, male orphan between the ages of six and ten years who was born in the City of Philadelphia, he was duly admitted to Girard College on January 31, 1902, two years and two months after his mother made application for his admission. He lived and studied at the school for nine years leaving in 1910.

Three pictures of Charlie Reitze, Jr., are known to have survived. The first is as an infant with his mother, Rachel; the second is as a school boy in his Girard College school uniform; and the third is as a young man in the company of his first cousin, Lucy Chambers.[215]

THE REST OF THE STORY. When Charlie, Jr., left Girard College in 1910 he probably went to live with his mother, Rachel, who rented rooms at 1312 Race Street.[216] Initially, Charlie, Jr., worked as a chauffeur. Eventually, he became an automobile mechanic and the manager of a garage.[217] He was still living at 1312 Race Street as late as 1920 with his mother, Rachel, and his step-father, William Maguire, a retired engineer who ran a fair-sized boarding house at that location.[218]

Charlie, Jr., eventually married a woman named Mary Kubick who predeceased him on July 2, 1964.[219] He died five years later on August 29, 1969, in Philadelphia.[220] He was 76 years old at the time of his death. Both Charlie, Jr., and his wife, Mary, are buried at Sunset Memorial

---

[215]The three pictures of Charlie Reitze, Jr., were in the possession of the late Josephine Thompson Marshall, 121 Reillywood Avenue, Haddonfield, New Jersey 08033-2201.

[216]1910 U.S. Census (population), Pennsylvania, Philadelphia County, City of Philadelphia, E.D. 149, Family Number 107, National Archives Microfilm Publication T624, Roll 1388.

[217]Employment Card for Charles A. Reitze, 1910-1950, Girard College, 2101 S. College Avenue, Philadelphia, Pennsylvania, 19121-4897.

[218]1920 U.S. Census (population), Pennsylvania, Philadelphia County, City of Philadelphia, E.D. 207, sheet 1, line 57, National Archives Microfilm Publication T625, Roll 1619.

[219]Obituary of Mary Reitz, *Philadelphia Inquirer*, Saturday, July 4, 1964, p. 10.

[220]Obituary of Charles A. Reitz, *Philadelphia Inquirer*, Sunday, August 31, 1969, Section 3, p. 9.

Park located in Somerton, Pennsylvania.[221] Sadly, the copper plate containing Charlie Jr.'s date of death has fallen off his headstone.[222] Charlie, Jr., and his wife, Mary, were survived by a son named John C. Reitz and a grandson named Kenneth C. Reitz.[223]

Christopher C. Reitze, Jr.

Christopher and Lucy's oldest child, Christopher C. Reitze, Jr., was born on September 9, 1855, in Woolwich Township, Gloucester County, New Jersey.[224,225] Known to his friends and family as Chris, he was 6 feet tall, over 200 pounds, strong, decisive, and athletic.

THE MARRIAGE OF CHRIS REITZE, JR., TO ELIZABETH HOFFNER. Chris Reitze, Jr., is believed to have married Elizabeth Hoffner on November 17, 1878, in Philadelphia. Although his mother, Lucy, recorded the marriage in the *Reitze Family Bible*, no corresponding entry has been found in the 1877 or 1878 Philadelphia Marriage Registers nor has the marriage been found

---

[221]Letter dated May 9, 1997, from Marie E. Cuthbertson, Office Manager, Sunset Memorial Park, P.O. Box 11508, County Line Road, Somerton, Pennsylvania, concerning the burial of Charles A. Reitz and Mary K. Reitz in Block E, Lot 369.

[222]Site visit to Sunset Memorial Park on June 22, 1997.

[223]Will of Charles A. Reitz, aka Reitze, # 3321, August 29, 1969, Register of Wills, Philadelphia, Pennsylvania.

[224]*The Reitze Family Bible - Latin Vulgate Version.* (New York: D & J Sadlier, 1844) was in the possession of the late Josephine Thompson Marshall, 121 Reillywood Avenue, Haddonfield, New Jersey 08033-2201.

[225]Birth of Christopher Reitze, New Jersey Births and Christenings, 1660-1980, Original Data: Gloucester County, New Jersey, Birth Records, Volume O, p. 103, line 28, Woolwich Township, FHL Microfilm Roll 584565 <<www.familysearch.org>>, downloaded July 21, 2017, says:

Name:	...
Birthplace:	Woolwich Township, Gloucester County
Birth Date:	09 September 1855
Father's Name:	Christopher ...
Mother's Name:	Lucy ...

in the New Jersey State Marriage Indexes.[226,227,228]

EARNING A LIVING. Chris Reitze, Jr., took seriously his responsibilities as a provider for his wife and children. He worked long and hard from the time he was very young. By the age of fifteen, he was working as a bar tender and living with James Wray and his family who operated a hotel and sold lager beer at 1417 Race Street, in the 10th Ward of the City of Philadelphia.[229,230] Presumably, he got his job through his father who previously had worked as a driver for the Bergdoll and Psotta Brewing Company and undoubtedly knew any number of people who could have given his young son a job tending bar.[231]

As he got older, Chris Reitze, Jr., joined the beer driver's union and took a job as a driver for the Bergner and Engel Brewing Company delivering barrels of beer to the hotels, saloons, and taverns in Philadelphia. This would have been steady work and the source of a good income as the Bergner and Engel Brewing Company was one of the larger breweries in Philadelphia. It was established in 1849 by Charles W. Bergner on 7th Street below Girard Avenue. In 1852, Gustavus Bergner took charge of the brewery. The business was small at that time with only twelve employees brewing about 7,000 barrels of beer a year. In 1870, however, Charles Engel entered into partnership with Gustavus Bergner. The Engel brewery at Fountain Green was combined with the Bergner brewery and the new larger operation was moved to the square lying between 31st and 32nd Streets and Thompson and Jefferson Streets in Brewerytown. The firm

---

[226]*The Reitze Family Bible - Latin Vulgate Version.* (New York: D & J Sadlier, 1844) was in the possession of the late Josephine Thompson Marshall, 121 Reillywood Avenue, Haddonfield, New Jersey 08033-2201.

[227]No Record of Registration # 951627, August 1997, Reitze/Hoffner Marriage, 1877, 1878 Marriage Registers, City of Philadelphia, Philadelphia City Archives, Philadelphia, Pennsylvania.

[228]New Jersey Marriage Indexes (1867-1878) and (1878-1900), New Jersey State Archives, Trenton, New Jersey.

[229]1870 U.S. Census (population), First Enumeration, Pennsylvania, Philadelphia County, City of Philadelphia, 10th Ward, page 353, National Archives Microfilm Publication M593, Roll 1395.

[230]1870 Philadelphia city directory.

[231]Based on a January 24, 2000, conversation with Elizabeth Wray (Wilson) Lutz, 71 Pinckney Drive, Coatesville, Pennsylvania 19320, it is thought that the Reitze family and the Wray family may have been related in that Mrs. Lutz's grandmother, Elizabeth C. (Reitze) Bustard, - who was Chris Reitze, Jr.'s oldest daughter - named her daughter Elizabeth Wray Bustard. This naming tradition, which began in 1906, has been maintained for three generations.

was officially incorporated in 1879 with numerous buildings, improved equipment, and a paid-in capital of nearly one-million dollars. At its new location, it employed 180 men in various capacities.[232] The brewery stables where Chris Reitze, Jr., reported to work every morning were located at 31st and Jefferson Street, just about four blocks away from his home.[233]

Toward the end of his life, Chris Reitze, Jr., was employed as a driver for F.A. Poth and Son, Inc., a brewery located just across the street from the Bergner and Engel brewery at 31st and Jefferson Streets.[234] Again, this brewery provided a good source of income and was conveniently located just a few blocks away from his home so that he could easily walk to work.

HEARTH AND HOME. Chris Reitze, Jr., probably lived his entire adult life in and around Brewerytown. In fact, two years after his marriage to Elizabeth Hoffner, he is documented in the 1880 census schedule living in the same house with people who are believed to have been members of his wife's family:

1621 N. 28th STREET:

Hofner (sic), Thomas	W M 56		brickmason	born in Penna.
-, Margaret	W F 40	wife	housekeeping	born in Penna.
-, Thomas	W M 11	son	at school	born in Penna.
-, George	W M 10	son	at school	born in Penna.
-, Herry (sic)	W M 7	son	at home	born in Penna.
-, Maggie	W F 3	dau	at home	born in Penna.
Dugale, Cristofer (sic)	W M 25		driving team	born in Penna.
-, Louisa	W F 24	wife	housekeeping	born in Penna.
-, Trevelana (sic)	W F 2	dau	at home	born in Penna.
Ritches, Christofer (sic)	W M 25		driving team	born in Penna. (sic)
-, Lizie (sic)	W F 20	wife	housekeeping	born in Penna.[235]

After 1880, Chris Reitze, Jr., and his family moved periodically, but they never strayed far from the vicinity of the breweries where Chris Reitze, Jr., is known to have worked. Their addresses as reported in the Philadelphia city directories are shown below:

1881	N. 28th n Columbia Ave	driver
1882	1244 N. 26th	driver
1883-1886	(no Reitze listed)	

---

[232]Scharf and Westcott, p. 2281.

[233]*Philadelphia Brewery Tour Book* (Lock Haven, Pennsylvania: Soy World, 1997), p. 33.

[234]Obituary of Christopher C. Reitze, *Philadelphia Public Ledger*, Saturday, March 9, 1907, p. 10.

[235]1880 U.S. Census (population), Pennsylvania, Philadelphia County, City of Philadelphia, E.D. 642, sheet 33, line 12, National Archives Microfilm Publication T9, Roll 1188.

1887-1888	1623 Marston	driver
1889	1631 Marston	driver
1890	1631 Marston	hostler
1891	1631 Marston	driver
1892	2714 Thompson	driver
1893	(not listed)	
1894-1900	2707 Thompson	driver
1906-1907	1330 N. 28th	driver

THE CHILDREN OF CHRIS REITZE, JR., AND ELIZABETH HOFFNER. In addition to acting as a father figure to his little sister, Josephine, Chris Reitze, Jr., and his wife, Elizabeth, had three children of their own - Elizabeth, Margaret and Christopher. The whole family was conveniently enumerated in the 1900 census schedule as follows:

2707 THOMPSON STREET:

Reitza, (sic) Christopher	Head W M Sep 1855 44	driver brewer	b. New Jersey
-, Elizabeth	Wife W F Oct 1861 38		b. Penna.
-, Margaret	Dau W F Dec 1882 17	umbrella maker	b. Penna.
-, Christopher	Son W M Sep 1885 14	umbrella maker	b. Penna.
Hoffner, Margaret	MIL W F Apr 1836 64		b. Penna.
-, Margaret	SIL W F Dec 1876 23	umbrella maker	b. Penna.

1307 CRANSTON STREET:

| Bustard, John A. | Head W M Sep 1867 32 | machinist | b. Penna. |
| -, Elizabeth C. | Wife W F Jun 1881 18 | | b. Penna[236] |

Chris Reitze, Jr.'s son, Christopher C. Reitze, I, married Helen C. Hoenigmann, his first wife, on September 28, 1908 at Zion German Presbyterian Church.[237,238] After the ceremony, the couple was presented with their marriage certificate which was signed by C. Theodor Albrecht, D.D., pastor of the church.[239] The Zion German Presbyterian Church was originally established as a mission by the Second German Presbyterian Church in 1878 specifically to serve the needs of the German community in the area around 28th and Mount Pleasant. The church itself was

---

[236]1900 U.S. Census (population), Pennsylvania, Philadelphia County, City of Philadelphia, E.D. 736, sheet 1, line 29, National Archives Microfilm Publication T623, Roll 1471.

[237]Affidavit of Applicant for Marriage License # 226148, April 27, 1908, (Christopher C. Reitze & Helen C. Hoenigmann), City of Philadelphia, Philadelphia City Archives, Philadelphia, Pennsylvania.

[238]Conversation on February 19, 1997, with the late Jeanne H. Reitze (widow of Harry E. Reitze, Sr.), 6 Pinewood Trail, Concord, New Hampshire 03301-5247.

[239]The original marriage certificate of Christopher K. (sic) Reitze and Helene (sic) C. Hoenigmann dated April 28, 1908, was in the possession of the late Jeanne H. Reitze (widow of Harry E. Reitze, Sr.), 6 Pinewood Trail, Concord, New Hampshire 03301-5247.

officially organized in 1882 and, in the early years, services were conducted entirely in German.[240] It was in this church that the Hoenigmann family worshiped and where Helen C. Hoenigmann was baptized on May 20, 1887.[241]

Chris Reitze, Jr.'s oldest daughter, Elizabeth Reitze, married John A. Bustard on June 28, 1899 and his younger daughter, Margaret Reitze, married Edward T. Burtis on June 19, 1901.[242,243] Both couples were married by the Reverend H.R. Myers, pastor of Trinity Baptist Church located at Poplar, West of 27th Street. This church was officially organized on May 16, 1886. The first pastor was the Reverend James Stifler, D.D., who presided for 11 years. Then, the Reverend H.R. Myers became pastor for 12 years. The origin of Trinity Baptist Church was in the Mission Sabbath School started under the direction of the Fifth Baptist Church in a hall over a stable on Taney Street, north of Poplar. The first service was held on Sunday, July 4, 1880. The work, which consisted of Sunday School and prayer meetings, was carried on in this hall until the fall of 1881 when the school moved into a new building on the corner of Pennock and Poplar Streets. Based on a church directory published in 1814, the Bustard and Burtis families were members of this church until at least that time. The church was closed in 1979.[244]

Chris Reitze, Jr.'s daughters are remembered fondly by their cousin, Josephine Thompson Marshall, who recalled that:

> I met his daughters many times and they were both fine Christian women.
> Maggie was very pretty with beautiful auburn hair and had a jolly disposition.

---

[240]Kenneth A. Hammonds, *Historical Directory of Presbyterian Churches and Presbyteries of Greater Philadelphia*, (Philadelphia, Pennsylvania: Presbyterian Historical Society, 1993), p. 77.

[241]The original baptismal certificate of Helene C. Hoenigmann dated May 20, 1887, was in the possession of the late Jeanne H. Reitze (widow of Harry E. Reitze, Sr.), 6 Pinewood Trail, Concord, New Hampshire 03301-5247.

[242]Affidavit of Applicant for Marriage License # 114693, June 28, 1899, (John A. Bustard & Elizabeth C. Reitze), City of Philadelphia, Philadelphia City Archives, Philadelphia, Pennsylvania.

[243]Affidavit of Applicant for Marriage License # 136919, June 11, 1901, (Edward T. Burtis & Margaret May Reitze), City of Philadelphia, Philadelphia City Archives, Philadelphia, Pennsylvania.

[244]Letter dated April 2, 2001, from Stuart W. Campbell, Director, American Baptist-Samuel Colgate Historical Library, 1106 S. Goodman Street, Rochester, New York 14620-2532.

Lizzie was quiet and a truly spiritual woman.[245]

Sadly, Elizabeth (Reitze) Bustard's spiritual strength was to be sorely tested twice in her life.

The first occasion was on April 16, 1927, when her oldest son, Edward John Bustard, was brutally murdered at the age of twenty-six.[246] His obituary appeared in the *Philadelphia Inquirer* and the *Philadelphia Public Ledger* on Monday, April 18, 1927, and Tuesday April 19, 1927, as follows:

> BUSTARD - April 16, Edward J., suddenly, beloved husband of Helen Bustard
> (nee Weber), and son of Elizabeth and John Bustard, aged 26. Relatives and
> friends, also the employees of the Pennsylvania and Jersey Bus Service, P.R.T.,
> are invited to attend funeral services, Wed., 2 P.M., at his parents' residence,
> 1728 N. 28th st. Int. Greenmount Cem. Viewing Tues., after 7 P.M.[247,248]

Having fatally shot Edward John Bustard, in broad daylight, at 28th and Oxford Streets, in front of several witnesses, the murderer, a man of recognized erratic temperament named William Conquest, fled the scene and escaped arrest.[249,250] He was captured some years later and extradited to Pennsylvania to stand trial.[251] Elizabeth (Reitze) Bustard testified at the trial that she did not want the murderer of her son to be put to death. On September 24, 1937, William Conquest pled guilty to murder in the first degree and was sentenced to life in prison at the

---

[245]Letter dated October 21, 1999, from the late Josephine Thompson Marshall, 121 Reillywood Avenue, Haddonfield, New Jersey 08033-2201.

[246]Death Certificate for Edward John Bustard, April 16, 1927, # 34688 & # 9017, Pennsylvania Division of Vital Statistics, New Castle, Pennsylvania 16103.

[247]Obituary for Edward J. Bustard, *Philadelphia Inquirer*, Monday, April 18, 1927, p. 19 and Tuesday, April 19, 1927, p. 27.

[248]Obituary for Edward J. Bustard, *Philadelphia Public Ledger*, Monday, April 18, 1927, p. 26 and Tuesday, April 19, 1927, p. 16.

[249]News Story and Photograph, *Philadelphia Inquirer*, Sunday, April 17, 1927, p. B-1.

[250]News Story, *Philadelphia Public Ledger*, Sunday, April 17, 1927, p. 2.

[251]Conversation on January 24, 2000, with Elizabeth Wray (Wilson) Lutz, 71 Pinckney Drive, Coatesville, Pennsylvania 19320.

Eastern State Penitentiary for his ruthless crime.[252,253,254,255]

The second time Elizabeth (Reitze) Bustard's spirituality was tested was when her younger son, Christopher C. Bustard, was lost at sea during World War II while serving in the U.S. Coast Guard as a Chief Machinist's Mate aboard the *Muskeget*. The *Muskeget* disappeared on September 9, 1942, about 400 nautical miles east of Newfoundland.

No bodies were ever recovered and the wreck was never found. A year later, on September 10, 1943, the U.S. Navy and U.S. Coast Guard officially declared all on board the *Muskeget* to have been killed in action. Only later did it become known that *U-755* had sunk her. The *Muskeget* was the only U.S. weather ship lost during World War II.

Christopher C. Bustard was posthumously awarded the Purple Heart Medal.[256] And, his name is inscribed on the East Coast Memorial dedicated to those men who gave their lives in the service of their Country during World War II, but whose remains have not been recovered and identified.

The memorial is situated in Battery Park near the southern tip of Manhattan Island in New York City. The memorial includes an 18-1/2 foot high bronze eagle atop a polished black granite base that bears the following inscription:

---

[252]Conversation on September 14, 1999, with the late Josephine Thompson Marshall, 121 Reillywood Avenue, Haddonfield, New Jersey 08033-2201.

[253]News Story, *Wilkes-Barre Times Leader, the Evening News*, Wilkes-Barre, Pennsylvania, Tuesday, September 25, 1934. P. 11 states:

> Philadelphia - William Conquest, 46, pleaded guilty to slaying Edward J.
> Bustard in a quarrel and was sentenced to life imprisonment.

[254]Death Certificate for William Conquest, January 17, 1956, # 9765, Pennsylvania Division of Vital Statistics, New Castle, Pennsylvania 16103, <<www.ancestry.com>>, downloaded August 12, 2017, states William Conquest died at the Farview State Hospital for the Criminally Insane now the State Correctional Institution (SCI) at Waymart.

[255]Philip Q. Roche, M.D., *The Criminal Mind ... A Study of Communication Between The Criminal Law and Psychiatry*, (New York: American Books - Stratford Press, Inc., 1958), p. 196-209.

[256]World War II & Korean Conflict Veterans Interred Overseas, <<www.ancestry.com>>, downloaded January 30, 2000.

1941-1945 * ERECTED BY THE UNITED STATES OF
AMERICA IN PROUD AND GRATEFUL REMEMBRANCE OF
HER SONS WHO GAVE THEIR LIVES IN HER SERVICE
AND WHO SLEEP IN THE AMERICAN COASTAL WATERS
OF THE ATLANTIC OCEAN * INTO THY HANDS O LORD[257]

LEISURE ACTIVITIES. In addition to dutifully fulfilling his family obligations as a loving husband, father, and son, Chris Reitze, Jr., is said to have been keenly interested in sports and athletic competition.

Family legend has it that Chris Reitze, Jr., belonged to the Vesper Boat Club, but his membership in that organization could not be confirmed.[258,259,260] Alternatively, he may have been a member of the Fairmount Rowing Association.[261] The following reports of the first and second annual regatta of the Fairmount Rowing Association make reference to his connection with that organization:

---

[257]Elizabeth Nishiura, Editor, *American Battle Monuments: A Guide to Military Cemeteries and Monuments Maintained by the American Battle Monuments Commission,* (Detroit, Michigan: Omnigraphics, Inc., 1989), p. 413.

[258]Conversation on August 12, 1995, with the late Josephine Thompson Marshall, 121 Reillywood Avenue, Haddonfield, New Jersey 08033-2201.

[259]Per conversation on August 12, 1995, with David H. Marshall, Jr., 121 Reillywood Avenue, Haddonfield, New Jersey 08033-2201, he believes that the member of the Vesper Boat Club was Chris Reitze's brother-in-law, Henry G. Douglass, whose name is said to appear on a plaque hanging on the wall of the club that lists the names of the founding fathers.

[260]Letter dated December 6, 1996, to Vesper Boat Club, Inc., # 10 Boathouse Row, Philadelphia, Pennsylvania 19130-2950 was never answered.

[261]Fairmount Rowing Association, <<www.fairmountrowing.org>>, downloaded March 28, 2000, states the present Fairmount Rowing Association is the incorporation of two original rowing clubs which merged in 1932, Fairmount at # 2 Boathouse Row founded in 1877 and Quaker City at # 3 Boathouse Row. Quaker City (the present entrance) was erected in 1858. The original Fairmount building, dating from 1860, is gone. The current Flemish-bonded brick structure was built in 1904 and is on the National Register of Historic Places. Fairmount and Quaker City originally attracted the predominantly blue-collar Fairmount neighborhood youths. In recent years, they have mostly been known as the premier club for Masters rowing in the mid-Atlantic region. Fairmount also boasts a small but excellent Juniors program, and even a few Elites. Fairmount is also home to the rowing programs of La Salle University, Wharton Crew, and Episcopal Academy.

> October 29, 1877 - The second and final day's races of the first annual regatta
> of the new Fairmount Rowing Association ... The first race was a six oar barge
> contest between the following: ... Fairmount - J. Popp, bow; G. Mitchell, J. Figgins,
> M. Tietze, F. Brownell, **C. Reitze**, stroke; J. Koetzel, coxswain.[262]

> October 5, 1878 - Second annual regatta of the Fairmount Rowing Association
> on the Schuylkill River, over the national course. Prize for single shells won by
> C. Hamilton in 11 minutes, 11-1/2 seconds; single shells, J. Schnall, 14 minutes,
> 46-1/4 seconds; double sculls, W. Tapper and **C. Reitze**, 12 minutes, 37-3/4
> seconds; four oared barges, Fairmount, 14 minutes, 10 seconds; six-oared
> barges, Washington, 10 minutes, 43-3/4 seconds.[263]

It is also said that Chris Reitze, Jr., may have belonged to the German Society of Pennsylvania located at 6th and Spring Garden.[264] The society was founded in 1764 to protect German immigrants from unscrupulous shipping agents and to ensure that immigrants were treated justly upon their arrival in Pennsylvania. It is the oldest German organization in America.[265]

Members of the German Society were also interested in preserving the cultural heritage of Germany. They did this by establishing a German library, sponsoring social activities, forming clubs, and founding singing and dancing groups as well as Turnvereine that cultivated gymnastics.

According to family legend, Chris Reitze, Jr., and his brother-in-law, William Scott Chambers, belonged to one of the gymnasiums sponsored by the German Society thus they were known as *turnvereins* - those who exercise. It is believed that the gymnasium to which they belonged was known as Turner Hall. It was located on the northeast corner of Broad and Columbia Streets. Turner Hall was built by the Philadelphia Turngemeinde, the local German

---

[262]News Story, "The First Annual Regatta," *Philadelphia Inquirer*, Monday, October 29, 1877, p 2.

[263]Rudolph J. Walther, compiler, *Happenings in Ye Olde Philadelphia, 1680-1900*, (Philadelphia, Pennsylvania: Walther Printing House, 1925), p. 63.

[264]Conversation on August 12, 1995, with David H. Marshall, Jr., 121 Reillywood Avenue, Haddonfield, New Jersey 08033-2201.

[265]The German Society of Pennsylvania, <<http://www.germansociety.org>>, downloaded December, 1996.

sports organization.[266] It was the scene of many sports events before the building was sold to Temple University in 1946. Those who exercised at Turner Hall were dedicated to the principle of a sound mind in a sound body, stressing gymnastics and other sports activities as well as encouraging singing, art and language classes.[267]

Apparently, exercise as a way of building strength, character, and discipline was first introduced in America by Karl Follen who opened a gymnasium at Harvard University in 1819 after fleeing his homeland in Germany on account of his political beliefs. By 1851, German-American gymnastics was so widespread that one-hundred gymnasiums had united in America as the Socialist Gymnasts' League and they were chosen to provide Abraham Lincoln's bodyguard at his inauguration in 1861.[268]

THE DEATH OF CHRIS REITZE, JR. After many years of hard work, Chris Reitze, Jr., died on Thursday, March 7, 1907, from acute nephritis and an enlarged liver.[269] He was only 51 years old.

His obituary, which appeared in the *Philadelphia Public Ledger* on Saturday, March 9, 1907, read as follows:

> REITZE - On March 7, 1907, CHRISTOPHER C., beloved husband of
> Elizabeth L. Reitze (nee Hoffner) and son of Lucy and the late Christopher
> Reitze. Relatives and friends also employees of F.A. Poth's Sons, Bergner and
> Engel Beneficial Society and the Beer Drivers' Union No. 132 are invited to
> attend the funeral services on Sunday at 2 p.m. at his late residence, 1330 North
> 28th St. Interment Northwood Cemetery.[270]

---

[266]Things That Aren't There Anymore - Temple University Edition. <<http://www.wrti.com/wrtifriend/things.html>>, August 15, 2017.

[267]The German Society of Pennsylvania, <<http://www.germansociety.org/our-history/>>, downloaded June 24, 2000.

[268]James Burke, "Connections," *Scientific American*, December 1996, p. 127.

[269]Death Certificate for Christopher Reitze, March 7, 1907, # 6778 & # 29110, Pennsylvania Division of Vital Statistics, New Castle, Pennsylvania 16103.

[270]Obituary of Christopher C. Reitze, *Philadelphia Public Ledger*, Saturday, March 9, 1907, p. 10.

The Oliver Bair Funeral Home handled the funeral.[271] No expense was spared.[272] Chris Reitze, Jr., was laid out neatly in the front parlor of his home in a large oak casket, 6 feet, 3 inches long, every bit of which was needed to accommodate his large frame. The Reverend Dr. Meyers (sic) officiated at the funeral for which three dozen chairs were provided to seat all the many people who came to pay their last respects.

Chris Reitze, Jr., was transported to Northwood Cemetery in a horse-drawn funeral hearse followed by eight coaches. Immediately behind the funeral hearse was the open coach filled to capacity with the myriad flower arrangements that were delivered to the house. Following the coach containing the flowers was the coach reserved for the immediate family including Chris Reitze, Jr.'s widow, Elizabeth, and his mother, Lucy. After that came the coach set aside for the pall bearers who were all close friends of the family and the rest of the mourners.

THE BURIAL OF CHRIS REITZE, JR. Christopher and Lucy's oldest son was buried in the Fairmount Section of Northwood Cemetery in a plot he had bought in August 1891.[273] At the conclusion of the graveside service, his casket was lowered into a polished cedar case. As it slowly disappeared from view, the plate inscription on his casket could be seen to read:

Christopher C. Reitze
September 9, 1855 - March 7, 1907

Chris Reitze, Jr., still rests today in the family plot at Northwood Cemetery. He was joined there on June 3, 1938, by his wife, Elizabeth (Hoffner) Reitze. The following notice of her death was placed in the Philadelphia Inquirer on Thursday, June 2, 1938:

> REITZE - May 31, ELIZABETH, beloved wife of the late Christopher Reitze (nee Hoffner). Relatives and friends, also D. of L. Council No. 108 are invited to attend funeral services, Fri., 2 P.M., at parlors of Joseph E. Hepp, 1320 N. 29th st. Viewing Thurs. eve. from 7 to 9. Int. Northwood Cemetery.[274]

---

[271]Oliver Bair Funeral Home Record for Christopher C. Reitze, March 10, 1907, Pennsylvania Historical Society, Philadelphia, Pennsylvania.

[272]The bill from Oliver H. Bair for this funeral was for $220.00 exclusive of the cost of the plot which had been purchased in 1891 and the cost of the headstone. The bill was to be paid by Elizabeth Reitze upon receipt of the insurance money from John Hancock ($180.00) and Prudential ($500.00). In the interim, a bond was posted to guarantee payment.

[273]Letter dated April 15, 1998, from Janet M. Leipert, Northwood Cemetery Company, 15th and Haines Streets, P.O. Box 5248, Philadelphia, Pennsylvania 19126, concerning burials in Fairmount Section, Lot 533 (Reitze, Bustard, Burtis, Knopp) and Ogontz Section, Lot 3 (Reitze, Hoenigmann, Freestone).

[274]Obituary of Elizabeth Reitze, *Philadelphia Inquirer*, Thursday, June 2, 1938, p. 29.

Also buried in the family plot at Northwood Cemetery are both his daughters, Elizabeth and Margaret, and their husbands; his baby grandson, Ellwood C. Burtis, who died of diphtheria in 1904 at the age of 11 months; and his wife's youngest sister, Margaret Hoffner Knopp. His son, Christopher C. Reitze, I, lies nearby in the Ogontz Section of the cemetery in a plot purchased by the Hoenigmann family in September 1912.[275] Buried with Christopher C. Reitze, I, are his first wife, Helen C. Hoenigmann; his second wife, Theresa (Reimold) Schaeffer; and several members of the Hoenigmann family.

John Francis Reitze

Known to all his children and grandchildren as Popie Reitze, John Francis Reitze was born October 30, 1869, in Philadelphia.[276,277] He was frequently sick as a child and missed a lot of school. As a consequence, he couldn't read or write very much more than his name.[278] Although he cared deeply for his children and his grandchildren, he seldom showed his emotions having learned from bitter experience to shield himself from the pain of losing the people he loved the most.

THE MARRIAGE OF POPIE REITZE AND MAGGIE MALLOY. When Popie Reitze met Maggie Malloy, it must have been love at first sight. Apparently, they met somewhere in the neighborhood as he was living at 2403 South Street with his mother, Lucy, his older brother, Charlie, and youngest sister, Josephine, and she was living at 2210 Wharton Street with her parents, Martin and Catharine (Kennedy) Malloy, and her brothers and sisters.

Then, in early 1893, shortly after the marriage of his older brother, Charlie; Popie Reitze, his mother, Lucy, and his sister, Josephine, moved to West Philadelphia. After they moved, Popie Reitze found that he missed Maggie, a lot. Apparently, they didn't lose touch entirely and, shortly before Maggie turned twenty-one years of age on Christmas day of 1895, Popie Reitze

---

[275]Letter dated April 15, 1998, from Janet M. Leipert, Northwood Cemetery Company, 15th and Haines Streets, P.O. Box 5248, Philadelphia, Pennsylvania 19126, concerning burials in Fairmount Section, Lot 533 (Reitze, Bustard, Burtis, Knopp) and Ogontz Section, Lot 3 (Reitze, Hoenigmann, Freestone).

[276]Conversation on February 23, 1998, with John J. Page, 2524 Lombard Street, Philadelphia, Pennsylvania 19146-1025.

[277]*The Reitze Family Bible - Latin Vulgate Version.* (New York: D & J Sadlier, 1844) was in the possession of the late Josephine Thompson Marshall, 121 Reillywood Avenue, Haddonfield, New Jersey 08033-2201.

[278]Conversation on November 29, 1996, with the late Josephine Thompson Marshall, 121 Reillywood Avenue, Haddonfield, New Jersey 08033-2201.

probably proposed.[279] Having secured Maggie's promise to marry and after having worked out the logistics of how to support a wife, Popie Reitze appeared before the Assistant Clerk of the Orphans' Court to swear out his application for a marriage license.[280] It read as follows:

> State of Pennsylvania
> Philadelphia County
>
>   Personally appeared John Francis Reitze who hereby requests the Clerk of the Orphans' Court for the said County, to issue a License for the Marriage of himself to Maggie Cecilia Malloy and who, being duly sworn according to law, doth depose and say; that he was born in Philadelphia on the 30th day of November A.D. 1871 (sic); that he resides at No. 886 N. 43-1/2 St., W. Phila.; that he is by occupation in braidworks; that he is not related by blood or marriage to the person whom he desires to marry; that he has not been married before; that Maggie C. Malloy whom he is about to marry, was born in Philadelphia on the 25th day of December A.D. 1873 (sic); that she resides at No. 2210 Wharton St., Phila; is by occupation a woolsorter; that she has not been married before; that he knows no reason why the said marriage may not be lawfully made.[281]
>
> Sworn and subscribed before me (the Assistant Clerk of the Orphans' Court), this 20th day of November A.D. 1895.
>
>   (signed) John F. Reitze

Popie Reitze and Maggie were married in her parish on November 27, 1895, at the rectory of St. Thomas' Roman Catholic Church by the Reverend F.P. Coyle.[282] Their witnesses were Alphonsus Eger and Margaret McCoy. The church, which was established in 1885, was located at 17th and Morris Streets just a short distance from Maggie's house on Wharton Street.

EARNING A LIVING. According to the Philadelphia city directories, Popie Reitze held a variety of jobs before he married Maggie Malloy ranging from a laborer (1891), to a segarmaker

---

[279]There is a discrepancy concerning the year when Margaret Malloy was born. The Affidavit of Applicant for Marriage License issued November 20, 1895, states that she was born December 25, 1873. Her death certificate states that she was born December 25, 1874.

[280]Affidavit of Applicant for Marriage License # 81373, November 20, 1895, (John Francis Reitze & Maggie Cecilia Malloy), City of Philadelphia, Philadelphia City Archives, Philadelphia, Pennsylvania.

[281]According to her death certificate, Margaret C. Reitze was born December 25, 1874.

[282]Letter dated March 14, 2000, from Christine Friend, Assistant Archivist, Philadelphia Archdiocesan Historical Research Center, 100 East Wynnewood Road, Wynnewood, Pennsylvania 19096-3001.

(sic) (1892, 1894), to a clerk (1893). After he got married, the Philadelphia city directories and the Federal census schedules show that he worked for many years as a fireman at an oil refinery.[283,284,285] According to family legend, the oil refinery where Popie Reitze worked was known as the Atlantic Petroleum Storage Company (aka the Atlantic refinery) which was located in the Point Breeze section of South Philadelphia.[286,287]

By the beginning of the 20th Century when Popie Reitze went to work for the Atlantic refinery, production at the oil refinery was way up as the invention of the internal-combustion engine and the growing popularity of the automobile ensured a steadily growing market for **gasoline**, especially once Henry Ford began mass production of the model T.[288] Apparently, the sky was the limit when it came to the availability of oil. To quote one authority of his time:

> There is as little need to worry about an oil shortage in the United States, as
> there is to worry about a shortage of coal - at least not for a few thousand years.
> No one has yet to come to a full realization of the inexhaustible natural resources
> of the United States, or of Pennsylvania. Henry Ford can multiply his "flivvers"
> by the million and there will still be gasoline enough produced in the United
> States to run all of them "there and back".[289]

Interestingly, the petroleum industry's original product was **kerosine** to be used as a substitute for whale oil whose price had skyrocketed in the 1850s due to the over-hunting of

---

[283]1906, 1907, 1908, 1909, 1911, 1915, 1916, 1917 Philadelphia city directories.

[284]1910 U.S. Census (population), Pennsylvania, Philadelphia County, City of Philadelphia, E.D. 869, Family Number 199, National Archives Microfilm Publication T624, Roll 1406.

[285]1920 U.S. Census (population), Pennsylvania, Philadelphia County, City of Philadelphia, E.D. 1265, sheet 9A, line 34, National Archives Microfilm Publication T625, Roll 1638.

[286]Conversation on February 23, 1998, with John J. Page, 2524 Lombard Street, Philadelphia, Pennsylvania 19146-1025.

[287]Philadelphia Energy Solutions, <<http://pes-companies.com>>, downloaded August 15,2017, states that Philadelphia Energy Solutions (PES) was formed in 2012 as a result of a partnership between The Carlyle Group and Sunoco Inc., which is a subsidiary of Energy Transfer Partners, L.P. family of companies.

[288]Jeremy Shere, *Renewable: The World-Changing Power of Alternative Energy*, (New York: St. Martin's Press, 2013), p. 29.

[289]George P. Donehoo, editor-in-chief, *Pennsylvania: A History*, (New York & Chicago: Lewis Historical Publishing Company, Inc., 1926), p. 1674.

whales. Thus, in the beginning, there were no uses for other petroleum products such as gasoline which were burned off or discarded. In the United States, the petroleum industry was controlled at first by small operators who owned an oil well or a refinery where kerosine was distilled from crude oil, distributed in barrels, and sold by the gallon in retail stores. By the late 1870s, however, John D. Rockefeller had purchased most of the nation's oil refineries and consolidated their operation in the hands of his own company then known as the Standard Oil Company (ESSO).[290]

Although Rockefeller was given credit by many people of his time for eliminating much of the fluctuation in the price of oil and all the crazy speculation which was once associated with the business, his monopoly of the oil industry was dissolved forever by enactment of the Sherman Anti-Trust Act of 1890.[291] Since then, the oil industry has been divided into three main branches: the large companies known as the "majors"; medium-sized companies called the "independents;" and a host of small producers, refiners, and distributors. When Popie Reitze worked at the Atlantic refinery in South Philadelphia it was an "independent" oil refinery in operation since 1870.

Working at an oil refinery was an exceedingly dangerous job in Popie Reitze's day as the threat of fire was great. Even today, with the myriad of Federal, state, and local laws and regulations governing the industry, the threat of a fire at an oil refinery continues to be a cause of major concern. In fact, according to the present owners of the facility where Popie Reitze once worked, the number one goal of Philadelphia Energy Solutions at the Philadelphia Refining Complex is the health and safety of their employees, customers, contractors and the communities that host their operations.[292]

Fortunately for the public, the approach to safety by the Philadelphia Refining Complex is proactive with an emphasis on continuous improvement and the prevention of problems before they occur. In the event of an emergency, they also have available highly trained and skilled emergency responders who are quickly able to initiate an effective response. In Popie Reitze's day, the Atlantic refinery's commitment to operate its facility in a manner that protected the health and safety of its employees and the surrounding community was probably more reactive than proactive. Thus, Popie Reitze's job as a fireman, which he undoubtedly fulfilled faithfully for the Atlantic refinery, was doubly difficult and in many ways more dangerous than the same job is today.

---

[290]Jeremy Shere, *Renewable: The World-Changing Power of Alternative Energy*, (New York: St. Martin's Press, 2013), p. 29.

[291]George P. Donehoo, editor-in-chief, *Pennsylvania: A History*, (New York & Chicago: Lewis Historical Publishing Company, Inc., 1926), p. 1674.

[292]Philadelphia Energy Solutions, <<http://pes-companies.com>>, downloaded August 15, 2017.

WINE MAKING. When Popie Reitze wasn't working as a fireman at the oil refinery he is said to have enjoyed making elderberry wine.[293] Reportedly, he indulged his passion regardless of the weather and picked elderberries even on the hottest day of the year. The American or Sweet Elderberry (S. canadensis) favored by Popie Reitze is a deciduous shrub that belongs to the honeysuckle family. In June, it produces large, flat plates of flowerheads known as umbrells. Its edible purplish-black berries hang from the umbrells and can be considered ripe when the clusters begin to turn upside down. To ensure the quality of his wine, Popie Reitze always gathered his elderberries when they were plump and in full color. Experience dictated that he never pick elderberries that were overripe.

After discarding any of the leaves, bark, or roots which are said to be poisonous, Popie Reitze carefully washed his elderberries. Satisfied that they were clean, he probably followed a recipe for making elderberry wine similar to the one described below:

Ingredients:
1lb Elderberries	1 gallon boiling water
3 lbs granulated sugar	"claret" yeast sachet
8 oz chopped raisins	juice of 1 lemon
juice of 1 orange	1 vitamin B tablet
1 tsp yeast nutrient	

Instructions:
With a fork, strip the elderberries from the umbrells into a suitably large primary fermentation vessel.
Add 8 oz chopped raisins, juice of 1 lemon, juice of 1 orange, 1 vitamin B tablet, and 1 tsp of yeast nutrient. Add the boiling water.
When cool enough to handle, squeeze the fruit with your hands to extract the juice. Set aside for 1 day to infuse.
Add 2-1/2 lbs sugar and activated yeast and leave covered for 3 days.
Stain off liquid into demijohns, top up with another 1/4 lb sugar in each and, if necessary, with cooled boiled water.
Leave to ferment in a warm (65-75 degree), dark place.
Rack off the lees (i.e., draw off the sediment) into a clean demijohn when bubbling has subsided. Rack again 6 weeks later.
Bottle in dark green bottles when the wine is clear (use a lamp to shine through to the other side) and there has been no activity for some time.
Mature for at least six months before drinking.[294]

Unfortunately, Popie Reitze's passion for making elderberry wine may have gotten the best of him in the end. The elderberry is a large, vigorous, spreading plant that grows best in full

---

[293]Conversation on June 28, 1999, with the late James G. Page, 6781 Ramundo Drive, Doraville, Georgia 30360.

[294]Paul Teclaff's' Elderberry Page, <<http://www.patch-work.demon.co.uk/elder.htm>>, copyright 1999 by Patch-Work Computer Services.

sun and wet soil. Apparently, in pursuit of the finest berries for his brew, Popie Reitze stayed out too long one day in the broiling sun picking elderberries in the open fields that ran down to the Schuylkill River below Elmwood Avenue in West Philadelphia. According to family legend, he suffered a serious sunstroke from which he never recovered fully.

THE DEATH OF MAGGIE (MALLOY) REITZE. Popie Reitze and Maggie were happily married for twenty-three years when Maggie was stricken with the Spanish influenza. It arrived in Philadelphia in mid-September of 1918 just as the Great War in Europe was slowly dragging to a close.[295]

Despite the epidemic raging in the city, Maggie had no notion of being sick. She had recently received a post card from her oldest son, George, who was serving with the United States forces in France, saying that soon he would be home.[296] She was relieved and happy that her son was safe. She was probably too busy concentrating on their long awaited family reunion to notice that anything was wrong. Then, before she knew it, she was flat on her back too ill to help herself. Her daughters tried desperately to nurse her back to health, but the unremitting fever raged within her body. Weak and exhausted, she died on Monday, October 14, 1918, a date that was seared forever in the brain of Popie Reitze as the worst day of his life.[297] She was not yet 44 years old.

Notice of Maggie's untimely passing initially appeared in the *Philadelphia Public Ledger* on Wednesday, October 16, 1918. It read as follows:

> REITZE - Oct 14, MARGARET wife of John F. Reitze (nee Malloy). Due notice of the funeral will be given Thurs., 9 a.m.[298]

Full notice of Maggie's death later appeared in the *Philadelphia Public Ledger* on Thursday, October 17, 1918, as follows:

> REITZE - Of influenza, Oct 14, MARGARET, wife of John F. Reitze (nee Malloy). Funeral private Sat 9 a.m. 2324 Morris st. Int. Holy Cross Cem.

According to the records of the Oliver Bair Funeral Home, Maggie was buried in her own

---

[295]News Story, *Philadelphia Inquirer*, Sunday, October 13, 1918, p. 15.

[296]The original post card is in the possession of John J. Page, 2524 Lombard Street, Philadelphia, Pennsylvania 19146-1025.

[297]Death Certificate for Margaret C. Reitze, October 14, 1918, # 151416 & # 33809, Pennsylvania Department of Vital Statistics, New Castle, Pennsylvania.

[298]Obituary of Margaret Reitze, *Philadelphia Public Ledger*, Wednesday, October 16, 1918, p. 20 and Thursday, October 17, 1918, p. 17.

dress, in an oak casket with silver handles and a satin lining.[299] There was a crucifix and silver plate on her casket that read:

Margaret Reitze
December 25, 1874 - October 14, 1918

No Solemn Requiem Mass was performed for Maggie at St. Edmond's Roman Catholic Church. And, none but the immediate family gathered at her grave at Holy Cross Cemetery to say their final farewells.[300] Both the city and the nation were in the midst of a national epidemic. As directed by the Pennsylvania State Board of Health and the City of Philadelphia Board of Health, all churches, schools, lodges, theaters, bar rooms, and clubs were closed. No public meetings were to be held.[301]

In spite of all these dramatic measures to assure the safety of the city's residents, 4,597 people died in Philadelphia of influenza or pneumonia the week ending October 19, 1918.[302] Sadly, Maggie (Malloy) Reitze was one of them.

THE FALL OF 1918. American society in the Fall of 1918 is best described by Katherine Anne Porter in her short-story, *Pale Horse, Pale Rider*:

> No more war, no more plague, only the dazed silence that follows the ceasing of
> heavy guns; noiseless houses with the shades drawn, empty streets, the dead cold
> light of tomorrow.

Undoubtedly, Popie Reitze was severely traumatized by the epidemic of Spanish influenza that struck the city in the Fall of 1918, an event that most people have long since forgotten. The fact is, it killed his wife and he probably never recovered from her death. He kept going to work and going through the motions of every day life, but he didn't care much about anything any more. He still had four children living at home including his youngest daughter, Elizabeth Mary Reitze, who was only thirteen years old when her mother died, but he just couldn't cope with the responsibilities of being both a father and a mother to his children. His

---

[299]Oliver Bair Funeral Home Record for Margaret Reitze, October 19, 1918, Pennsylvania Historical Society, Philadelphia, Pennsylvania.

[300]Letter dated August 27, 1999, from Veronica T. Johnson, Assistant Director, Catholic Cemeteries Office, 111 South 38th Street, Philadelphia, Pennsylvania 19104-3179, regarding the burial of Margaret Rutze (sic) at Holy Cross Cemetery in Section 1, Range 14, Lot 21 owned by Catharine Malloy.

[301]News Story, *Philadelphia* Inquirer, Wednesday, October 16, 1918, p. 7.

[302]Alfred W. Crosby, *America's Forgotten Pandemic: The Influenza of 1918*, (New York: Cambridge University Press, 1989), p. 86.

world was fast collapsing all around him.

THE MARRIAGE OF POPIE REITZE AND EMILY MALLOY. As things continued to deteriorate in the Reitze household, Popie Reitze's mother-in-law, Catharine (Kennedy) Malloy, came up with what she thought was a good idea. It seems that her youngest daughter, Emily Malloy Murphy, had been widowed on April 4, 1919, and left with three young children to support - two boys and a girl.[303] She proposed that Popie Reitze and his widowed sister-in-law, Emily, get married and consolidate their households into one family at 2324 Morris Street.

According to family legend, Popie Reitze was unsure about the advisability of the marriage. For one, he was twenty years older than his sister-in-law, Emily, and, secondly, her deceased husband, John F. Murphy, appears to have been a tough act to follows as he was quite active in a number of fraternal and beneficial associations and he was also a member of the Holy Name Society of St. Edmond's Church.

Regardless of his continuing concerns, after a certain amount of prodding, Catharine (Kennedy) Malloy finally got her way and the widowed couple was married in 1921, probably at the rectory of St. Edmond's Church located at 2130 S. 21st Street.[304]

THE SPIRITUAL LIFE OF POPIE REITZE. Sadly, marriage did not improve Popie Reitze's disposition or demeanor. He remained withdrawn, detached, cold, and seemingly uncaring. He didn't have much to say to anyone in the family. He never smiled. He never embraced his children. He never played with his grandchildren or lovingly reached out to them in any way. They all attributed his unusual behavior to what they believed was his strict Quaker upbringing. More likely it was due to the tragic loss of his beloved wife, Maggie. Even after his conversion to Catholicism which took place about sixteen years after he married his second wife, Emily, Popie Reitze apparently never found any peace within himself.[305]

WHOSE HOUSE IS IT, ANYWAY. Even though Popie Reitze had next to no formal education and may have been severely depressed for most of his life after the death of his first wife, Maggie, he wasn't stupid. He owned his own home at 2324 Morris Street. His second wife, Emily, owned her house a few doors away at 2314 Morris Street. Reportedly, she inherited her house in 1919 upon the death of her first husband, John F. Murphy.

---

[303]Obituary of John F. Murphy, *Philadelphia Public Ledger*, Sunday, April 6, 1919, p. 15; Monday, April 7, 1919, p. 12; and Tuesday, April 8, 1919, p. 22.

[304]Conversation on February 23, 1998, with John J. Page, 2524 Lombard Street, Philadelphia, Pennsylvania 19146-1025.

[305]Conversation on February 23, 1998, with John J. Page, 2524 Lombard Street, Philadelphia, Pennsylvania 19146-1025.

After Popie Reitze married his widowed sister-in-law, Emily, she and her children moved into his house at 2324 Morris Street and she rented her house. Over the years, Emily, subtly (or not so subtly) suggested at various times that Popie Reitze put his house in both their names. He suggested to her that she make the first move by putting his name on the title to her house. She demurred and Popie Reitze was reportedly struck with a terminal case of inertia on this subject. Not surprisingly, the change in the title to his house never occurred on his watch.

The big surprise to the heirs of Popie Reitze including his son, John Francis Reitze, Jr., was the discovery after their father's death that, much to their chagrin, their late step-mother (and aunt), Emily, had quietly transferred the title of Popie Reitze's house to one of her sons for the paltry sum of one dollar. Legal wrangling ensued, the sale was invalidated, and ownership of the house passed, as it rightfully should, to Popie Reitze's namesake, John Francis Reitze, Jr.[306]

THE DEATH OF EMILY (MALLOY) REITZE. After thirty-one years of marriage to Popie Reitze, Emily (Malloy) Murphy Reitze died on May 4, 1951, at the age of 62. Her obituary appeared in the *Philadelphia Inquirer* on Sunday, May 6, 1951, as follows:

> REITZE-MURPHY - May 4, 1951, EMILY C. (nee Malloy), wife of John F.
> Reitze. Relatives and friends are invited to attend funeral, Tuesday, 8:30 a.m.,
> from her late residence 2324 Morris street. Solemn Requiem Mass, St.
> Edmond's Church, 10 A.M. Int. Holy Cross Cem. Friends may call Monday
> evening.[307]

On the morning of her burial, a funeral mass was performed for Emily (Malloy) Murphy Reitze at her parish church, St. Edmond's, located at 21st and Snyder Avenue. At the conclusion of the funeral mass, she was transported by hearse to Holy Cross Cemetery. There she was laid to rest in the Malloy Family Plot beside her first husband, John F. Murphy; her parents, Martin and Catharine (Kennedy) Malloy; her older sister, Maggie (Malloy) Reitze; and seven other of her brothers and sisters.[308]

THE DEATH OF POPIE REITZE. Popie Reitze carried on with great difficulty for another four years after the death of his second wife, Emily. Toward the end, he was stooped over and somewhat senile from picking all those elderberries in the hot sun. As was his custom, he kept

---

[306]Conversation on February 28, 1998, with John J. Page, 2524 Lombard Street, Philadelphia, Pennsylvania 19146-1025.

[307]Obituary of Emily C. Reitze-Murphy, *Philadelphia Inquirer*, Sunday, May 6, 1951, Section B, p. 19.

[308]Letter dated August 27, 1999, from Veronica T. Johnson, Assistant Director, Catholic Cemeteries Office, 111 South 38th Street, Philadelphia, Pennsylvania 19104-3179, regarding the burial of Emily Reitze at Holy Cross Cemetery in Section 1, Range 14, Lot 21 owned by Catharine Malloy.

his thoughts to himself. He even gave up playing pinochle, his favorite card game. He died February 15, 1955, at the age of 85 from myocarditis and arteriosclerosis.[309]

As the end approached, his son, John Francis Reitze, Jr., summoned Popie Reitze's youngest daughter, Elizabeth Mary (Reitze) Page, and his grandson, John J. Page, to Popie Reitze's bedside. Just as they arrived at the house, he took his last breath. He was finally at peace. Carefully, his two children and his grandson straightened out Popie Reitze's crooked body. Then, they dressed him. Only after those two tasks had been accomplished to the complete satisfaction of everyone present did they notify the doctor and the Oliver Bair Funeral Home that Popie Reitze was dead.[310]

His obituary appeared in the *Philadelphia Inquirer* on Thursday, February 17, 1955. It read as follows:

> REITZE - February 15, 1955, JOHN F., husband of the late Emily Malloy Reitze
> of 2324 Morris st. Relatives and friends are invited to the funeral on Friday at
> 8:30 A.M. from Oliver Bair's, 1820 Chestnut st. Solemn Requiem Mass at
> St. Edmond's Church, 10 A.M. Int. Holy Cross Cem. Friends may call
> Thursday evening.[311]

At the conclusion of his funeral mass, Popie Reitze was transported to Holy Cross Cemetery where he was laid to rest in a family plot apart from his beloved first wife, Maggie, and his oldest son, George B. Reitze, a veteran of World War I, who had died on January 29, 1934.[312,313]

Two years later, Popie Reitze was joined in the family plot at Holy Cross Cemetery by his

---

[309]Death Certificate for John F. Reitze, February 15, 1955, # 3251, Pennsylvania Division of Vital Statistics, New Castle, Pennsylvania.

[310]Conversation on September 12, 1999, with John J. Page, 2524 Lombard Street, Philadelphia, Pennsylvania 19146-1025.

[311]Obituary of John F. Reitze, *Philadelphia Inquirer*, Thursday, February 17, 1955, p 29.

[312]Letter dated August 25, 1997, from Veronica T. Johnson, Assistant Director, Catholic Cemeteries Office, 111 South 38th Street, Philadelphia, Pennsylvania 19104-3179, regarding the burial of John F. Reitze, Elizabeth M. Page, and John F. Reitze, Jr., at Holy Cross Cemetery in Section 15, Range 3, Lot 7 owned by Pauline Kelly.

[313]Letter dated September 20, 1999, from Veronica T. Johnson, Assistant Director, Catholic Cemeteries Office, 111 South 38th Street, Philadelphia, Pennsylvania 19104-3179, regarding the burial of George B. Reitz (sic) at Holy Cross Cemetery in Section 3, Range 3, Lot 30 owned by Henry Laverty.

youngest daughter, Elizabeth Mary (Reitze) Page, who died on April 27, 1957.[314] Her headstone, which was installed by her sons, John J. Page and James G. Page, is the only memorial marking the grave. Eighteen years later, on February 20, 1975, Popie Reitze's namesake, John Francis Reitze, Jr., was buried there, too.[315]

TIME MOVES ON. Popie Reitze's oldest daughter, Lucy Elizabeth (Reitze) Bach (named after Popie Reitze's mother, Lucy), died June 14, 1980, in Alameda, California.[316] She is buried in the Golden Gate National Cemetery in San Bruno, California, alongside her husband, Sgt. Joshua Leon Bach, who died May 21, 1951.[317,318] Her son, Jay Leon Bach, is buried nearby in the same national cemetery.[319] He was a World War II U.S. Navy aviation cadet who was killed on May 28, 1943, when his airplane crashed during flight training in Plumas County, California.[320]

Popie Reitze's last surviving daughter was Catherine Irene (Reitze) Kelly. She died March 21, 1995, at the age of 91 while she was living at the West Caldwell Care Center in West Caldwell, Essex County, New Jersey.[321] She was buried in Holy Sepulchre Cemetery in Totowa, New Jersey.

---

[314]Obituary of Elizabeth M. Page, *Philadelphia Inquirer*, Wednesday, May 1, 1957, p. 51.

[315]Obituary of John Reitze, *Philadelphia Inquirer*, Sunday, February 23, 1975, p. 21H.

[316]Obituary of Lucy Elizabeth Bach, *The Oakland Tribune*, Tuesday, June 17, 1980, p. A8.

[317]Letter dated June 24, 1998, from Gloria C. Gamez, Director, Department of Veterans Affairs, Golden Gate National Cemetery, 1300 Sneath Lane, San Bruno, California, 94066 concerning the burials of Joshua L. Bach and Lucy E. Bach in Section M, Grave 1810 and Jay Leon Bach in Section H, Grave 3755.

[318]Obituary of Joshua Leon Bach, *The Oakland Tribune*, Wednesday, May 23, 1951, p. E39.

[319]Letter dated June 24, 1998, from Gloria C. Gamez, Director, Department of Veterans Affairs, Golden Gate National Cemetery, 1300 Sneath Lane, San Bruno, California, 94066 concerning the burials of Joshua L. Bach and Lucy E. Bach in Section M, Grave 1810 and Jay Leon Bach in Section H, Grave 3755.

[320]News Story, *Feather River Bulletin*, Thursday, June 3, 1943, p. 1, California State Library, Sacramento, California.

[321]Death Certificate for Catherine I. Kelly, March 21, 1995, # 0014639, New Jersey State Department of Health, Trenton, New Jersey.

Known to all her nieces and nephews as Aunt Lizzie, Christopher and Lucy's oldest surviving daughter was born December 1, 1863, at 2819 Coates Street (now Fairmount Avenue).[322,323,324] She was short and stout, extremely frugal, and determined to live to be one-hundred years old. She is also said to have been active in the Presbyterian Church. Over the course of 97 years, she outlasted two husbands, all but one of her siblings, and a parrot that delighted her nieces and nephews whenever they came to visit.

EDWARD J. COLLINS. Aunt Lizzie's first husband was a man named Edward J. Collins. He was about four years older than Aunt Lizzie.

Although family legend has it that Edward J. Collins was Irish Catholic his actual family origins remain obscure except that he, his said sister, Sarah (Collins) Douglass, and his said brother, Charles Collins, all reported in the 1880 census schedule that they and their parents were born in Pennsylvania.[325] Another interesting fact about Edward J. Collins is that, as shown below, his said sister, Sarah, was married to George W. Douglass, whose younger half-brother, Henry G. Douglass, later became Aunt Lizzie's second husband. The enumeration was as follows:

3639 LUDLOW STREET:

Douglass, George	W M 42	fireman	b in Penna.
-, Sarah	W F 38 wife	keeping house	b in Penna.
Collins, Edward	W M 21 BIL(sic)	shipping clerk	b in Penna.
-, Charles	W M 40 BIL	typecaster	b in Penna.[326]

At the time Aunt Lizzie met her first husband, she was living at home with her mother,

---

[322]*The Reitze Family Bible - Latin Vulgate Version.* (New York: D & J Sadlier, 1844) was in the possession of the late Josephine Thompson Marshall, 121 Reillywood Avenue, Haddonfield, New Jersey 08033-2201.

[323]1863 Birth Register, Volume 6, page 130, (Elizabeth REES - December 1, 1863), City of Philadelphia, Philadelphia City Archives, Philadelphia, Pennsylvania.

[324]Jefferson M. Moak, *Philadelphia Street Name Changes*, (Philadelphia, Pennsylvania: Chestnut Hill Almanac, 1996), p. 26, says that Coates Street was renamed Fairmount Avenue in 1873.

[325]Conversation on August 12, 1995, with the late Josephine Thompson Marshall, 121 Reillywood Avenue, Haddonfield, New Jersey 08033-2201.

[326]1880 U.S. Census (population), Pennsylvania, Philadelphia County, City of Philadelphia, E.D. 570, sheet 6, line 28, National Archives Microfilm Publication T9, Roll 1186.

Lucy, at 3214 St. James Place and working in a chemical factory.[327] Compared to working in the factory, marrying Edward J. Collins probably looked pretty appealing.

In 1882, there were about 40 factories in Philadelphia manufacturing all sorts of chemicals under conditions that most likely would be considered extremely hazardous today. Chemical factories in Philadelphia manufactured sulfuric, muriatic, and nitric acids, as well as alum, ammonia, sulphate, animal charcoal, coal-tar products, chemical fertilizers, paints and colors, soaps, white lead, and pharmaceutical preparations.[328] Exactly where Aunt Lizzie worked or what kind of chemicals she was inhaling or absorbing through her skin on a daily basis is unknown. Whatever was in the air in that factory, one thing for sure is that it couldn't have been very good for Aunt Lizzie's health.

THE MARRIAGE OF AUNT LIZZIE TO EDWARD J. COLLINS. Aunt Lizzie's sworn deposition dated July 20, 1891, says she married Edward J. Collins on November 7, 1882, at St. James Roman Catholic Church at 38th and Chestnut Streets.[329,330] The marriage was not recorded by her mother, Lucy, in the *Reitze Family Bible* nor was her mother present at the ceremony.[331]

MARRY IN HASTE, REPENT AT LEISURE. In a sworn statement dated July 20, 1891, Aunt Lizzie said that:

> Immediately after the marriage we went to live at my mother's 3214 St. James Street; lived there about a year and four months. From my mother's we went to live at No. 7 [Somers] Place (near 37th and Market Streets); lived there about eight months. From there I moved to 36th and Aspen Streets; lived there about four months. From there I moved to 115 Mechanics Street, Camden, N.J.; lived

---

[327]1880 U.S. Census (population), Pennsylvania, Philadelphia County, City of Philadelphia, E.D. 582, sheet 31, line 34, National Archives Microfilm Publication T9, Roll 1186

[328]Scharf and Westcott, p. 2277.

[329]Lizzie Collins v Edward J. Collins, CP # 3, January Term 1891, Case # 31, Court of Common Pleas of Philadelphia County, Certifications Unit, Room 266, City Hall, Philadelphia, Pennsylvania 19107.

[330]Letter dated March 14, 2000, from Christine Friend, Assistant Archivist, Philadelphia Archdiocesan Historical Research Center, 100 East Wynnewood Road, Wynnewood, Pennsylvania 19096-3001 states that the Collins/Reitze marriage could not be located in any of the following parish records between the years 1878 and 1884: St. James, St. Agatha, St. Patrick, or St. John the Evangelist.

[331]Elizabeth M. Collins v Edward J. Collins, CP # 3, January Term 1891, Case # 31, Court of Common Pleas of Philadelphia County, Certifications Unit, Room 266, City Hall, Philadelphia, Pennsylvania 19107.

there about 3 or 4 months. From there we came to 3234 St. James Street, West
Philadelphia. We lived there until February 8, 1887, when I was forced to
withdraw.[332]

During the course of their marriage, Edward J. Collins appears to have worked as a
typesetter as he was listed variously in the Philadelphia city directories as a typefounder,
typecaster, typemaker, compositor and caster.[333] Aunt Lizzie claimed in her sworn statement that
her husband told her he made between $15 and $18 per week working at Johnson's Type
Foundry.[334] Evidently, he changed employer from time to time as he was working for the
MacKeller, Smith & Jordan Type Foundry located at 608 Sansom Street at the time of their
divorce. Printing and publishing was an important business enterprise in Philadelphia in those
days. There were, in fact, many printing and publishing houses in existence at the time that
provided a good income for skilled workers like Edward J. Collins.

Regrettably, Edward J. Collins' personal conduct was such that Aunt Lizzie's married life
was completely miserable. She stated in her sworn statement that he was a drunk, he would not
give her enough money to keep the house, and he beat her.[335] Her account of the sorry state of
her marriage was corroborated by her mother, Lucy, and her best friend, Sallie Keenan (who later
became the first wife of William Scott Chambers).

Aunt Lizzie also reported in her sworn statement that it was during the course of her
marriage to Edward J. Collins that she gave birth to a child that was born in December 1883,

---

[332]Elizabeth M. Collins v Edward J. Collins, CP # 3, January Term 1891, Case # 31,
Court of Common Pleas of Philadelphia County, Certifications Unit, Room 266, City Hall,
Philadelphia, Pennsylvania 19107.

[333]1881-1893 Philadelphia city directories.

1881	typefounder, h 3639 Ludlow
1882	typecaster, 3639 Ludlow
1884	typemaker, h 3639 Ludlow
1885	compositor, h 3205 St. James
1886	typemaker, h 3234 St. James
1887	caster, h 3234 St. James
1891	typecaster, h 3419 Ludlow
1893	caster, h 3339 Ludlow

[334]Elizabeth M. Collins v Edward J. Collins, CP # 3, January Term 1891, Case # 31,
Court of Common Pleas of Philadelphia County, Certifications Unit, Room 266, City Hall,
Philadelphia, Pennsylvania 19107.

[335]Elizabeth M. Collins v Edward J. Collins, CP # 3, January Term 1891, Case # 31,
Court of Common Pleas of Philadelphia County, Certifications Unit, Room 266, City Hall,
Philadelphia, Pennsylvania 19107.

thirteen months after they were married.[336] Further, she said that there was only one child born of the marriage and that the child died right after birth only living twenty-four hours.[337,338] Doubtlessly, Aunt Lizzie mourned the loss of her child all the rest of her life. In a poignant letter she wrote to her grandnephew and his wife in 1947, just after the birth of their first child, Aunt Lizzie said how happy she was to hear about the birth of the baby and how much she wished her baby, a little boy, had survived, but that he was born all blue and could not live.[339]

After living apart from Edward J. Collins for four years (which time included one very short-lived attempt at a reconciliation), Aunt Lizzie filed for divorce in the Philadelphia Court of Common Pleas.[340] Even after having been served personally with notice of the divorce petition pending against him, Edward J. Collins did not appear to contest the divorce action. The decree was final on October 3, 1891, on the grounds of desertion.

----

[336]Elizabeth M. Collins v Edward J. Collins, CP # 3, January Term 1891, Case # 31, Court of Common Pleas of Philadelphia County, Certifications Unit, Room 266, City Hall, Philadelphia, Pennsylvania 19107.

[337]A burial record for the child could not be found in the following sources:

> Philadelphia Cemetery Returns, 1883, Week Ending 1 December (New Philadelphia - Z) thru 23 December (A -Blockley Baptist), FHL Microfilm Roll 2069144.

> Philadelphia Cemetery Returns, 1883, Week Ending 20 December (Cathedral - Z) thru 1884 Week Ending 5 January (A - Laurel Hill), FHL Microfilm Roll 2069249.

[338]The following inconclusive burial record for an unknown male infant was found in the Philadelphia Cemetery Returns, 1884, Week Ending 5 January, FHL Microfilm Roll 2069249:

Name	Unknown Infant
Event Type	Found Dead
Event Date	19 Dec 1883
Event Place	Philadelphia, Philadelphia, Pennsylvania
Gender	Full Term Male
Race	White
Age	0
Birth Year (Estimated)	1883
Burial Date	29 December 1883
Burial Place	Potter's Field

[339]Conversation on September 16, 1999, with the late William Scott Chambers, 325 N.W. 95th Avenue, Plantation, Florida 33324-7021.

[340]Elizabeth M. Collins v Edward J. Collins, CP # 3, January Term 1891, Case # 31, Court of Common Pleas of Philadelphia County, Certifications Unit, Room 266, City Hall, Philadelphia, Pennsylvania 19107.

During the course of their separation, Aunt Lizzie lived with her mother at 21st and South Streets in South Philadelphia. After her divorce, she lived at 503 S. 23rd Street just around the corner from her mother, Lucy, and her siblings, Charles, John, and Josephine, who had moved to 2403 South Street.[341] Her ex-husband, Edward J. Collins, appears to have moved in with George W. and Sarah (Collins) Douglass who were then living at 3339 Filbert Street in West Philadelphia. He was still working at the same job as a caster.[342]

HENRY G. DOUGLASS. Aunt Lizzie's second husband was Henry Grafe Douglass who was known to all his nieces and nephews as Uncle Harry. Aunt Lizzie considered Uncle Harry to be "a good catch" as he had money and was kind and generous to Aunt Lizzie and all the members of her family.[343] He may have paid for the lawyer that handled Aunt Lizzie's divorce and he may even have helped his mother-in-law, Lucy, pay for an 18 karat gold diamond ring that she gave to her daughter, Josephine, for her sixteenth birthday.

From an analysis of census schedules, city directories, and death certificates, it appears that Uncle Harry was the son of Henry G. Douglass (Sr.) and his second wife, Sarah Ashton.[344,345] His father was born in Pennsylvania and his mother was born in New Jersey.[346] In the 1850 census, the Douglass family was enumerated in West Philadelphia where Uncle Harry's father operated an inn:

Henry G. Douglass	30	Inn Keeper	b in Penna.
Sarah	33		b in Penna. (sic)
George W.	[12]		b in Penna.
Charles	9		b in Penna.
Joseph [T.]	7		b in Penna.

---

[341]1892 Philadelphia city directory.

[342]1893 Philadelphia city directory.

[343]Conversation on August 12, 1995, with the late Josephine Thompson Marshall, 121 Reillywood Avenue, Haddonfield, New Jersey 08033-2201.

[344]Death Certificate for Harry Douglass, June 10, 1932, Lakeland, Gloucester Township, Camden County, New Jersey, State of New Jersey - Bureau of Vital Statistics, New Jersey State Archives, Trenton, New Jersey states that his mother's name was Sarah Ashton.

[345]Death Certificate for Kate A. McLaughlin, July 26, 1917, Hopewell Township, Cumberland County, New Jersey, State of New Jersey - Bureau of Vital Statistics, New Jersey State Archives, Trenton, New Jersey states that her mother's name was Sarah Ashton.

[346]See Appendix F, *The Douglass Family.*

Catharine   3   b in Penna.[347]

Uncle Harry was born on July 9, 1854.[348,349] He was the younger of the two children of Henry G. Douglass (Sr.) and Sarah Ashton.

Sometime after Uncle Harry was born, his father went West in search of gold.[350] It is unknown whether Uncle Harry's father set out alone or in a group. It is also unknown whether he took a sailing ship to California via the Straits of Magellan or whether he traveled by railroad to St. Louis, Missouri, which in those days was used as a jumping off point by many men for their long journey West across the prairie and the plains into the Rocky Mountains. By whatever means he may have traveled, the journey West probably presented Uncle Harry's father with severe hardships and dangers beyond anything he could have envisioned before he left home. Eventually, he reached California where he died on November 25, 1858.[351,352]

---

[347]1850 U.S. Census (population), Pennsylvania, Philadelphia County, West Philadelphia, page 501, National Archives Microfilm Publication M432, Roll 823.

[348]Affidavit of Applicant for Marriage License # 51028, April 19, 1892, (Henry G. Douglass & Lizzie Reitze), City of Philadelphia, Philadelphia City Archives, Philadelphia, Pennsylvania says his date of birth was July 9, 1854.

[349]Death Certificate for Harry Douglass, June 10, 1932, Lakeland, Gloucester Township, Camden County, New Jersey, State of New Jersey - Bureau of Vital Statistics, New Jersey State Archives, Trenton, New Jersey says his date of birth was July 30, 1853.

[350]E-mail dated December 12, 1997, from the late William Scott Chambers, 325 N.W. 95th Avenue, Plantation, Florida 33324-7021.

[351]Death of Henry Douglass, November 25, 1858, Stockton, San Joaquin County, California. Henry Douglass, Stockton State Hospital Commitment Register 1852-1862, p. 346, California State Hospital Records, 1856-1923, <<www.ancestry.com>>, downloaded January 2, 2017.

> Henry Douglass - Committed by M. C. Blake Co. Judge of San Francisco. Is a native of Penn. 42 yrs of age, says that he is married. Has been insane two weeks, cause of insanity unknown. Has no property. Admitted June 2d 1858. Died Nov 25th of marasmus. Grave No. 22. New G. Yd.

[352]Letter dated October 21, 1999, from the late Josephine Thompson Marshall, 121 Reillywood Avenue, Haddonfield, New Jersey 08033-2201 says she once found a newspaper clipping stored in a small jar at her grandmother's house that said Uncle Harry's father died in California (somewhere just outside of San Francisco). Much later, when she once again looked for the newspaper clipping, it had completely disintegrated. As far as she could recall, the clipping merely stated his death. She also said Aunt Lizzie gave her a $1.00 gold piece dated

After the death of Uncle Harry's father, Uncle Harry's mother, Sarah, began running a boarding house with the help of her sister, Mary Ashton. Thus, on the eve of the Civil War, the entire family was enumerated, together, in the 1860 census schedule in West Philadelphia as follows:

Sarah Douglass	35 (sic)	Boardinghouse Keeper	b in New Jersey
Catharine	14		b in Penna.
Henry	7		b in Penna.
Joseph	15		b in Penna.
Charles	20		b in Penna.
George	23	Mariner	b in Penna.
Mary Ashton	45		b in New Jersey [353,354]

The whereabouts of Uncle Harry are unclear immediately after the end of the Civil War, but he reemerges in the first enumeration of the 1870 census still living with his mother, Sarah, his sister, Kate, and his aunt, Mary Ashton:

Douglass, Sarah	56 F W		b in New Jersey
-, Kate	23 F W	Sales Lady	b in Penna.
-, Harry	18 M W	App to Augermaker	b in Penna.
Ashton, Mary	57 F W	At home	b in New Jersey [355]

Based on information contained in the second enumeration of the 1870 census, their street address was 7 Steinmetz Place. [356]

____

1864 (sic) and a tiny 25 cent gold piece which Aunt Lizzie said Uncle Harry's father sent home from California for his son, Harry, "the baby of the family."

[353] 1860 U.S. Census (population), Pennsylvania, Philadelphia County, City of Philadelphia, 24th Ward, page 999, National Archives Microfilm Publication M635, Roll 1175.

[354] 1861-1862 Philadelphia city directories state:

| 1861 | Douglass, Sarah, widow Henry, Chestnut ab Moore |
| 1862 | Douglass, Sarah, widow, 3 Lancaster av ab 32d (son, Charles G., at that address, too) |

[355] 1870 U.S. Census (population), First Enumeration, Pennsylvania, Philadelphia County, City of Philadelphia, Ward 27, page 75, National Archives Microfilm Publication M593, Roll 1445.

[356] 1870 U.S. Census (population), Second Enumeration, Pennsylvania, Philadelphia County, City of Philadelphia, Ward 27, page 141B, National Archives Microfilm Publication M593, Roll 1443, says:

#7 [STEINMETZ PLACE]
    Douglas (sic), C. (sic)   60 (sic) M (sic)

Then tragedy struck again. Within a year, Uncle Harry and Kate lost both their aunt, Mary Ashton, and their mother, Sarah (Ashton) Douglass, who died on December 30, 1870, and July [20], 1871, respectively.[357,358] Initially, Uncle Harry and Kate, are likely to have joined their half-brother, George W. Douglass, who was living at 9 Steinmetz Place in 1874. Then, according to the 1875 and 1876 Philadelphia city directories, they seem to have lived at 3625 Ludlow Street with their half-brother, Charles G. Douglass.

About fourteen years later, Uncle Harry's sister, Kate, finally got married. Then, on April 15, 1885, through sheer luck or dogged determination, Uncle Harry got a big break because he was appointed to the position of hoseman for the Philadelphia Fire Department.[359] His first assignment was with Engine Company Number 30 located at the rear of 3546 Germantown Avenue. In 1886, he was reassigned to Engine Company Number 16 located at 51st and Lancaster Avenue. On June 23, 1896, this engine company relocated to a new station on Belmont Avenue below Girard Avenue.

THE MARRIAGE OF AUNT LIZZIE AND UNCLE HARRY. Exactly how Aunt Lizzie met Uncle Harry is unknown, but she may have gotten to know him through her first husband, Edward J. Collins, whose said sister, Sarah Collins, was married to Uncle Harry's oldest brother, George W. Douglass. In fact, from an examination of the Philadelphia city directories, there appears to have been a long association between the Collins and the Douglass families going

---

-, C.	22 F
-, H.M. (sic)	15 M
Ashton, M.	70 (sic) F

[357]Obituary of Mary Ashton, *Philadelphia Public Ledger*, Monday, January 2, 1871, Philadelphia, Pennsylvania, <<www.genealogybank.com>>, downloaded January 1, 2017.

> On the 30th ult, MARY ASHTON in the [60th] year of her age. The relatives and friends
> of the family are respectfully invited to attend the funeral from her sister's residence, Mrs.
> Sarah A. Douglass, No. 7 Steinmetz Place, West. Phila. this (Monday) afternoon at 2
> o'clock.

[358]Obituary of Sarah Douglass, *Philadelphia Public Ledger*, Friday, July 21, 1871, Philadelphia, Pennsylvania, <<www.genealogybank.com>>, downloaded January 1, 2017.

> On the [20th] inst., Mrs. Sarah Douglass, wife of the late Henry G. Douglass in
> the 53rd year of her age.

> The relatives and friends of the family and also the [Siloam] Lodge No. 11 [N of
> L] are respectfully invited to attend the funeral from her late residence, No. 7
> Steinmetz Place, West Phila., on Sunday at one o'clock. To proceed to Mount
> Moriah Cemetery.

[359]Letter dated September 1, 1999, from F.F. Daniel J. Kenney, Archivist, Historian, Fireman's Hall, 147 N. 2nd Street, Philadelphia, Pennsylvania 19106-2010.

back to at least 1863 when both families lived in the vicinity of 31st and Ludlow Streets in West Philadelphia.

Regardless of how they may have met, the record indicates that Uncle Harry appeared at the courthouse and filed an application for a marriage license on April 19, 1892.[360] It read as follows:

State of Pennsylvania
Philadelphia County

Personally appeared Henry Graffe (sic) Douglass who hereby requests the Clerk of the Orphans' Court for the said County, to issue a License for the Marriage of himself to Lizzie Reitze and who, being duly sworn according to law, doth depose and say; that he was born in Phila. on the 9th day of July A.D. 1854; that he resides at No. 826 N. 46th St., Phila.; that he is by occupation fireman, that he is not related by blood or marriage to the person whom he desires to marry; that he has not been married before; that Lizzie Reitze whom he is about to marry, was born in Phila. on the --- day of (age 27 years) A.D. 18 --; that she resides at No. 2403 South St., Phila.; no occupation; that she has been once married before, and the marriage was dissolved by divorce - Lizzie Collins vs Edwd J. Collins, Phil. C.P. No. 3, [June 7, 91], No. 31. Decree Oct. 3/91 - Grounds "desertion"; that he knows no reason why the said marriage may not be lawfully made.

Sworn and subscribed before me (the Assistant Clerk of the Orphans' Court), this 19th day of April A.D. 1892.

(signed) Henry G. Douglass

Aunt Lizzie and Uncle Harry were married six days later on Monday, April 25, 1892, by the Reverend William Tracy, Minister of the Gospel at Christ Memorial, a Reformed Episcopal Church located on the corner of Chestnut and South 43rd Street.[361] According to Aunt Lizzie's grandniece, Josephine Thompson Marshall, she remembers seeing a clipping that appeared in one of the local newspapers concerning Aunt Lizzie's wedding reception.[362]

Although no mention of the wedding reception could be found in the *Philadelphia Public*

---

[360]Affidavit of Applicant for Marriage License # 51028, April 19, 1892, (Henry G. Douglass & Lizzie Reitze), City of Philadelphia, Philadelphia City Archives, Philadelphia, Pennsylvania.

[361]1892 Philadelphia city directory.

[362]Letter dated October 21, 1999, from the late Josephine Thompson Marshall, 121 Reillywood Avenue, Haddonfield, New Jersey 08033-2201 says that the clipping has long since disappeared.

Ledger or the *Philadelphia Inquirer*, a copy of the news story was later located among family papers. It read as follows in its entirety:

A WEDDING RECEPTION

Mr. And Mrs. H. Douglas Receive Their Friends

A wedding reception was given by Mr. and Mrs. Harry Douglas at the residence of Mrs. [...] Reitze, the brides mother, 2408 South Street, which was a brilliant affair. The bride whose [as] beautiful as well as accomplished, welcomed her many friends in a most hospitable manner. During the evening many talented ladies and gentleman participated in dancing and singing which was very much enjoyed. Congratulations were showered upon the happy couple, and every good fortune wished them on their journey through life.

The wedding guests included: Mrs. Reitze, Mr. McLaughlin and wife. George Hoskins and wife, Charles Reitze and Miss R. Kelly, E. Bushell and Miss Mary Maloy, John Reitze and Miss Maggie Maloy, John Wilson and Miss M. Mitchell, J. Young and wife, Charles O'Donnell and Miss Josie Reitze, Charles Holliday and Miss M. Lovett, J.R. Smith: Assistant Engineer of the Fire Department, William Black: Foreman of No. 1 P.F. Department, George F. Nellins, Charles Hoskins, the accomplished Miss May Evans, Samuel Linn and Miss Emma Carter, Harry Evans and Miss Eva Gray, Frank Gunn, Martin Kesler, Eddie Moore, Thomas Nolan, Ida Collins, John Jones, Martin Erb, J. Kennedy and Miss Alice Deveny, P. Fagan, Miss Lillian Cheston, Mr. McMahon, P. Clarke and Philadelphia's favorite comedian, Harvey Earle. This gentleman deserves much credit for the manner in which he worked to please the guests. The music was furnished by Professor Murry.[363]

AUNT LIZZIE AND UNCLE HARRY'S MARRIED LIFE TOGETHER. After they were married, Aunt Lizzie moved from South Philadelphia to 886 N. 43-1/2 Street in West Philadelphia where Uncle Harry lived as he needed to be close to the firehouse where he worked as a fireman. A year later, after Aunt Lizzie's brother, Charlie Reitze, married, her mother, Lucy, her brother, John, and her sister, Josephine, moved to West Philadelphia, too. Eventually, John and Josephine married and Aunt Lizzie, Uncle Harry, and Aunt Lizzie's mother, Lucy, moved to 4242 Lancaster Avenue.[364]

When Uncle Harry was not working as a fireman, he is said to have been active in

---

[363]E-mail dated January 2, 2011, from David H. Marshall, Jr., 121 Reillywood Avenue, Haddonfield, New Jersey 08033-2201, transmitting a transcription of the Wedding Announcement of Harry Douglas (sic) and Elizabeth Reitze.

[364]1900 U.S. Census (population), Pennsylvania, Philadelphia County, City of Philadelphia, E.D. 568, sheet 1, line 88, National Archives Microfilm Publication T623, Roll 1466.

Republican politics.[365] He also may have been a member of the Vesper Boat Club located at # 10 Boathouse Row in Philadelphia where a plaque is said to hang on the wall of the club that lists his name as one of the founding fathers.[366]

After Uncle Harry retired from the Philadelphia Fire Department on August 1, 1905, he and Aunt Lizzie moved to Gloucester City, Camden County, New Jersey, where they bought a large house at 15 Thompson Avenue which they owned free and clear.[367,368] He continued to be involved in local Republican politics and, after women won the right to vote through passage of the Nineteenth Amendment to the Constitution in 1920, Aunt Lizzie served as a local area committeewoman for the Republican Party.[369] She also served as a member of the Gloucester Board of Health.[370]

As was her usual custom, Aunt Lizzie also took pains to keep in touch with other members of the family including her mother's brothers and sisters - the Devlins - and the descendants of her father's sisters - the Wicks/Weeks and the Westcotts/Wolcotts.[371]

GIFTS AND INHERITANCES. According to family legend, there came a day when Aunt Lizzie notified her nephew, Henry Grafe Chambers, to present himself at her house to collect his

---

[365]Obituary of Henry G. Douglas (sic), *Camden Courier Post*, Monday, June 13, 1932, p. 2.

[366]Conversation on August 12, 1995, with David H. Marshall, Jr., 121 Reillywood Avenue, Haddonfield, New Jersey 08033-2201.

[367]Letter dated September 1, 1999, from F.F. Daniel J. Kenney, Archivist, Historian, Fireman's Hall, 147 N. 2nd Street, Philadelphia, Pennsylvania 19106-2010.

[368]1910 U.S. Census (population), New Jersey, Camden County, Gloucester City, E.D. 98, sheet 7B, line 61, Family Number 143, National Archives Microfilm Publication T624, Roll 872.

[369]Conversation on September 14, 1999, with the late Josephine Thompson Marshall, 121 Reillywood Avenue, Haddonfield, New Jersey 08033-2201.

[370]Obituary of Henry G. Douglas (sic), *Camden Courier Post*, Monday, June 13, 1932, p. 2.

[371]Conversation on September 14, 1999, with the late Josephine Thompson Marshall, 121 Reillywood Avenue, Haddonfield, New Jersey 08033-2201 in which she recalled that in the mid-1930s after she graduated from high school she was interviewed for a job by an executive at the Sherwin-Williams Paint Company in downtown Philadelphia. He did not hire her because he said that his last two secretaries had resigned after getting married and she "looked too eligible." Later, she learned from Aunt Lizzie that the man who interviewed her was married to one of the descendants of Christopher Reitze's sisters.

inheritance as she wanted to give it to him while she was still alive. Aunt Lizzie's nephew, named after Uncle Harry by Aunt Lizzie's sister, Josephine (Reitze) Chambers, appeared at the appointed hour to collect his legacy. Surprisingly, Aunt Lizzie's gift turned out to be an antique porcelain water pitcher, wash bowl, and tooth brush holder. Although the nature of the gift was unusual, her nephew accepted it with grace, and took it home where he presented it to his wife. Reportedly, they both had a good laugh after which they dutifully put the gift on display.[372] Aunt Lizzie also gave her nephew the Civil War U.S. Cavalry discharge papers of his granduncle, John Henry Devlin, and the Civil War U.S. Navy pension certificate of George W. Douglass, Uncle Harry's oldest brother.[373]

Aunt Lizzie also gave (or promised to give) her niece, Elizabeth Mary Reitze, a pair of diamond earrings. Elizabeth Mary Reitze was the youngest daughter of Aunt Lizzie's brother, John Reitze, who had named his daughter after his older sister.   Apparently, Elizabeth Mary Reitze visited Aunt Lizzie often and they got along well despite her mischievous efforts to teach Aunt Lizzie's parrot to recite provocative verse. Unfortunately, Elizabeth Mary Reitze predeceased Aunt Lizzie. After her death in 1957, her oldest sister, Lucy Elizabeth (Reitze) Bach, asked Aunt Lizzie whether she could have the diamond earrings. Whatever the answer from Aunt Lizzie, the present whereabouts of the diamond earrings are unknown.[374]

Aunt Lizzie didn't forget her grandniece, Josephine Thompson Marshall, either. She gave her the *Reitze Family Bible* and a speller (copyrighted 1844) that belonged to one of the Devlin sisters. She also gave her grandniece a scraf that once belonged to Annie Oakley. According to family legend, Uncle Harry's brother (possibly Charles G. Douglass who was a Sergeant on the Philadelphia Police Department) once acted as an official escort to Annie Oakley. At the conclusion of her stay in the city, Annie Oakley gave Uncle Harry's brother her scarf in appreciation for showing her around town.[375]

Aunt Lizzie also offered her grandniece a quantity of cemetery deeds which her grandniece respectfully declined to accept at the time and which Aunt Lizzie took with her when she moved to the Presbyterian Home. Subsequently, Aunt Lizzie gave the cemetery plot deeds to

---

[372]The antique porcelain water pitcher, wash bowl, and tooth brush holder are in the possession of Kathryn C. Torpey, 5035 Domain Place, Alexandria, Virginia 22311-5066.

[373]These documents are in the possession of Kathryn C. Torpey, 5035 Domain Place, Alexandria, Virginia 22311-5066.

[374]Conversation on February 23, 1998, with John J. Page, 2524 Lombard Street, Philadelphia, Pennsylvania, 19146-1025.

[375]The scarf given to Charles G. Douglass by Annie Oakley was in the possession of the late Josephine Thompson Marshall, 121 Reillywood Avenue, Haddonfield, New Jersey 08033-2201.

the Presbyterian Home in Haddonfield. Among them may have been the deed to the plot at Fernwood Cemetery where Aunt Lizzie's mother, Lucy, was buried and the deed to the plot at Glenwood Cemetery where Christopher Reitze and five of the children who did not survive their infancy were buried. When Aunt Lizzie's grandniece asked the Presbyterian Home about the deeds after Aunt Lizzie died, she was told they were turned over to the Synod.[376]

THE DEATH AND BURIAL OF UNCLE HARRY. Uncle Harry died from uremia on June 10, 1932, just seventeen days after Aunt Lizzie admitted him to the Camden County Mental Hospital in Lakeland, Gloucester Township, Camden County, New Jersey.[377] He was 78 years old and in the end stages of chronic nephritis. Despite her best efforts, Aunt Lizzie, who was 69 years old, was no longer able to take care of him at home.[378]

Uncle Harry's obituary appeared in the *Camden Courier Post* on Monday, June 13, 1932. It read as follows:

> HENRY G. DOUGLAS (sic) - The funeral of Henry G. Douglas (sic), husband of Mrs. Elizabeth Douglas (sic), active in Republican politics, will be held tomorrow afternoon at his late home, 15 Thompson avenue, Gloucester. Burial will be in Lawnview Cemetery, Fox Chase, Philadelphia. He died Friday. His wife was a former member of the Gloucester Board of Health.[379]

Uncle Harry was buried at Lawnview Cemetery in a plot that had been purchased jointly by Aunt Lizzie and Uncle Harry's sister, Kate A. McLaughlin. The first to be buried in the plot was his brother-in-law, William P. McLaughlin, and then his sister, Kate A. McLaughlin.[380] After their deaths, a large, heavy, headstone was placed on the grave which read:

---

[376]Letter dated October 21, 1999, from the late Josephine Thompson Marshall, 121 Reillywood Avenue, Haddonfield, New Jersey 08033-2201.

[377]Death Certificate for Harry Douglass, June 10, 1932, Lakeland, Gloucester Township, Camden County, New Jersey, State of New Jersey - Bureau of Vital Statistics, New Jersey State Archives, Trenton, New Jersey.

[378]Conversation on April 14, 1997, with the late Josephine Thompson Marshall, 121 Reillywood Avenue, Haddonfield, New Jersey 08033-2201.

[379]Obituary of Henry G. Douglas (sic), *Camden Courier Post*, Monday, June 13, 1932, p. 2.

[380]Letter dated February 18, 1997, from Karen L. Crawford, Lawnview Cemetery, 500 Huntingdon Pike, Rockledge, Pennsylvania 19046, regarding burials in Lot 340, Fox Chase Lawn Section, belonging to Kate A. McLaughlin (deceased) and Mrs. Harry Douglass.

MacLAUGHLIN (sic)

1853 William P. 1915
his wife
1847 Kate A. 1917

After Uncle Harry was buried, Aunt Lizzie commissioned a stonemason to add his epitaph to the headstone. It read as follows:

1854 Henry G. Douglass 1932

THE PRESBYTERIAN HOMES OF NEW JERSEY. After Aunt Lizzie was widowed, she stayed on at 15 Thompson Avenue until about 1935. Several of her nieces and nephews continued to visit her on a regular basis taking the train from Camden after first having crossed the Delaware River from Philadelphia on a ferry.[381]

Finally, the big four bedroom house in Gloucester City just a short half block walk from the railroad tracks became too much for Aunt Lizzie to handle so she appears to have converted it to a multi-family rental property.[382] She then appears to have moved about a mile away to 821 Middlesex Street, Gloucester City, Camden County, New Jersey. There she became a lodger in the home of Albert and Delcinia Slater.[383]

Later, she moved to the Presbyterian Home in Belvidere, Warren County, New Jersey. According to family legend, Aunt Lizzie transferred the title to her house in Gloucester City to the Presbyterian Homes of New Jersey in exchange for life care.

Apparently, the Presbyterian Home in Belvidere was entirely to Aunt Lizzie's liking and must have met her needs substantially as she was still living there as late as March 1948 when she sent a birthday card to her great-grandniece, Kathryn Judith Chambers, on the occasion of her first birthday. The birthday card contained the following short hand-written note addressed to her great-grandniece's mother:

---

[381]Conversation on November 29, 1996, with the late Josephine Thompson Marshall, 121 Reillywood Avenue, Haddonfield, New Jersey 08033-2201.

[382]1940 U.S. Census (population), New Jersey, Camden County, Gloucester City, Ward 3, E.D. 4-51, page 61B, lines 53-56, families 238-239, National Archives Microfilm Publication T627, Roll 2321.

[383]1940 U.S. Census (population), New Jersey, Camden County, Gloucester City, Ward 1, E.D. 4-41, page 4A, line 31, family 77, National Archives Microfilm Publication T627, Roll 2321.

85

Belvidere, N.J.

Dear Gloria,

Enclosed you will find $1.00 for your darling on her first birthday from me, Aunt Lizzie. Hope you are all well. We have a guest from Princeton, a Miss Murray. She says she was at your wedding. Give my love to Billie and love to you and Judy. Wishing her many birthdays.

Aunt Lizzie Douglass[384]

Later, a second Presbyterian Home was built in Haddonfield, Camden County, New Jersey. Aunt Lizzie transferred to that facility as it was closer to where she had lived in Gloucester City.[385]

THE DEATH OF AUNT LIZZIE. Aunt Lizzie died at the Presbyterian Home in Haddonfield on April 14, 1961, at the age of 97, her ambition to live to be one-hundred years old thwarted by a fatal attack of auricular fibrillation.[386]

Her obituary appeared in the *Camden Courier Post* on Saturday, April 15, 1961. It read as follows:

> DOUGLASS - On April 14, 1961, Elizabeth, widow of Harry G. of the Presbyterian Home, formerly of Gloucester, N.J. Relatives and friends of the family are invited to attend the funeral services on Monday at 1:30 p.m. at Stretch Funeral Home, 8 Kings Highway, West Haddonfield. Interment at Lawnview Cemetery, Fox Chase, PA.[387]

Aunt Lizzie was buried at Lawnview Cemetery in the same plot as her husband, Uncle Harry, and her in-laws, William and Kate (Douglass) McLaughlin.

---

[384]Birthday card from Aunt Lizzie Douglass is in the possession of Kathryn C. Torpey, 5035 Domain Place, Alexandria, Virginia 22311-5066.

[385]Conversation on September 14, 1999, with the late Josephine Thompson Marshall, 121 Reillywood Avenue, Haddonfield, New Jersey 08033-2201.

[386]Death Certificate for Elizabeth Douglass, April 14, 1961, Haddonfield Borough, Camden County, New Jersey, State Department of Health of New Jersey, Trenton, New Jersey. Note: It is unclear when Aunt Lizzie entered the Presbyterian Home in Haddonfield. Her death certificate issued on April 14, 1961, states *"length of stay in this place 18 years,"* which could be in error given that the birthday card she sent in March 1948 states *"Belvidere, N.J."*

[387]Obituary of Elizabeth Douglass, *Camden Courier Post*, Saturday, April 15, 1961, p. 13.

For some reason, Aunt Lizzie's name was not added to the large headstone that marks the grave. Josephine Thompson Marshall, the only one of Aunt Lizzie's surviving nieces or nephews who can actually remember attending her funeral, recalls that:

> I remember it well. After all, I visited her often and saw her through her final illness. I had no say as the Home was in charge of her affairs. I did go over and pick out her clothes and a special pair of earrings. The Home saw that the funeral was very well done. My husband and I also attended her funeral as did several former friends and neighbors. As far as I know, she left no will, having nothing I know of to leave. And why there is no date on her tombstone, that was up to the Home - I had no say.[388]

Josephine Irene Reitze

Christopher and Lucy's youngest daughter, Josephine Irene Reitze, was born July 4, 1877, at 2721 Scott Street.[389,390] She was a remarkable woman with a terrific sense of humor who loved vacations and hated her first name preferring instead to be called Jo or Josey by her family and close friends. Her grandchildren always referred to her as Nannie. She was strongly decisive as a child and as an adult. She was married for fifty-four years to William Scott Chambers known to everyone in the family as Grandpop Chambers. For as long as she lived, she was respected as the family matriarch and much loved as a wife, mother, and grandmother.

THE MARRIAGE OF NANNIE AND GRANDPOP CHAMBERS. Although there is no family legend concerning how Nannie and Grandpop Chambers met, he always said that the first time he laid eyes on her she was walking across the Gray's Ferry Bridge. Even though Nannie was only twelve years old at the time, she must have made a powerful impression on Grandpop Chambers because, later, he was able to describe accurately exactly what she was wearing on that fateful day.[391]

---

[388]Letter dated October 21, 1999, from the late Josephine Thompson Marshall, 121 Reillywood Avenue, Haddonfield, New Jersey 08033-2201.

[389]1877 Birth Register, p. 181, (Josephine REIZ - July 4, 1877), City of Philadelphia, Philadelphia City Archives, Philadelphia, Pennsylvania.

[390]Jefferson M. Moak, *Philadelphia Street Name Changes*, (Philadelphia, Pennsylvania: Chestnut Hill Almanac, 1996), p. 94, says that Scott Street from 27th to 28th Streets, north of Poplar, was changed to George Street in 1897.

[391]Conversation on September 14, 1999, with the late Josephine Thompson Marshall, 121 Reillywood Avenue, Haddonfield, New Jersey 08033-2201.

Nannie and Grandpop Chambers may not actually have meet until sometime in 1894.[392]
Grandpop Chambers was ten years older than Nannie and a recent widower. Her mother, Lucy,
ever mindful of potential marital catastrophes, forewarned her youngest daughter about the perils
of marrying an older man, especially a widower.[393] Throwing caution to the wind, Nannie
decided to take the plunge anyway. Grandpop Chambers gave Nannie a lovely engagement ring
of which she was very proud. Although the diamond was small, the setting was exquisite - what
was then known as a rose setting.[394]

After they became officially engaged, Grandpop Chambers appeared before the Assistant
Clerk of the Orphans Court of the City of Philadelphia on March 27, 1896, to swear out an
affidavit for a marriage license.[395] It read as follows:

> State of Pennsylvania
> Philadelphia County
>
> Personally appeared William Scott Chambers who hereby requests the
> Clerk of the Orphans' Court for the said County, to issue a License for the
> Marriage of himself to Josephine Irene Reitze and who, being duly sworn
> according to law, doth depose and say: that he was born in Phila. on the 5th day
> of June A.D. 1867; that he resides at No. 3223 Marston St.. W. Phila.;[396] that he
> is by occupation fireman B. & O. R. R., that he is not related by blood or
> marriage to the person whom he desires to marry; that he has once been married
> before, and the marriage was dissolved by death about 1894 - in Phila; that
> Josephine I. Reitze whom he is about to marry, was born in Phila. on the 4th day
> of July A.D. 1874 (sic); that she resides at No. 4230 Lancaster Ave., W. Phila.;
> is by occupation domestic; that she has not been married before, that he knows
> no reason why the said marriage may not be lawfully made.

---

[392]Grandpop Chambers' first wife - Sallie (White) Keenan - was best friends with
Nannie's older sister - Elizabeth (Reitze) Douglass - thus it is supposed that Nannie probably met
Grandpop Chambers sometime during his first marriage which only lasted seven months as his
first wife was terminally ill with consumption at the time of their marriage.

[393]Conversation (date unknown) with the late William Scott Chambers, 325 N.W. 95th
Avenue, Plantation, Florida 33324-7021.

[394]The engagement ring was in the possession of the late Josephine Thompson Marshall,
121 Reillywood Avenue, Haddonfield, New Jersey 08033-2201.

[395]Affidavit of Applicant for Marriage License # 84108, March 27, 1896, (William Scott
Chambers & Josephine Irene Reitze), City of Philadelphia, Philadelphia City Archives,
Philadelphia, Pennsylvania.

[396]Jefferson M. Moak, *Philadelphia Street Name Changes*, (Philadelphia, Pennsylvania:
Chestnut Hill Almanac, 1996), p. 69, says that Marston Street between the Schuylkill River and
33rd Street, south of Pine Street, was changed to Lombard Street in 1897.

Sworn and subscribed before me (the Assistant Clerk of the Orphans' Court),
this 27th day of March A.D. 1896.

(signed) William Scott Chambers

Having fibbed about Nannie's age to make her twenty-one thus skirting the official "red-tape" requirement for a parent's written permission to marry, Nannie and Grandpop Chambers were united in marriage on March 30, 1896, by the Reverend Jacob G. Walker, Minister of the Gospel at the Mantua Baptist Church located on the corner of Fairmount Avenue and North 40th Street in West Philadelphia.[397]

MARRIED LIFE IN WEST PHILADELPHIA. A marriage announcement appeared in the *Philadelphia Inquirer* on April 4, 1896. It read as follows:

MARRIED

CHAMBERS - REITZE - On March 30, 1896, by J.G. Walker, D.D., William S. Chambers and Miss Josephine I. Reitze, all of West Philadelphia.[398]

After they were married, Nannie and Grandpop Chambers lived briefly with his family, but Nannie reported that all the Chambers snored, loudly, and she couldn't get any sleep so she and Grandpop Chambers set up housekeeping in a home of their own located at 1234 S. 34th Street in the Gray's Ferry neighborhood of Philadelphia.[399]

Both of their children were born at the house on 34th Street. Her son, Henry Grafe Chambers, who was named after Nannie's brother-in-law, Henry Grafe Douglass, was born first on January 8, 1897.[400] The birth was attended by Doctor L.P. Lampen, M.D., of 618 N. 40th Street. Her daughter, Lucy Elizabeth Chambers, who was named after Nannie's mother, was

---

[397]Although the Affidavit of Applicant for Marriage License contains a notation that the marriage occurred at Williamsen's Baptist Church at 44th and Westminster Avenue, the 1896 Philadelphia city directory states that the Rev. J.G. Walker was the minister of the Mantua Baptist Church at N 40th c Fairmount Avenue.

[398]Notice of Marriage, *Philadelphia Inquirer*, Saturday, April 4, 1896, p. 9, <<www.newspapers.com>>, downloaded August 11, 2017.

[399]Conversation on September 14, 1999, with the late Josephine Thompson Marshall, 121 Reillywood Avenue, Haddonfield, New Jersey 08033-2201.

[400]Original birth certificate of Henry Graef (sic) Chambers, No. C52220, January 8, 1897, Philadelphia, Pennsylvania, is in the possession of Kathryn C. Torpey, 5035 Domain Place, Alexandria, Virginia, 22311-5066.

born the very next year on March 11, 1898.[401] Nannie reported to her granddaughter, Josephine Thompson Marshall, that the baby was born with a mysterious film over her eyes. Apparently, the doctor quickly cut the membrane with his cufflinks to keep the baby from going blind. Nannie also told her granddaughter that she had a third child that was stillborn. She said she was almost nine months pregnant when she lost the baby. Apparently, she was getting off the trolley when it suddenly lurched forward. She lost her balance and fell. The baby was born dead that night. Nannie told her granddaughter that the child's face haunted her all the rest of her life.[402]

Nannie didn't have to work after she got married because Grandpop Chambers was well paid by the railroad. Gone were the days when she had to work at the cigar factory and occasionally help her mother dress dead bodies for the Oliver Bair Funeral Home. Instead, she was free to devote herself to keeping house and raising her children.

According to her granddaughter, Nannie was an excellent cook. Many of her recipes came from her mother, Lucy. When her son, Harry, got married, Nannie taught her daughter-in-law, Mary Ann Chambers, how to cook. Nannie's pie crusts were renowned. She was especially proud of her pumpkin pie and her mincemeat pie which was liberally laced with whisky. She also made a fine walnut cake that was always in demand especially when the First United Presbyterian Church at 52nd and Chester Avenue held bake sales to raise money during World War II. While she was not particularly interested in canning fruits and vegetables, she did make tasty jelly and elderberry wine. On Thanksgiving Day, she served all her specialities on her best china including a roasted turkey prepared with her special mix of herbs and spices, bread stuffing, cauliflower in cheese sauce, and an array of fancy salads which she took delight in serving to her family long before serving salads was popular with most women.[403]   At the end of the meal, everyone was treated to an assortment of Nannie's delicious pies.[404]

Like many railroad families, Nannie and Grandpop Chambers enjoyed eating raw oysters whenever their son, Harry, who was also a fireman and an engineer on the railroad, brought home big bags of fresh oysters from the Jersey shore. They would pile the oysters on the kitchen table,

----

[401]Although no record of the birth of Lucy Elizabeth Chambers was found in the 1898 Birth Register for the City of Philadelphia, the birth is recorded in the Christian Methodist Episcopal Church Records, 1897 to 1926, Philadelphia, Pennsylvania, Genealogical Society of Pennsylvania, Philadelphia, Pennsylvania, Microfilm Roll XX342:8.

[402]Conversation on September 14, 1999, with the late Josephine Thompson Marshall, 121 Reillywood Avenue, Haddonfield, New Jersey 08033-2201.

[403]The complete set of china is in the possession of Kathryn C. Torpey, 5035 Domain Place, Alexandria, Virginia 22311-5066.

[404]Conversation on September 14, 1999, with the late Josephine Thompson Marshall, 121 Reillywood Avenue, Haddonfield, New Jersey 08033-2201.

cut them open with a sharp knife, and swallow them whole right out of the shell. Although Nannie is reported not to have been a drinker of hard liquor, she was known to have occasionally washed down her raw oysters with a glass of beer.[405]

Despite her large frame, Nannie was a graceful and stylish lady. Both she and her daughter, Lucy, were always very well dressed. In fact, she and her daughter enjoyed shopping for clothes together at Bonwit-Teller, and they had hats made a Gimbles. They also liked to accessorize their outfits with jewelry such as Nannie's beautiful black jet necklace and the earrings she made out of buttons from one of her mother's dresses.[406,407] Reportedly, Nannie and her daughter had many a good time shopping together. After her daughter died, Nannie carried on the family tradition with her granddaughter, an activity they both enjoyed immensely.[408]

Nannie was also an excellent seamstress. She had a Singer sewing machine that she used to make dresses for herself, her daughter, and her granddaughter. In fact, there was a children's fancy dress shop on Walnut Street in downtown Philadelphia where Nannie shopped for the latest in children's fashions. After she bought a dress, she would use her ingenuity to copy the pattern, altering each garment slightly at the neckline or the sleeves to make a lovely assortment of dresses for her granddaughter. Although Nannie was not particularly interested in tatting, crocheting, or knitting, she excelled in delicate needlework and alterations. Such was her skill that she even tailored her daughter's wool coat with sealskin trim so that it fit her granddaughter beautifully.[409] Nannie made sure that her granddaughter, Josephine, always felt like one of the best dressed children in the neighborhood.[410]

LEISURE ACTIVITIES. Much of Nannie's leisure time was devoted to projects in support of Grandpop Chambers' local labor union activities. She was an active member of the local

---

[405]Conversation on September 14, 1999, with the late William Scott Chambers, 325 N.W. 95th Avenue, Plantation, Florida 33324-7021.

[406]The black jet necklace is in the possession of Cynthia Scott Chambers, 1450 S.W. 70th Avenue, Plantation, Florida 33317.

[407]The earrings are in the possession of Kathryn C. Torpey, 5035 Domain Place, Alexandria, Virginia 22311-5066.

[408]Letter dated October 21, 1999, from the late Josephine Thompson Marshall, 121 Reillywood Avenue, Haddonfield, New Jersey 08033-2201.

[409]Conversation on September 14, 1999, with the late Josephine Thompson Marshall, 121 Reillywood Avenue, Haddonfield, New Jersey 08033-2201.

[410]Conversation on September 14, 1999, with the late Josephine Thompson Marshall, 121 Reillywood Avenue, Haddonfield, New Jersey 08033-2201.

ladies' auxiliary of the Brotherhood of Locomotive Firemen and Enginemen known as the Pride of William Penn Lodge # 433.[411] According to family legend, Nannie even served as President of the ladies auxiliary for one term.[412] The ladies' auxiliary was primarily a social organization. Several times a year, they gave covered dish suppers and fancy dress parties at the Union Hall to which the whole family including children and grandchildren were invited to attend. They also gave costume parties at Halloween for the children.[413]

Reportedly, Nannie loved vacations. According to her granddaughter, Josephine Thompson Marshall, every year, Nannie arranged for her family to go to the Jersey shore for the whole month of August. They always rented a large apartment at the southern end of Wildwood near Wildwood Crest where the family could get away from the heat of the city and enjoy the sun, sand, and surf undisturbed.[414]

She also liked to travel. In 1922, Grandpop Chambers was elected local representative to the 29th National Convention of the Brotherhood of Locomotive Firemen and Enginemen. The convention was to be held in Houston, Texas, from May 8 to June 8, 1922.[415] As Nannie was an active member of the ladies auxiliary, she wanted to attend the convention with Grandpop Chambers. According to family legend, she asked her son and daughter-in-law, Harry and Mary Ann Chambers, who lived a few doors away, to take care of her granddaughter (their niece) who was in kindergarten at the time. Having made arrangements for the care of her granddaughter, Nannie packed their bags and she and Grandpop Chambers set out on their great adventure - a three month, round-trip journey by train across America. After the convention was over, Nannie and Grandpop Chambers toured the West. Among the many sights they saw on their travels were the Alamo, Hollywood, Catalina Island, and Pike's Peak. Nannie is reported to have sent back many postcards during the trip. According to her granddaughter, Nannie must have had dyslexia as the messages on the postcards were riddled with misspellings. It seems that Nannie spelled

---

[411]Obituary of Josephine I. Chambers, *Philadelphia Inquirer*, Saturday, May 5, 1962, p. 7.

[412]Conversation on April 27, 1996, with the late William Scott Chambers, 325 N.W. 95th Avenue, Plantation, Florida 33324-7021.

[413]Conversation on September 18, 1999, with the late William Scott Chambers, 325 N.W. 95th Avenue, Plantation, Florida 33324-7021.

[414]Conversation on September 14, 1999, with the late Josephine Thompson Marshall, 121 Reillywood Avenue, Haddonfield, New Jersey 08033-2201.

[415]United Transportation Union - A History of the Brotherhood of Locomotive Firemen and Enginemen (http://www.utu.org/history/history2.htm), copyright 1997.

just about everything phonetically.[416]

Nannie is even reported to have kept in touch with the political process. Apparently, whenever the Republican National Convention came to town which it did on June 24-28, 1940, and June 21-25, 1948, Nannie and her friends are said to have particularly enjoyed attending the candidates' speeches.[417]

FRIENDS AND FAMILY. Nannie also enjoyed spending time with friends and family. She kept in close touch with her older sister, Lizzie (Reitze) Douglass and she was visited frequently by her nieces, Elizabeth (Reitze) Bustard and Margaret (Reitze) Burtis, the daughters of Nannie's oldest brother, Chris, Jr. Occasionally, Nannie and her daughter, Lucy, visited her nephew, Charlie Reitze, Jr., at Girard College where he had been enrolled by his mother after his father died. From time to time, she also saw her brother, John Reitze and his first wife, Maggie.

Nannie and Grandpop Chambers also enjoyed attending all kinds of social events in the neighborhood. One of the most fabulous celebrations was probably the 50th wedding anniversary celebration of Nannie's aunt and uncle, Charles and Isabella (Devlin) Smith, the sister and brother-in- law of Nannie's mother, Lucy (Devlin) Reitze. According to the article that appeared in the *Philadelphia Public Ledger*, the happy couple was married on August 15, 1855, and celebrated their Golden Wedding Anniversary in the company of about twenty-five friends and relatives.[418,419] The party was held at their home, 55 N. 38th Street, which was said to have been

---

[416]Conversation on September 14, 1999, with the late Josephine Thompson Marshall, 121 Reillywood Avenue, Haddonfield, New Jersey 08033-2201.

[417]Conversation on September 14, 1999, with the late Josephine Thompson Marshall, 121 Reillywood Avenue, Haddonfield, New Jersey 08033-2201.

[418]News Story, *Philadelphia Public Ledger*, Wednesday, August 16, 1905, p. 6.

Anniversary of Their Marriage

Mr. and Mrs. George (sic) Smith celebrated their golden wedding last evening at their home at 55 North Thirty-eighth street. The house was prettily decorated. Mr. and Mrs. Smith were married in this city on August 15 (sic), 1855, and have spent their entire married life here. Mr. Smith was born in Germany, but came to this country when 20 years of age. Mrs. Smith is the mother of fourteen children, eight of whom are living.
Their guests included:

Harry Douglass	Mrs. T.H. Oliver
Mrs. Harry Douglass	James Devlin
William Chambers	Mrs. James Devlin
Mrs. William Chambers	Miss Natalie Devlin
John Foley	Joseph McGuire
Mrs. John Foley	Mrs. Joseph McGuire
Joseph Smith	The Misses Foley

prettily decorated for the occasion. Also attending the festivities were Harry and Lizzie (Reitze) Douglass, Nannie's sister and brother-in-law.

THE DEATH OF NANNIE'S DAUGHTER. Perhaps the worst tragedy that Nannie had to endure was the death of her daughter, Lucy. According to Nannie's granddaughter, Josephine Thompson Marshall, it all began one day when Nannie and Lucy were downtown shopping and Lucy hit her elbow on the door at Wanamakers Department Store. The bruise would not heal. She went to the doctor who misdiagnosed her problem as rheumatism and put her arm in a cast.

While Lucy was struggling to recover from her illness, her husband, William Thompson, was commissioned as a First Lieutenant in the U.S. Army Air Corps and told to report for duty at a military base in Mount Clements, Michigan. After he, his wife, Lucy, and their baby daughter, Josephine, arrived in Mount Clements, Lucy became much sicker. A doctor who lived next door told William Thompson that his wife, Lucy, was seriously ill and should be sent home to her parents immediately for treatment. Reluctantly, the family separated and Lucy and her baby daughter returned to Philadelphia.

After Lucy arrived home, it was determined by doctors that she had tuberculosis arthritis a painful swelling of the bone usually found in the joints. The condition is caused by a tubercular infection in the bone. Small growths known as tubercles grow rapidly in the bone tissue and die thus destroying the tissue and creating cavities in the bone. The skin remains white over the affected area due to an increase in the size of the bone.[420]

Although Lucy was treated at the University of Pennsylvania Hospital, there was no cure for tuberculosis in those days and the infection spread to her spine. Fighting anemia, fever, and emaciation, Lucy grew weaker every day. There was nothing anyone could do to save her. She died on Friday, November 22, 1918.[421] Nannie and Grandpop Chambers were devastated by the

---

Mrs. Joseph Smith	The Misses Donahue
George Smith	Edward McBride
Mrs. George Smith	Charles Donahue
Joseph McShean	Miss Anna Beatty
Mrs. Joseph McShean	Miss Helen Reilly
Miss Quigley	

[419]Notice of Marriage, *Philadelphia Public Ledger*, Tuesday, August 21 1855, p. 2.

On the 14th of August by Rev. P. Rafferty at St. Francis Church Mr. Charles Smith to Miss Isabella Devlin all of this city.

[420]Jeanette L. Jerger, M.D., *A Medical Miscellaney for Genealogists*, (Bowie, Maryland: Heritage Books, Inc., 1995), p. 162.

[421]Conversation on September 14, 1999, with the late Josephine Thompson Marshall, 121 Reillywood Avenue, Haddonfield, New Jersey 08033-2201.

death of their daughter.

Notice of Lucy's death initially appeared in the *Philadelphia Public Ledger* on Saturday, November 23, 1918. It read as follows:

> THOMPSON - Nov 22, LUCY ELIZABETH, wife of William Thompson and daughter of W.S. and Josephine Chambers, aged 20. Notice of funeral later.[422]

The following full notice of Lucy's death later appeared in both the *Philadelphia Public Ledger* and the *Philadelphia Inquirer* for several additional days:

> THOMPSON - Nov 22, LUCY ELIZABETH, wife of William Thompson and daughter of W.S. and Josephine Chambers, aged 20. Relatives and friends are invited to services, Tues., 2 p.m., 5334 Greenway ave. Int. Mt. Moriah Cem. Friends may call Mon., 7:30 to 9:30 p.m.[423,424]

A somber funeral service for Lucy was officiated by the Reverend Samuel C. Carter, minister of the Woodland Avenue Methodist Episcopal Church located at the corner of 50th and Woodland Avenue.[425] After the service, Lucy was transported by hearse, followed by a wagon full of flowers and seven coaches, to Mount Moriah Cemetery where she was laid to rest in a plot purchased by her father.[426,427] The plate inscription on her casket read:

> Lucy Elizabeth Thompson
> March 11, 1898 - November 22, 1918

---

[422]Obituary of Lucy Elizabeth Thompson, *Philadelphia Public Ledger*, Saturday, November 23, 1918, p. 17.

[423]Obituary of Lucy Elizabeth Thompson, *Philadelphia Public Ledger*, Sunday, November 24, 1918, p. 4; Monday, November 25, 1918, p. 17; and Tuesday, November 26, 1918, p. 16.

[424]Obituary for Lucy Elizabeth Thompson, *Philadelphia Inquirer*, Monday, November 25, 1918, p. 15 and Tuesday, November 26, 1918, p. 15.

[425]Oliver Bair Funeral Home Record for Lucy Elizabeth Thompson, November 26, 1918, Pennsylvania Historical Society, Philadelphia, Pennsylvania.

[426]Oliver Bair Funeral Home Record for Lucy Elizabeth Thompson, November 26, 1918, Pennsylvania Historical Society, Philadelphia, Pennsylvania.

[427]The original deed for the plot at Mount Moriah Cemetery (10 Middle Part of South Part, Range 7, Section E) is in the possession of the Kathryn C. Torpey, 5035 Domain Place, Alexandria, Virginia, 22311-5066.

The large headstone that marks her grave was purchased by her husband, William Thompson.[428]

RAISING A GRANDCHILD. After Lucy died, her husband, William Thompson, returned to his military duty station where he remained until the end of the war. His daughter, Josephine, remained in Philadelphia with Nannie and Grandpop Chambers. Having lost her daughter, Nannie was determined not to lose her granddaughter. At the end of World War I, when William Thompson was finally able to return to Philadelphia, he realized immediately that Nannie had made a long-term commitment to raising her granddaughter. Out of respect for Nannie's dedication and devotion to his child, William Thompson deferred to his mother-in-law's judgement. Thus, Nannie raised her granddaughter.[429]

Josephine Thompson Marshall recalls growing up in her grandmother's home:

> Nannie was an intelligent woman, but a poor speller. We now know dyslexia runs in the family. However, she was a whiz at math and handled all the family finances. I do not believe that all the education she had was three years in the convent school with the nuns. When did she learn to read? She knew her Bible through and through. She was an avid newspaper reader waiting impatiently for the *Evening Bulletin* to arrive at 3:00 PM - always dressed in a clean afternoon house dress, with her breastpin and her pearl earrings.
>
> I remember her reading me stories from a handsome, large, color-illustrated book. How she and I cried over "Little Nell" and "The Little Match Girl". It was *Charles Dickens' Stories for Children*. The book probably originated in Aunt Lizzie's store and had been read to my mother and Uncle Harry.
>
> Nannie took after her hardworking mother. She was extremely generous and kind. She worked diligently for her church and during World War II, the ladies spent many hours making bandages and preparing first-aid kits, knitting sweaters, and raising money any way they could. They sent out Christmas baskets to the poor, and they cooked dinners for the church to raise money. They also had a good time.
>
> During the depression, Nannie anonymously sent baskets of food to out-of-work railroaders. She made clothes for friends of mine, especially for special occasions, and always made them seem a special present.
>
> Our house must have had a mysterious sign on it. From out of nowhere (especially during the depression) men appeared asking for food and Nannie fed them warm meals, privately, behind the column of the porch where they could not be seen by anyone.

---

[428]Conversation on March 21, 1995, with the late Josephine Thompson Marshall, 121 Reillywood Avenue, Haddonfield, New Jersey 08033-2201.

[429]Conversation on March 21, 1995, with the late Josephine Thompson Marshall, 121 Reillywood Avenue, Haddonfield, New Jersey 08033-2201.

When the Little Sisters of the Poor took their Annual Block Collection, they had
lunch at our house (the only Protestants on the block), and left with their arms
laden with jellies and other goodies.

She was called Jo or Josey by her family and close friends. Her nieces and
nephews called her Aunt Josey. I was the one who began calling her Nannie
and, of course, Bill and Tom followed. She was referred to as "Your Nannie" by
the other kids. I remember the mailman calling her Nannie and she complained
to me that she seemed to be Nannie to the world.

But don't think she was an angel - we all knew to avoid her temper. She was
funny and could tell wonderful tales. Occasionally, her language was salty, but
she was always the center of the group. When I had meetings at my house, the
girls all pleaded with her to stay. She would get a few laughs and then knew
when to go.

My children adored her. They eagerly awaited her arrival and, when they were
small, my daughter, Lucy, would always ask, "Nannie, when are you going
home?" meaning, please stay as long as possible.[430]

NANNIE'S HEALTH. Having successfully raised two children, suffered the death of her
beloved daughter, Lucy, and, then, raised her granddaughter, Josephine, Nannie was ready for a
rest, but there was no rest in sight. It was 1942 and World War II was raging in both Europe and
the Pacific.

On top of being anxious about the safety of her two grandsons - William Scott Chambers
and Thomas Wallace Chambers - who were both away at war, one in the U.S. Merchant Marine
and the other in the U.S. Army, Nannie's only granddaughter, Josephine, whom she had raised
after the death of her daughter, was soon to be married. Her granddaughter's finacee, David
Harrington Marshall, was also away during the war serving the country as an Army Chief
Warrant Officer.

High stress combined with a bad heart resulted in Nannie having a major heart attack
followed soon thereafter by a gallbladder operation.[431] Her granddaughter postponed her
wedding while Nannie recovered. Then, the worst happened, and Nannie discovered that she had
a lump the size of an egg under one of her breasts.

According to Doctor Lehman, Nannie's only option was a radical mastectomy. From all
accounts, it was a terrible operation. She was in the hospital at the Women's Medical College of
Philadelphia for one month where she had radium treatments three times a week. After that, she

---

[430]Letter dated October 21, 1999, from the late Josephine Thompson Marshall, 121
Reillywood Avenue, Haddonfield, New Jersey 08033-2201.

[431]Conversation on September 14, 1999, with the late Josephine Thompson Marshall, 121
Reillywood Avenue, Haddonfield, New Jersey 08033-2201.

had to return to the hospital twice a year for follow-up treatment. While the operation may have saved Nannie's life, it left her horribly scarred and with an enlarged arm which she usually kept wrapped in a towel or resting on a pillow.[432]

THE DEATH OF GRANDPOP CHAMBERS. William Scott Chambers died on February 5, 1950. He was 83 years old and had been in poor health for some time. Nannie took care of him at home until the end. They were happily married for fifty-four years. He was a handsome guy when she married him and he was a loyal and steadfast husband, father, and grandfather all the years they were together. Despite her mother's warning about the risks of marrying an older man, Nannie had no regrets. They were right for each other.

Grandpop Chambers obituary appeared in the *Philadelphia Inquirer* on Monday, February 6, 1950. It read as follows:

> CHAMBERS - Of 5313 Yocum st., Feb 5, WILLIAM S., husband of Josephine I. Relatives and friends also Lodge 319 B. of L. E. and F. are invited to services Wed. at 2 P.M., from Barker's 5413 Chester ave. Int. private. Viewing Tues. 7 to 9 P.M.[433]

Nannie buried Grandpop Chambers at Mount Moriah Cemetery alongside their daughter, Lucy.

NANNIE'S SPIRITUAL LIFE. Nannie's granddaughter, Josephine Thompson Marshall, recalls that Nannie said she attended Bethany Memorial Presbyterian Church (somewhere close to home) as a child and as a teenager. Nannie said the church was mentored by John Wanamaker (founder of Wanamaker's Department Store) and that it was the religious and social center of the area.[434,435]

---

[432]Conversation on September 14, 1999, with the late Josephine Thompson Marshall, 121 Reillywood Avenue, Haddonfield, New Jersey 08033-2201.

[433]Obituary of William S. Chambers, *Philadelphia Inquirer*, Monday, February 6, 1950, p. 24.

[434]Letter dated October 21, 1999, from the late Josephine Thompson Marshall, 121 Reillywood Avenue, Haddonfield, New Jersey 08033-2201.

[435]Kenneth A. Hammonds, *Historical Directory of Presbyterian Churches and Presbyteries of Greater Philadelphia Related to the Presbyterian Church (USA) and to its Antecedents 1690-1990*, (Philadelphia, Pennsylvania: Presbyterian Historical Society, 1993), p. 63, says that in February, 1858, John Wanamaker and E. H. Toland, a missionary of the American Sunday School Union, rented a room at 2135 South Street and the following Sunday began a Sunday school known as the Bethany Mission School. In a short time, the whole room was filled with pupils, so in July, 1858, a tent was erected on South Street west of 21st Street to

Although no record has been found of Nannie's baptism, the Session Minutes of Bethany Presbyterian Church indicate that on January 18, 1891, Josephine Reitz (sic) appeared before the Session, was examined as to her Christian experience and, having made a satisfactory profession of her faith in the Lord Jesus Christ, was duly admitted to the fellowship of the church.[436] Nannie would have been thirteen years old at the time.

Reportedly, Nannie enjoyed attending services at the church. Apparently, she also enjoyed combining her spirituality with her well known penchant for mischievousness as she told her granddaughter that, as a youngster, she once used a pea shooter from the balcony of Bethany Presbyterian Church to hit an elderly parishioner in the back of the head during Sunday services. He soon found out who she was and where she lived as he is said to have chased her all the way up the steps to her house in an unsuccessful effort to mete out justice.[437]

Later, after their children were born, Nannie and Grandpop Chambers had them both baptized by the Reverend S.G. Grove, minister of the Christian Methodist Episcopal Church located on Christian Street near 24th Street. According to the baptismal records of the church, the baptisms took place on June 20, 1898, at their residence, 1234 S. 34th Street.[438] Later, Nannie and Grandpop Chambers are reported to have attended the Woodland Avenue Methodist Episcopal Church located at the corner of 50th and Woodland Avenue.[439] Their children, Harry and Lucy, are thought to have attended Sunday school services there, too.[440] In 1918, during the influenza

---

provide more room. This led to the construction of a chapel for year round use. The chapel later became Bethany Memorial Presbyterian Church. The Church broke ground for a new building at the corner of 22nd and Bainbridge Streets in the spring of 1866. It was dedicated on February 13, 1868. A second building was added in 1874. Besides worship services, Sunday school, youth activities and adult organizations, Bethany Memorial maintained a medical dispensary, a Building and Loan Association, a Penny Savings Bank, a Friendly Inn, and Bethany College.

[436]Bethany Presbyterian Church Records, 1861 to 1899, Philadelphia, Pennsylvania, FHL Microfilm Roll 0912991.

[437]Conversation on May 24, 2001, with the late Josephine Thompson Marshall, 121 Reillywood Avenue, Haddonfield, New Jersey 08033-2201.

[438]Christian Methodist Episcopal Church Records, 1897 to 1926, Philadelphia, Pennsylvania, Genealogical Society of Pennsylvania, Philadelphia, Pennsylvania, Microfilm Roll XX342:8.

[439]Conversation on September 14, 1999, with the late Josephine Thompson Marshall, 121 Reillywood Avenue, Haddonfield, New Jersey 08033-2201.

[440]Conversation on April 27, 1996, with the late William Scott Chambers, 325 N.W. 95th Avenue, Plantation, Florida 33324-7021.

epidemic that gripped the city, Nannie made arrangements for her granddaughter and her son-in-law, William Thompson, to be baptized. Although it is not clear exactly who performed the baptisms, Nannie's granddaughter recalls being told that the baptisms took place at their home, 5334 Greenway Avenue.[441]

After the death of her daughter, Nannie is said to have gradually stopped attending church regularly until the next door neighbors began taking her granddaughter, Josephine, to the First United Presbyterian Church at 52nd and Chester Avenue.[442] Thereafter, the whole family (including Nannie's son, Harry and his family) attended the First United Presbyterian Church. In fact, Nannie's granddaughter, Josephine Thompson Marshall, was married in that church and her children were baptized there, too.[443]

Toward the end of her life, Nannie appears to have changed religious affiliation once again after she began attending services in the chapel of the Evangelical Home . It was there that Nannie came to know the Reverend I. James Bobst who was greatly loved by everyone and became like a second son to her.[444,445]

THE EVANGELICAL HOME. Shortly after Grandpop Chambers died, Nannie entered the Evangelical Home at 8401 Roosevelt Boulevard.

The German Evangelical Home for Aged (as it was first known) was founded in 1888 by German speaking persons who were members of the Evangelical Church, a Protestant denomination. The first residents were admitted to the Home in 1890. During its first 30 years, the Evangelical Home was supervised by Deaconess Minnie Scheidt. From 1929 forward, clergymen of the Evangelical Church became administrators of the Home and in 1938, the Reverend I. James Bobst was named to this position which he held until his death in 1967. In 1968, following years of study, planning, and preparation, the Evangelical Church, the

---

[441]Conversation on May 24, 2001, with the late Josephine Thompson Marshall, 121 Reillywood Avenue, Haddonfield, New Jersey 08033-2201.

[442]Conversation on November 29, 1996, with the late Josephine Thompson Marshall, 121 Reillywood Avenue, Haddonfield, New Jersey 08033-2201.

[443]Letter dated October 21, 1999, from the late Josephine Thompson Marshall, 121 Reillywood Avenue, Haddonfield, New Jersey 08033-2201.

[444]Letter dated November 26, 1999, from Reverend Harold J. Schieck, administrator emeritus of Evangelical Manor, 8401 Roosevelt Boulevard, # A501, Philadelphia, Pennsylvania 19152.

[445]Conversation on September 14, 1999, with the late Josephine Thompson Marshall, 121 Reillywood Avenue, Haddonfield, New Jersey 08033-2201.

Evangelical United Brethren Church, and the Methodist Church merged into the United Methodist Church. Thus, the Evangelical Home (now known as Evangelical Manor) came under the auspices of the Eastern Pennsylvania Conference of the United Methodist Church.[446]

According to her granddaughter, Josephine Thompson Marshall, Nannie's widow's pension from the railroad was only about $100 a month which was not sufficient to meet her personal needs and take care of a house so she and her neighbor, Mrs. Sarah Rule who lived at 5310 Greenway Avenue, contacted the Evangelical Home and made arrangements to move. In return for life care at the Evangelical Home, Nannie agreed to give them her house at 5313 Yocum Street which was at that time worth about $2,500. According to family legend, all of the arrangements were in place before Nannie's son, Harry, got word that his mother was moving. Reportedly, he was fit to be tied and privately embarrassed that some people might think that his mother was moving into a Home because of his inability or unwillingness to provide for her in her old age.[447]

Apparently, nothing could have been further from the truth which was that Nannie had a decisive personality and invariably made up her own mind about what she was going to do. Her granddaughter, Josephine Thompson Marshall, recalls that:

> Aunt Mary Chambers called me to try to dissuade Nannie from going into the Home. I spent an afternoon reasoning with Nannie, but she was determined to go. One reason she gave me was that Aunt Mary and Uncle Harry were finally living a life of their own (their oldest son, Bill, was married and living in Cuba and their younger son, Tom, was in the service) and she didn't want to come live with me with those "two little kids". I called the Home in her presence and talked with the Reverend Bobst and he said the Home very much wanted Nannie as he felt she would be an asset, but if she didn't come then, her name would go to the bottom of the list. Later, when Uncle Harry and I visited Nannie after one of her long illnesses, he said to me, "It was the best move of her life." She truly received loving care at the Evangelical Home.[448]

Not surprisingly, Nannie and Mrs. Rule enjoyed living at the Evangelical Home. Each of them had her own room on the second floor with a big breezy window. It was there that Nannie regaled her great-grandchildren with stories about her wild and wooly childhood.

---

[446]Letter dated November 26, 1999, from Reverend Harold J. Schieck, administrator emeritus of Evangelical Manor, 8401 Roosevelt Boulevard, # A501, Philadelphia, Pennsylvania 19152.

[447]Conversation on September 18, 1999, with the late William Scott Chambers, 325 N.W. 95th Avenue, Plantation, Florida 33324-7021.

[448]Letter dated October 21, 1999, from the late Josephine Thompson Marshall, 121 Reillywood Avenue, Haddonfield, New Jersey 08033-2201.

Since Nannie and Mrs. Rule could come and go whenever they chose as long as they were in good health, they used their widow's railroad passes to travel to New York City whenever the occasion presented itself. They even went to see Guy Lombardo play and had a great time except that Nannie, who didn't drink hard liquor, always waited in the hotel lobby whenever Mrs. Rule decided to have a cocktail in the lounge.

THE DEATH OF NANNIE CHAMBERS. Nannie died on May 3, 1962, of chronic myocarditis and arteriosclerotic cardio muscular disease.[449] According to her granddaughter, her final illness lasted about three months. Nannie spent much of that time in the infirmary at the Evangelical Home where the Reverend Bobst made sure she was assigned to the best room that was available close to the nurses station.[450] Her granddaughter visited her there every other day bringing her food and other goodies.

On the day that Nannie died, her granddaughter arrived at the infirmary too late to be with her grandmother in her final hour. The Reverend Bobst assured Nannie's granddaughter that she had nothing to be ashamed of in not being present when Nannie died because she had always been very faithful to Nannie throughout her entire life. He also said, that for him personally, the last three months of Nannie's life were a most beautiful experience in that he had been privileged to know her enduring spirit and cheerfulness.

Nannie's obituary appeared in the *Philadelphia Inquirer* on Saturday, May 5, 1962. It read as follows:

> CHAMBERS - May 3, 1962, JOSEPHINE I. (nee Reitze), of the Evangelical Home, widow of William S. Chambers (aged 84 years). Relatives, friends and members of Pride of William Penn Lodge # 433, B. L. F. E., are invited to services, Mon., 1 P.M., at Hackman Bros., Inc., 905-07 W. Lehigh ave., where friends may call Sun. eve. Int. Mt. Moriah Cemetery.[451]

---

[449]Death Certificate for Josephine Irene Chambers, May 3, 1962, # not shown, Pennsylvania Division of Vital Statistics, New Castle, Pennsylvania.

[450]Letter dated October 23, 1999, from Reverend Harold J. Schieck, administrator emeritus of Evangelical Manor, 8401 Roosevelt Boulevard, # A501, Philadelphia, Pennsylvania 19152 says that "Record keeping at Evangelical Manor 45 years ago and earlier are hard to find.... Thus, in an old notebook from the then nurse in the then Evangelical Manor Infirmary, lists your great-grandmother, Josephine Chambers, as Discharged by Death, May 3, 1962.... I regret that our old records are almost nonexistent.... I regret I cannot give you more specific information concerning your great-grandmother."

[451]Obituary of Josephine I. Chambers, *Philadelphia Inquirer*, Saturday, May 5, 1962, p. 7.

The funeral service was officiated by the Reverend Bobst.[452] At the conclusion of the service, Nannie was transported to Mount Moriah Cemetery where she was buried in the same plot as her husband, her daughter, Lucy; and her son, Harry, who died on November 11, 1953.[453]

GIFTS AND BEQUESTS. Although Nannie did not leave a will, she did leave her New Testament to her only surviving grandson, William Scott Chambers.[454] She also confided in her granddaughter, Josephine, that she had hidden $200 under one of the drawers in her room and that her granddaughter was to take the money after Nannie died. Of the $200 that Nannie had saved, her granddaughter divided $150 evenly between herself, Mary Ann Chambers (the widow of Nannie's son, Harry), and Florence Chambers (the widow of Nannie's grandson, Thomas Wallace Chambers).

The remainder of the money she used to purchase two brass candlesticks which were given to the Reverend Bobst for use in the chapel of the Evangelical Home in memory of Nannie Chambers.[455] Reportedly, the Memorial Candlesticks, as well as other items in memory of the Reverend Bobst, are still very much a part of Evangelical Manor's chapel services.[456]

------

[452]Funeral Card in Memory of Josephine I. Chambers is in the possession of Kathryn C. Torpey, 5035 Domain Place, Alexandria, Virginia 33211-5066.

[453]Obituary of Harry G. Chambers, *Philadelphia Inquirer*, Thursday, November 12, 1953, p. 41.

[454]The New Testament was in the possession of the late William Scott Chambers, 325 N.W. 95th Avenue, Plantation, Florida 33324-7021.

[455]Conversation on September 14, 1999, with the late Josephine Thompson Marshall, 121 Reillywood Avenue, Haddonfield, New Jersey 08033-2201.

[456]Letter dated November 26, 1999, from Reverend Harold J. Schieck, administrator emeritus of Evangelical Manor, 8401 Roosevelt Boulevard, # A501, Philadelphia, Pennsylvania 19152.

United States of America.

Be it Remembered, That at a Court of NISI PRIUS, holden by one of the Justices of the SUPREME COURT of Pennsylvania, at Philadelphia, in and for the Eastern District, a Court of Record in the United States of America, on the *Twenty Eighth* day of *September* in the year of our Lord one thousand eight hundred and sixty- *Eight* *Christopher Reitze* a native of *Germany* exhibited a Petition praying to be admitted to become a CITIZEN OF THE UNITED STATES, and it appearing to said Court that he had declared on *oath* before the Prothonotary of said Court, on the *28th* day of *September* A. D. *1868*, that it was bona fide his intention to become a Citizen of the United States, and to renounce forever all allegiance and fidelity to any foreign Prince, Potentate, State or Sovereignty whatsoever, and particularly to the *Grand Duke of Hesse Cassel* of whom he was at that time a subject; and the said *Christopher Reitze* having on his solemn *oath* declared and also made proof thereof agreeably to law, to the satisfaction of the Court, that he had resided within the limits and under the jurisdiction of the United States of America three years next preceding his arriving at the age of twenty-one years, and continued to reside therein at the time of making his application : that including the three years of his minority he had resided one year and upwards, last past, within the State of Pennsylvania, and within the limits and under the jurisdiction of the United States five years and upwards, and that during the three years next preceding it had been bona fide his intention to become a Citizen of the United States, and that during that time he had behaved as a man of good moral character, attached to the principles of the CONSTITUTION OF THE UNITED STATES; and well disposed to the good order and happiness of the same ; and having declared on his solemn *oath* before the said Court, that he would support the CONSTITUTION OF THE UNITED STATES, and that he did absolutely and entirely renounce and abjure all allegiance and fidelity to every foreign prince, potentate, state and sovereignty whatsoever, and particularly to the *Grand Duke of Hesse Cassel.* of whom he was before a subject. And having in all respects complied with the laws in regard to Naturalization, in his case made and provided, Thereupon the Court admitted the said *Christopher Reitze* to become a citizen of the United States, and ordered all the proceedings aforesaid to be recorded by the Prothonotary of said court, which was done accordingly.

In Witness Whereof, I have hereunto set my hand and affixed the seal of said Court at Philadelphia, this *28th* day of *September* in the year one thousand eight hundred and sixty- *Eight,* and of the INDEPENDENCE of the United States of America the *Ninety third,*

James Ross Snowden
Prothonotary

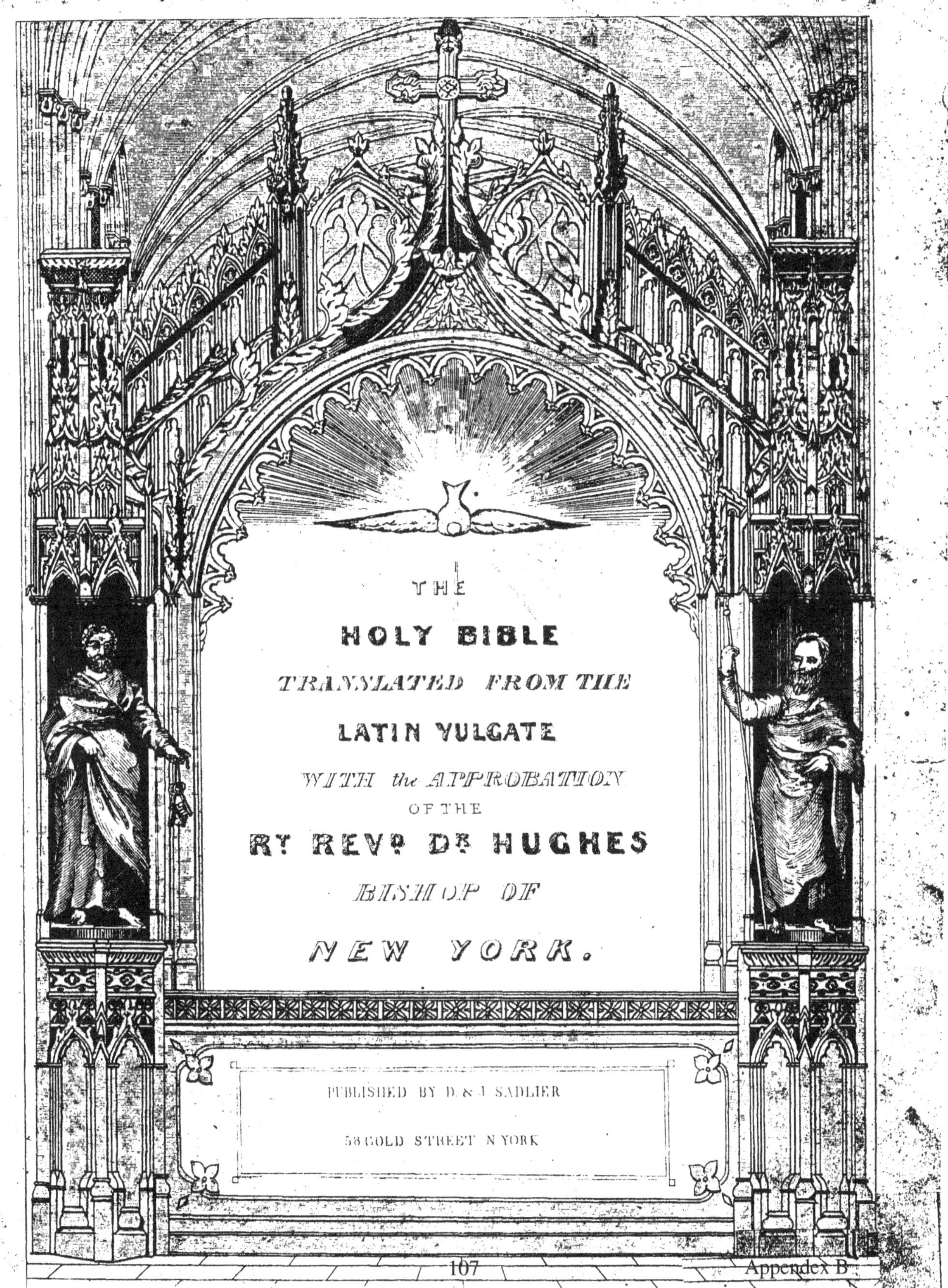

THE
HOLY BIBLE
TRANSLATED FROM THE
LATIN VULGATE
WITH the APPROBATION
OF THE
RT REVD DR HUGHES
BISHOP OF
NEW YORK.
PUBLISHED BY D. & J. SADLIER
58 GOLD STREET N YORK

Appendex B

THE
HOLY BIBLE,

TRANSLATED FROM

THE LATIN VULGATE:

DILIGENTLY COMPARED WITH

THE HEBREW, GREEK, AND OTHER EDITIONS, IN VARIOUS LANGUAGES.

THE OLD TESTAMENT WAS FIRST PUBLISHED BY THE ENGLISH COLLEGE AT DOWAY, A. D. 1609:
AND THE NEW TESTAMENT, BY THE ENGLISH COLLEGE AT RHEIMS, A. D. 1582.

WITH

ANNOTATIONS, BY THE REV. DR. CHALLONER; TOGETHER WITH REFERENCES, AND AN HISTORICAL AND CHRONOLOGICAL INDEX.

REVISED AND CORRECTED ACCORDING TO THE CLEMENTINE EDITION OF THE SCRIPTURES.
WITH THE APPROBATION OF THE RIGHT REV. BISHOP HUGHES.

With a number of Steel Engravings.

NEW-YORK:

PUBLISHED BY D. & J. SADLIER,
NO. 58 GOLD, AND 221 BLEECKER STREET.

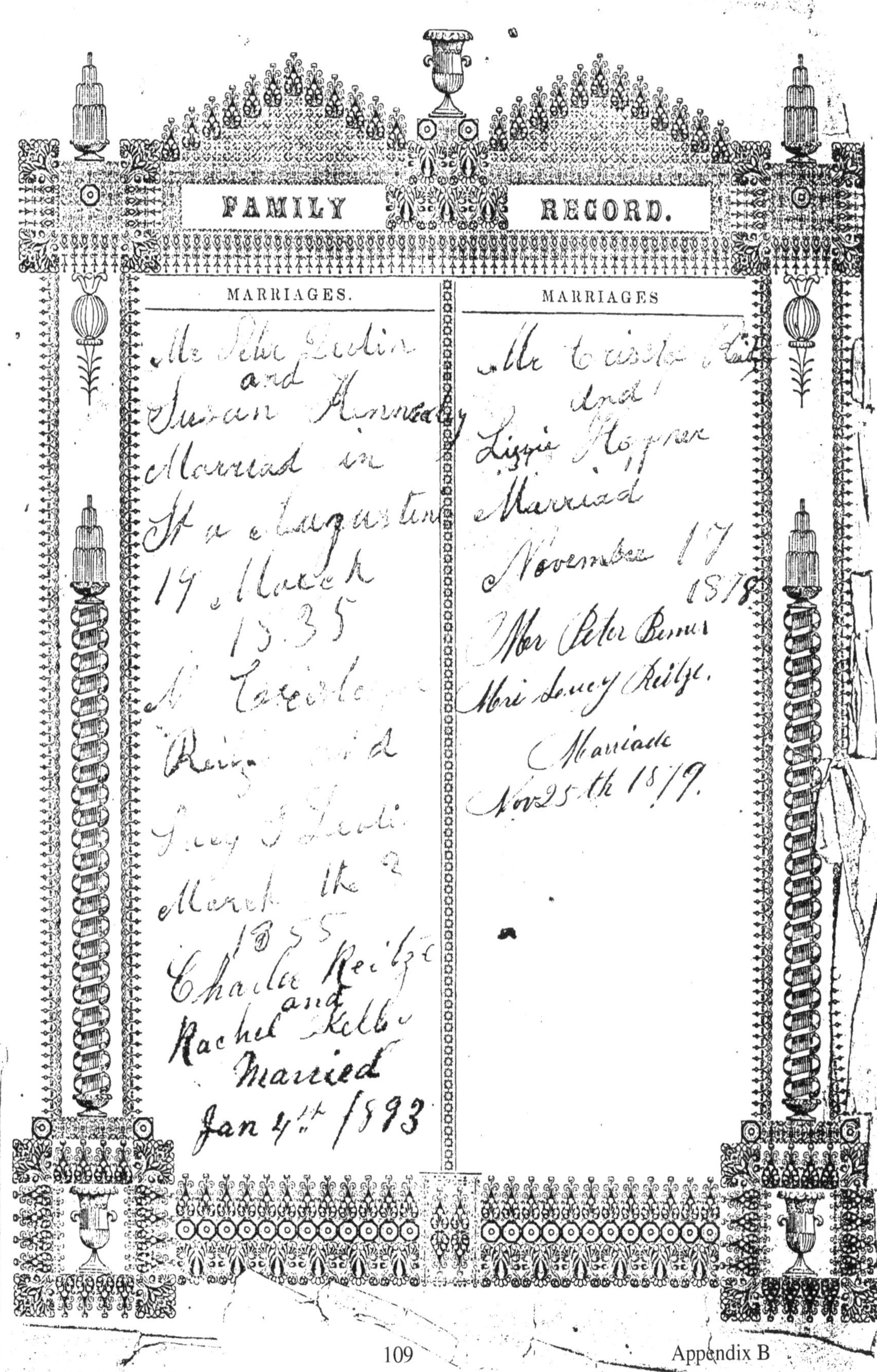

FAMILY   RECORD.
MARRIAGES.
MARRIAGES
Mr Peter Leslie
and
Susan Kennedy
Married in
St augustine
17 March
1835
Reid
Married
November 17
1878
Mr Peter Burns
Mrs Lucy Reitze
Married
Nov 25th 1879
Lizzie Hopper
Charles Reitze
and
Rachel Kelly
Married
Jan 4th 1893

FAMILY RECORD.

BIRTHS.	BIRTHS.
Cristopper Reitze Born September 7 1855.	John Reitze Borne the 30 October 1869.
Susen Reitze Born December the 1. 1859	Maggie Reitze Born 15 July 1875
Henry Reitze Borne Januar the 9. 1861	Coney Reitze Born the 12 of March 1876
Lizzie Reitze Born the 1. Decem 1863	Josey Reitze Born July 4 1877
Charley Reitze Born Febery the 7. 1866	[illegible] an Lucy July an Elley 1873

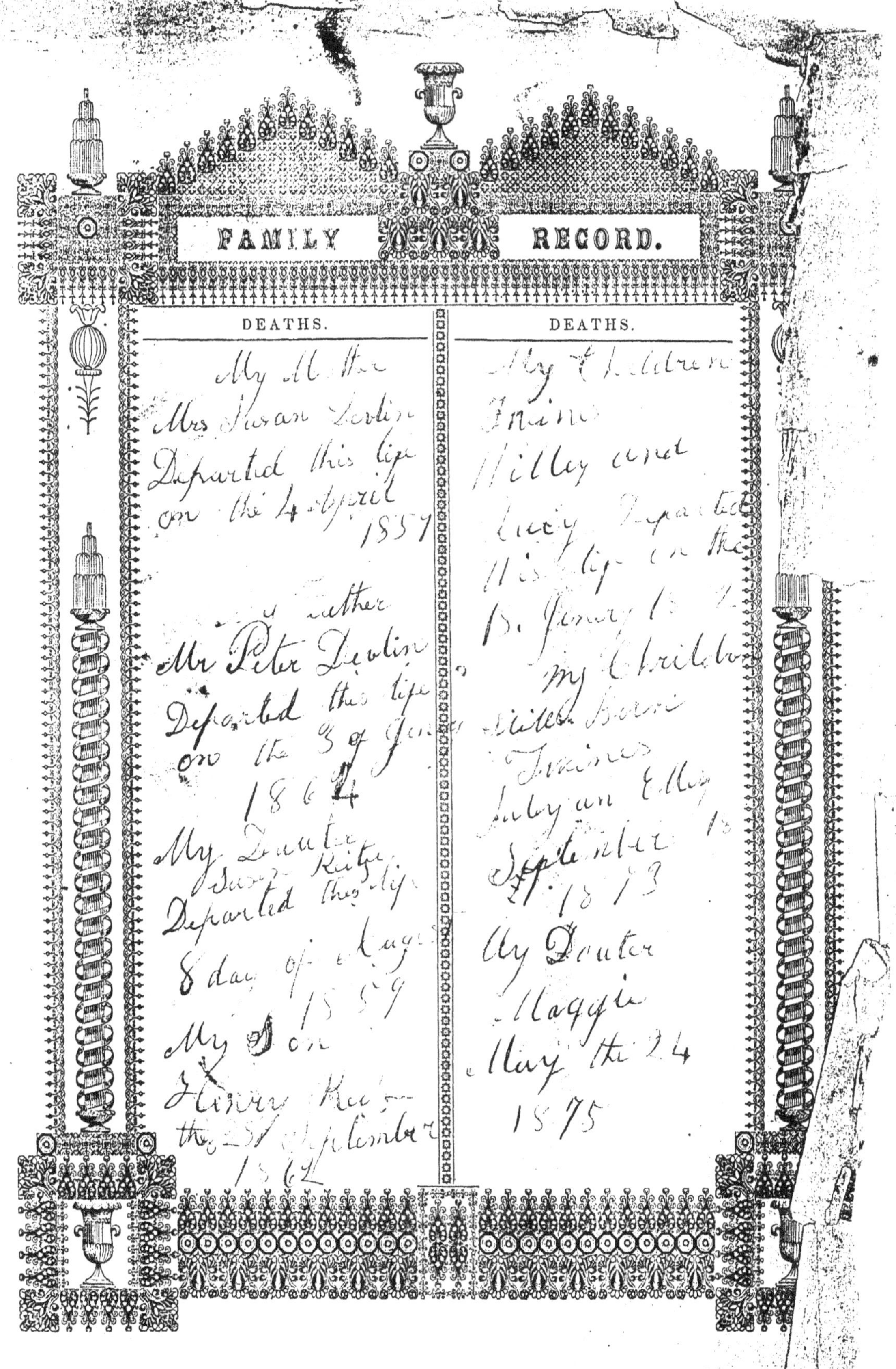

FAMILY RECORD.
DEATHS.
DEATHS.
My Mother
Mrs Susan Devlin
Departed this life
on the 4 April
1857

My Father
Mr Peter Devlin
Departed this life
on the 3 of June
1864
My Daughter
Susan Keith
Departed this life
8 day of Aug
1859
My Son
Henry Keith
the 2? September
1862
My Children
Minnie
Willey and
Lucy Departed
this life on the
13 January
my Children
still born
Twines
July an Ellen
September 13
1873
My Daughter
Maggie
May the 24
1875

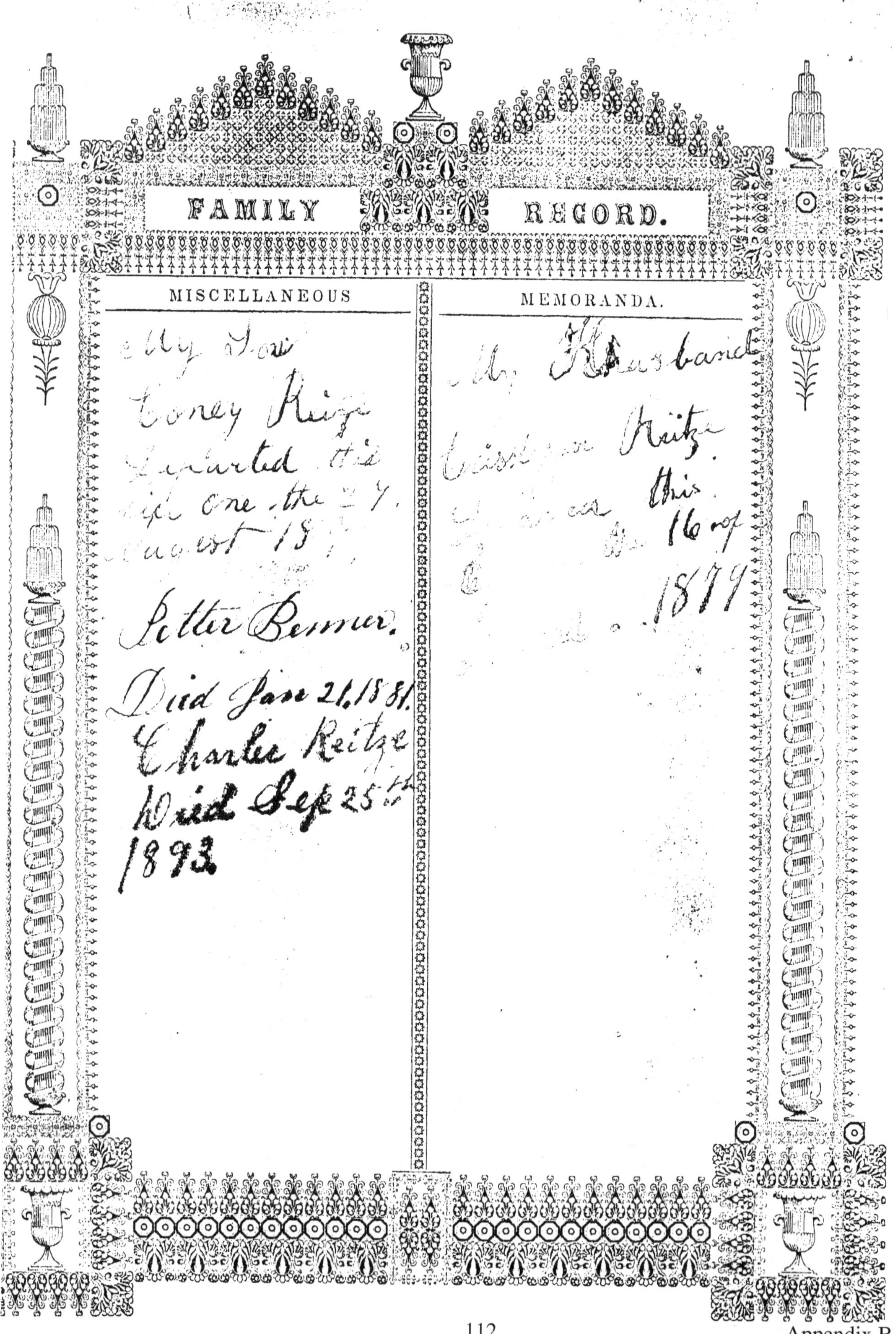

FAMILY RECORD.
MISCELLANEOUS
MEMORANDA.

Descendants of Christopher Reitze

Generation 1

1. CHRISTOPHER[1] REITZE was born on 12 Mar 1824 in Bottendorf, Kurhessen, Hesse-Cassel, Germany. He died on 16 Apr 1879 in Philadelphia, Pennsylvania. He married Lucy S. Devlin, daughter of Peter Devlin and Susan Kennedy on 03 Mar 1855 in Philadelphia Pennsylvania. She was born on 12 Jun 1836 in Philadelphia, Pennsylvania. She died on 07 May 1909 in Gloucester City, Camden County, New Jersey.

Christopher Reitze and Lucy S. Devlin had the following children:

2. i. CHRISTOPHER C.[2] REITZE JR. was born on 09 Sep 1855 in Woolwich Township, Gloucester County, New Jersey. He died on 07 Mar 1907 in Philadelphia, Pennsylvania. He married Elizabeth L. Hoffner, daughter of Thomas Hoffner and Margaret on 17 Nov 1878. She was born in Oct 1861 in Pennsylvania. She died on 31 May 1938 in Philadelphia, Pennsylvania.

   ii. SUSAN R. REITZE was born on 12 Jan 1859. She died on 08 Aug 1859 in Philadelphia, Pennsylvania.

   iii. HENRY REITZE was born on 09 Jan 1861 in Philadelphia, Pennsylvania. He died on 28 Aug 1862 in Philadelphia, Pennsylvania.

3. iv. ELIZABETH M. REITZE was born on 01 Dec 1863 in Philadelphia, Pennsylvania. She died on 14 Apr 1961 in Haddonfield, Camden County, New Jersey. She married (1) EDWARD J. COLLINS, son of John Collins and Rose on 07 Nov 1882 in Philadelphia, Pennsylvania. He was born in 1859 in Pennsylvania. He died on 23 Jun 1893 in Philadelphia Pennsylvania. She married (2) HENRY GRAFE DOUGLASS, son of Henry G. Douglass and Sarah Ashton on 25 Apr 1892 in Philadelphia, Pennsylvania. He was born on 09 Jul 1854 in Philadelphia, Pennsylvania. He died on 10 Jun 1932 in Lakeland, Gloucester Township, Camden County, New Jersey.

4. v. CHARLES ARCHIBALD REITZE SR. was born on 07 Feb 1866 in Philadelphia, Pennsylvania. He died on 25 Sep 1893 in Philadelphia, Pennsylvania. He married Rachel M. Kelly on 04 Jan 1893 in Philadelphia, Pennsylvania. She was born about 1869 in Scotland.

5. vi. JOHN FRANCIS REITZE SR. was born on 30 Oct 1869 in Philadelphia, Pennsylvania. He died on 15 Feb 1955 in Philadelphia, Pennsylvania. He married (1) MARGARET CECILIA MALLOY, daughter of Martin Malloy and Catherine Kennedy on 27 Nov 1895 in Philadelphia, Pennsylvania. She was born on 25 Dec 1873 in Philadelphia, Pennsylvania. She died on 14 Oct 1918 in Philadelphia, Pennsylvania. He married (2) EMILY "EMMA" C. MALLOY, daughter of Martin Malloy and Catherine Kennedy in 1921. She was born in Oct 1888 in Pennsylvania. She died on 04 May 1951 in Philadelphia, Pennsylvania.

   vii. LUCY (TWIN) REITZE was born on 16 Mar 1872 in Philadelphia, Pennsylvania. She died on 16 Mar 1872 in Philadelphia, Pennsylvania.

   viii. WILLIAM (TWIN) REITZE was born on 16 Mar 1872 in Philadelphia, Pennsylvania. He died on 17 Mar 1872 in Philadelphia, Pennsylvania.

ix.   ELLEN (TWIN) REITZE was born on 18 Sep 1873. She died on 18 Sep 1873.

x.   JULIE (TWIN) REITZE was born on 18 Sep 1873. She died on 18 Sep 1873.

xi.   MAGGIE REITZE was born on 15 Jul 1874 in Philadelphia, Pennsylvania. She died on 20 May 1875 in Philadelphia, Pennsylvania.

xii.   CONRAD REITZE was born on 12 Mar 1876 in Philadelphia, Pennsylvania. He died on 23 Aug 1877 in Philadelphia, Pennsylvania.

6.   xiii.   JOSEPHINE IRENE REITZE was born on 04 Jul 1877 in Philadelphia, Pennsylvania. She died on 03 May 1962 in Philadelphia, Pennsylvania. She married William Scott Chambers, son of George Washington Chambers and Annie Adam Edwards on 30 Mar 1896 in Philadelphia, Pennsylvania. He was born on 05 Jun 1867 in Philadelphia, Pennsylvania. He died on 05 Feb 1950 in Philadelphia, Pennsylvania.

Generation 2

2.   CHRISTOPHER C.[2] REITZE JR. (Christopher[1]) was born on 09 Sep 1855 in Woolwich Township, Gloucester County, New Jersey. He died on 07 Mar 1907 in Philadelphia, Pennsylvania. He married Elizabeth L. Hoffner, daughter of Thomas Hoffner and Margaret on 17 Nov 1878. She was born in Oct 1861 in Pennsylvania. She died on 31 May 1938 in Philadelphia, Pennsylvania.

Christopher C. Reitze Jr. and Elizabeth L. Hoffner had the following children:

7.   i.   ELIZABETH C.[3] REITZE was born on 02 Jun 1881 in Philadelphia, Pennsylvania. She died on 10 Sep 1971 in Downingtown, Uwchlan Township, Chester County, Pennsylvania 19380. She married John A. Bustard on 28 Jun 1899 in Philadelphia, Pennsylvania. He was born in Sep 1867 in Philadelphia, Pennsylvania. He died on 22 May 1934 in Philadelphia, Pennsylvania.

8.   ii.   MARGARET MAY REITZE was born on 02 Oct 1882 in Philadelphia, Pennsylvania. She died on 06 Jun 1959 in Gloucester Township, Camden County, New Jersey. She married Edward Taylor Burtis, son of Ellwood Burtis and Louise Diemer on 19 Jun 1901 in Philadelphia, Pennsylvania. He was born on 18 Dec 1871 in Philadelphia, Pennsylvania. He died on 23 Nov 1956 in Franklin Township, Gloucester County, New Jersey.

9.   iii.   CHRISTOPHER CARL REITZE I was born on 15 Sep 1885 in Philadelphia, Pennsylvania. He died on 04 Jul 1942 in Philadelphia, Pennsylvania. He married (1) HELEN C. HOENIGMANN, daughter of Peter Hoenigmann and Kathrina [Caroline Rose] on 29 Apr 1908 in Philadelphia, Pennsylvania. She was born on 20 May 1887 in Philadelphia, Pennsylvania. She died on 28 Jul 1923 in Philadelphia, Pennsylvania. He married (2) THERESA "TESS" REIMOLD, daughter of Conrad Reimold in 1924 in Philadelphia, Philadelphia County, Pennsylvania. She was born in Dec 1882 in Pennsylvania. She died on 18 Jul 1943 in Philadelphia, Pennsylvania.

3.   **ELIZABETH M.**[2] **REITZE** (Christopher[1]) was born on 01 Dec 1863 in Philadelphia, Pennsylvania. She died on 14 Apr 1961 in Haddonfield, Camden County, New Jersey. She married (1) **EDWARD J. COLLINS**, son of John Collins and Rose on 07 Nov 1882 in Philadelphia, Pennsylvania. He was born in 1859 in Pennsylvania. He died on 23 Jun 1893 in Philadelphia Pennsylvania. She married (2) **HENRY GRAFE DOUGLASS**, son of Henry G. Douglass and Sarah Ashton on 25 Apr 1892 in Philadelphia, Pennsylvania. He was born on 09 Jul 1854 in Philadelphia, Pennsylvania. He died on 10 Jun 1932 in Lakeland, Gloucester Township, Camden County, New Jersey.

Edward J. Collins and Elizabeth M. Reitze had the following child:
    i.   BABY[3] COLLINS was born on 18 Dec 1883 in Philadelphia Pennsylvania. He died on 19 Dec 1883 in Philadelphia Pennsylvania.

4.   **CHARLES ARCHIBALD**[2] **REITZE SR.** (Christopher[1]) was born on 07 Feb 1866 in Philadelphia, Pennsylvania. He died on 25 Sep 1893 in Philadelphia, Pennsylvania. He married Rachel M. Kelly on 04 Jan 1893 in Philadelphia, Pennsylvania. She was born about 1869 in Scotland.

Charles Archibald Reitze Sr. and Rachel M. Kelly had the following child:
10.   i.   CHARLES ARCHIBALD[3] REITZE JR. was born on 06 Nov 1893 in Philadelphia, Pennsylvania. He died on 29 Aug 1969 in Philadelphia, Pennsylvania. He married MARY KUBICK. She was born on 04 Jul 1897 in Philadelphia, Pennsylvania. She died on 02 Jul 1964 in Philadelphia, Pennsylvania.

5.   **JOHN FRANCIS**[2] **REITZE SR.** (Christopher[1]) was born on 30 Oct 1869 in Philadelphia, Pennsylvania. He died on 15 Feb 1955 in Philadelphia, Pennsylvania. He married (1) **MARGARET CECILIA MALLOY**, daughter of Martin Malloy and Catherine Kennedy on 27 Nov 1895 in Philadelphia, Pennsylvania. She was born on 25 Dec 1873 in Philadelphia, Pennsylvania. She died on 14 Oct 1918 in Philadelphia, Pennsylvania. He married (2) **EMILY "EMMA" C. MALLOY**, daughter of Martin Malloy and Catherine Kennedy in 1921. She was born in Oct 1888 in Pennsylvania. She died on 04 May 1951 in Philadelphia, Pennsylvania.

John Francis Reitze Sr. and Margaret Cecilia Malloy had the following children:
11.   i.   GEORGE B.[3] REITZE was born on 08 Aug 1896 in Philadelphia, Pennsylvania. He died about 27 Jan 1934 in Philadelphia, Pennsylvania. He married Isabel Smith in 1924 in Philadelphia, Philadelphia County, Pennsylvania. She was born on 30 Jun 1899. She died about 31 Dec 1978.

12.   ii.   LUCY ELIZABETH REITZE was born on 27 Nov 1897 in Pennsylvania. She died on 14 Jun 1980 in Alameda, California 94501. She married Joshua Leon Bach, son of William P. Bach and Mary B. Yurgey in 1917 in Philadelphia, Philadelphia County, Pennsylvania. He was born on 21 Apr 1890 in Pottstown, Pennsylvania. He died on 21 May 1951 in Alameda, California 94501.

    iii.   JOHN FRANCIS REITZE JR. was born on 23 Nov 1901 in Pennsylvania. He died on 20 Feb 1975 in Philadelphia, Pennsylvania.

13.   iv.   CATHERINE IRENE REITZE was born on 04 Sep 1903 in Philadelphia, Pennsylvania. She died on 21 Mar 1995 in West Caldwell, Essex County, New Jersey. She married Frank John Kelly in 1925 in Philadelphia, Philadelphia County,

Pennsylvania.

14.   v.   ELIZABETH MARY REITZE was born on 01 Sep 1905 in Philadelphia, Pennsylvania. She died on 27 Apr 1957 in Philadelphia, Pennsylvania. She married John Joseph Page Sr. in Sep 1925 in Philadelphia, Pennsylvania. He was born on 12 Oct 1902 in Philadelphia, Pennsylvania. He died on 17 Jan 1971 in Philadelphia, Pennsylvania.

6.   JOSEPHINE IRENE[2] REITZE (Christopher[1]) was born on 04 Jul 1877 in Philadelphia, Pennsylvania. She died on 03 May 1962 in Philadelphia, Pennsylvania. She married William Scott Chambers, son of George Washington Chambers and Annie Adam Edwards on 30 Mar 1896 in Philadelphia, Pennsylvania. He was born on 05 Jun 1867 in Philadelphia, Pennsylvania. He died on 05 Feb 1950 in Philadelphia, Pennsylvania.

William Scott Chambers and Josephine Irene Reitze had the following children:

15.   i.   HENRY GRAFE[3] CHAMBERS was born on 08 Jan 1897 in Philadelphia, Pennsylvania. He died on 11 Nov 1953 in Collingswood, Camden County, New Jersey. He married Mary Ann McCauley, daughter of Thomas McCauley and Mary Ann Wallace on 30 Jul 1918 in Philadelphia, Pennsylvania. She was born on 07 Jul 1892 in Philadelphia, Pennsylvania. She died on 08 Aug 1984 in Burlington Township, Burlington County, New Jersey.

16.   ii.   LUCY ELIZABETH CHAMBERS was born on 11 Mar 1898 in Philadelphia, Pennsylvania. She died on 22 Nov 1918 in Philadelphia, Pennsylvania. She married William Thompson, son of William Thompson and Hester Carrick on 12 Jun 1915 in Elkton, Cecil County, Maryland. He was born on 28 May 1891 in Pennsylvania. He died on 19 Jun 1965 in Philadelphia, Pennsylvania.

Generation 3

7.   ELIZABETH C.[3] REITZE (Christopher C.[2] Jr., Christopher[1]) was born on 02 Jun 1881 in Philadelphia, Pennsylvania. She died on 10 Sep 1971 in Downingtown, Uwchlan Township, Chester County, Pennsylvania 19380. She married John A. Bustard on 28 Jun 1899 in Philadelphia, Pennsylvania. He was born in Sep 1867 in Philadelphia, Pennsylvania. He died on 22 May 1934 in Philadelphia, Pennsylvania.

John A. Bustard and Elizabeth C. Reitze had the following children:

i.   EDWARD JOHN[4] BUSTARD was born on 15 Jan 1901 in Philadelphia, Pennsylvania. He died on 16 Apr 1927 in Philadelphia, Pennsylvania. He married Helen Weber about Aug 1926 in Philadelphia, Pennsylvania.

ii.   CHRISTOPHER C. BUSTARD was born on 03 Jul 1904 in Philadelphia, Pennsylvania. He died on 10 Sep 1942 in North Atlantic Ocean (World War II). He married Dora Rhettenbock in 1927 in Philadelphia, Philadelphia County, Pennsylvania. She was born on 25 Mar 1906. She died on 02 Sep 1972.

iii.   ELIZABETH WRAY BUSTARD was born on 02 May 1906 in Philadelphia, Pennsylvania. She died on 30 May 1981 in Downingtown, Uwchlan Township, Chester County, Pennsylvania. She married ROBERT WILSON. He was born in 1901 in Montana. He died on 02 Aug 1959 in Butte, Silver Bow, Montana.

8. **MARGARET MAY[3] REITZE** (Christopher C.[2] Jr., Christopher[1]) was born on 02 Oct 1882 in
    Philadelphia, Pennsylvania. She died on 06 Jun 1959 in Gloucester Township, Camden County,
    New Jersey. She married Edward Taylor Burtis, son of Ellwood Burtis and Louise Diemer on 19
    Jun 1901 in Philadelphia, Pennsylvania. He was born on 18 Dec 1871 in Philadelphia,
    Pennsylvania. He died on 23 Nov 1956 in Franklin Township, Gloucester County, New Jersey.

    Edward Taylor Burtis and Margaret May Reitze had the following children:

    i.   ELLWOOD C.[4] BURTIS was born in Apr 1903 in Philadelphia, Pennsylvania. He died
         on 27 Mar 1904 in Philadelphia, Pennsylvania.

    ii. MILDRED BURTIS was born in 1907 in Philadelphia, Pennsylvania. She married LEON
         MCCOY SR..

    iii. ELSIE BURTIS was born on 03 May 1910. She died on 24 Sep 1999 in Leesburg,
         Florida. She married (1) ARNOLD J. BRYAN in 1927 in Philadelphia, Philadelphia
         County, Pennsylvania. He was born in 1910. He died on 15 Feb 1972. She married
         (2) HAIG SAHAG MEDZARENTZ about 1977. He was born on 23 Feb 1923 in
         Philadelphia, Pennsylvania. He died on 03 Jun 2015 in Bushnell, Florida.

    iv. ELIZABETH BURTIS was born on 04 Aug 1914. She died on 05 May 1961. She
         married Howard Prince Sr. on 23 Mar 1934. He was born on 30 Jul 1912. He died
         on 18 Nov 1961.

9. **CHRISTOPHER CARL[3] REITZE I** (Christopher C.[2] Jr., Christopher[1]) was born on 15 Sep 1885 in
    Philadelphia, Pennsylvania. He died on 04 Jul 1942 in Philadelphia, Pennsylvania. He married (1)
    HELEN C. HOENIGMANN, daughter of Peter Hoenigmann and Kathrina [Caroline Rose] on 29 Apr
    1908 in Philadelphia, Pennsylvania. She was born on 20 May 1887 in Philadelphia, Pennsylvania.
    She died on 28 Jul 1923 in Philadelphia, Pennsylvania. He married (2) **THERESA "TESS" REIMOLD**,
    daughter of Conrad Reimold in 1924 in Philadelphia, Philadelphia County, Pennsylvania. She was
    born in Dec 1882 in Pennsylvania. She died on 18 Jul 1943 in Philadelphia, Pennsylvania.

    Christopher Carl Reitze I and Helen C. Hoenigmann had the following children:

    i.   CHRISTOPHER CARL[4] REITZE II was born on 19 Nov 1909 in Philadelphia,
         Pennsylvania. He died on 05 Feb 1985 in Pittsburgh, Allegheny County,
         Pennsylvania. He married (1) MARGARET MCFADDEN on 15 May 1930 in
         Philadelphia, Pennsylvania. She was born on 02 Jan 1906. She died on 20 May
         1973 in Pittsburgh, Allegheny County, Pennsylvania. He married (2) HELEN
         SHOEMAKER after 1973.

    ii. HARRY EDWIN REITZE SR. was born on 19 Jun 1919 in Philadelphia, Pennsylvania.
         He died on 16 Sep 1999 in Concord, New Hampshire. He married Jeanne Helene
         Chamberland on 12 Sep 1959 in Philadelphia, Pennsylvania. She was born on 07
         Jan 1927 in Manchester, New Hampshire. She died on 25 Jun 2009.

10. **CHARLES ARCHIBALD[3] REITZE JR.** (Charles Archibald[2] Sr., Christopher[1]) was born on 06 Nov 1893
    in Philadelphia, Pennsylvania. He died on 29 Aug 1969 in Philadelphia, Pennsylvania. He married
    MARY KUBICK. She was born on 04 Jul 1897 in Philadelphia, Pennsylvania. She died on 02 Jul

1964 in Philadelphia, Pennsylvania.

Charles Archibald Reitze Jr. and Mary Kubick had the following child:

    i.   JOHN C.[4] REITZ was born on 18 Nov 1928 in Philadelphia, Pennsylvania. He died on 01 Dec 1972. He married ELEANOR M. She was born on 09 Jul 1925. She died on 08 Jan 1995.

11.   GEORGE B.[3] REITZE (John Francis[2] Sr., Christopher[1]) was born on 08 Aug 1896 in Philadelphia, Pennsylvania. He died about 27 Jan 1934 in Philadelphia, Pennsylvania. He married Isabel Smith in 1924 in Philadelphia, Philadelphia County, Pennsylvania. She was born on 30 Jun 1899. She died about 31 Dec 1978.

George B. Reitze and Isabel Smith had the following child:

    i.   GEORGE J.[4] REITZE was born on 26 Dec 1926 in Philadelphia, Pennsylvania. He died about 19 Sep 1983 in Delaware County, PA 19063. He married ANNE HAEFFNER.

12.   LUCY ELIZABETH[3] REITZE (John Francis[2] Sr., Christopher[1]) was born on 27 Nov 1897 in Pennsylvania. She died on 14 Jun 1980 in Alameda, California 94501. She married Joshua Leon Bach, son of William P. Bach and Mary B. Yurgey in 1917 in Philadelphia, Philadelphia County, Pennsylvania. He was born on 21 Apr 1890 in Pottstown, Pennsylvania. He died on 21 May 1951 in Alameda, California 94501.

Joshua Leon Bach and Lucy Elizabeth Reitze had the following children:

    i.   JAY LEON[4] BACH was born on 14 Dec 1922 in Baltimore, Maryland. He died on 28 May 1943 in Plumas County, California (World War II).

    ii.   LOUIS BACH was born on 31 Oct 1927 in Baltimore, Maryland. He died on 21 Sep 1985 in Sonoma County, California.

13.   CATHERINE IRENE[3] REITZE (John Francis[2] Sr., Christopher[1]) was born on 04 Sep 1903 in Philadelphia, Pennsylvania. She died on 21 Mar 1995 in West Caldwell, Essex County, New Jersey. She married Frank John Kelly in 1925 in Philadelphia, Philadelphia County, Pennsylvania.

Frank John Kelly and Catherine Irene Reitze had the following children:

    i.   FRANK[4] KELLY JR. was born on 29 Apr 1926 in Philadelphia, Pennsylvania. He died on 31 Oct 1993 in Jupiter, Palm Beach County, FL 33477. He married GRACE. He married SECOND WIFE.

    ii.   MARGARET KELLY was born on 17 Jun 1927 in Philadelphia, Pennsylvania. She married HERBERT BURNS.

14.   ELIZABETH MARY[3] REITZE (John Francis[2] Sr., Christopher[1]) was born on 01 Sep 1905 in Philadelphia, Pennsylvania. She died on 27 Apr 1957 in Philadelphia, Pennsylvania. She married John Joseph Page Sr. in Sep 1925 in Philadelphia, Pennsylvania. He was born on 12 Oct 1902 in Philadelphia, Pennsylvania. He died on 17 Jan 1971 in Philadelphia, Pennsylvania.

John Joseph Page Sr. and Elizabeth Mary Reitze had the following children:

    i.   JOHN JOSEPH[4] PAGE JR. was born on 15 Sep 1926 in Philadelphia, Pennsylvania.

    ii.   JAMES GEORGE PAGE was born on 16 Aug 1933 in Philadelphia, Pennsylvania. He died on 13 Jan 2003 in Doraville, Georgia. He married Barbara Summerill on 06 Oct 1962 in Philadelphia, Pennsylvania. She was born on 01 Feb 1941 in Philadelphia, Pennsylvania.

15.   HENRY GRAFE[3] CHAMBERS (Josephine Irene[2] Reitze, Christopher[1] Reitze) was born on 08 Jan 1897 in Philadelphia, Pennsylvania. He died on 11 Nov 1953 in Collingswood, Camden County, New Jersey. He married Mary Ann McCauley, daughter of Thomas McCauley and Mary Ann Wallace on 30 Jul 1918 in Philadelphia, Pennsylvania. She was born on 07 Jul 1892 in Philadelphia, Pennsylvania. She died on 08 Aug 1984 in Burlington Township, Burlington County, New Jersey.

Henry Grafe Chambers and Mary Ann McCauley had the following children:

    i.   WILLIAM SCOTT[4] CHAMBERS was born on 25 Feb 1921 in Philadelphia, Pennsylvania. He died on 08 Feb 2014 in Plantation Broward County Florida. He married Gloria Ann Freda, daughter of Guerino Angelo Maria Freda and Filomena M. Quaresima on 26 Jan 1946 in Princeton, Mercer County, New Jersey. She was born on 06 Mar 1921 in Princeton, Mercer County, New Jersey. She died on 28 Aug 1987 in Portsmouth, Virginia.

    ii.   THOMAS WALLACE CHAMBERS was born on 25 Mar 1923 in Philadelphia, Pennsylvania. He died on 06 Oct 1955 in Stateburg, Sumter County, South Carolina. He married Florence Clark, daughter of James Freeman Clark and Anna Lee on 31 May 1948 in New Castle, New Castle County, Delaware. She was born on 13 Apr 1930 in Haddonfield, Camden County, New Jersey. She died on 16 Feb 2016 in Churchville, Bucks County, Pennsylvania.

16.   LUCY ELIZABETH[3] CHAMBERS (Josephine Irene[2] Reitze, Christopher[1] Reitze) was born on 11 Mar 1898 in Philadelphia, Pennsylvania. She died on 22 Nov 1918 in Philadelphia, Pennsylvania. She married William Thompson, son of William Thompson and Hester Carrick on 12 Jun 1915 in Elkton, Cecil County, Maryland. He was born on 28 May 1891 in Pennsylvania. He died on 19 Jun 1965 in Philadelphia, Pennsylvania.

William Thompson and Lucy Elizabeth Chambers had the following child:

    i.   JOSEPHINE HESTER[4] THOMPSON was born on 10 May 1916 in Philadelphia, Pennsylvania. She died on 06 Oct 2008 in Haddonfield, Camden County, New Jersey. She married David Harrington Marshall Sr., son of Thomas Marshall on 13 Jun 1942 in Philadelphia, Pennsylvania. He was born on 27 Jun 1912 in Philadelphia, Pennsylvania. He died on 02 Nov 2009 in Newark, Delaware.

THE BENNER FAMILY

by Kathryn C. Torpey

Lucy (Devlin) Reitze married Peter Benner as her second husband on November 25, 1879. Tracing Peter Benner's ancestry was determined to be important because, according to family legend, he and Lucy (Devlin) Reitze were childhood sweethearts.

Benner was a fairly common surname in Philadelphia in the 1800s. Despite the difficulties of researching the Benner family, the analysis and correlation of evidence in original and derivative sources leads to the conclusion that Peter Benner was the son of Henry and Mary (Buser) Benner and the grandson of Peter and Sarah Benner.

PETER AND SARAH BENNER
(Peter Benner's Grandparents)

Peter Benner (the elder) is said to have been the son of Martin Benner whose estate he administered in 1791.[1,2,3,4]

Peter Benner (the elder) and his brother, Matthias Benner, were master brickmakers who owned a brick making establishment at Schuylkill 2nd and Cedar Streets (now known as 21st and South). Apparently, Peter Benner (the elder) did fairly well in the brick making business. He was known to have employed six men and two boys in his brickyard in 1820 to whom he paid upwards of $1,300 in annual wages which is said to have been more than 60% of his "contingent

---

[1]National Society Sons of the American Revolution, Membership Applications, 1889-1970, Roland Benner Barrett, National # 30780, State # 880 (Michigan), Patriot Martin Benner, <<www.ancestry.com>>, downloaded February 2, 2017.

[2]*Benner families of Philadelphia, Pennsylvania: especially the family of Henry Benner (1777-1857)*, Call Number FC Be, Historical Society of Pennsylvania, Philadelphia, Pennsylvania.

[3]*The Matthias & Johanna Benner family of Phila. Including Henry C. Benner and his family of Washington, D.C.,* compiled by Barbara B. Ford (Rev. 1986), Call Number FC Be, Historical Society of Pennsylvania, Philadelphia, Pennsylvania.

[4]Estate of Martin Benner, March 1, 1791, Administration File No. 22, 1791, Book 1, p 240, Philadelphia, Pennsylvania, <<www.ancestry.com>>, downloaded May 23, 2017.

expenses."[5]

In addition to brick making, Peter Benner (the elder) and Matthias Benner owned two adjacent lots (19' x 120') at 13th and Spruce Streets which they bought on July 28, 1796 for 80 pounds each.[6] Both men appear to have married women named Sarah and they both appear to have built their homes adjacent to one another on their lots that fronted on the 1300 block of Spruce Street.

After a long life of hard work, Peter Benner (the elder), died "in Spruce above 13th St" on June 29, 1838, from rheumatism.[7] His obituary, which appeared in the *Philadelphia Public Ledger* on Monday, July 2, 1838, read as follows:

> On the 29th ult., Mr. Peter Benner in the 73rd year of his age.[8]

His wife, Sarah Benner, died two years later on June 1, 1840, from congestion of the lungs.[9] Her obituary, which appeared in the *Philadelphia Public Ledger* on Thursday, June 4, 1840, read as follows:

> On the 2nd (sic) inst., Mrs. Sarah Benner in the 80th year of her age. Friends and
> acquaintances of the family are invited to attend the funeral from her late
> residence Spruce Street above Thirteenth this afternoon at 4 o'clock without

---

[5]Donna J. Rilling, *Making Houses, Crafting Capitalism - Builders in Philadelphia 1790-1850*, (Philadelphia, Pennsylvania: University of Pennsylvania Press, 2001), p. 108.

[6]*Genealogies of Pennsylvania Families From the Pennsylvania Genealogical Magazine*, (Baltimore, Maryland: Genealogical Publishing Company, 1982), Volume I (Arnold - Hertzel), 354 (also see fn 42 re: Deed Book, D-59, 229, 233: 28 July 1796, Elizabeth Cornman *et al* to Mathias (sic) Benner and Peter Benner), and 355, <<www.ancestry.com>>, downloaded February 11, 2017.

[7]Philadelphia, Pennsylvania, City Registration of Deaths, 1803-1903, FHL Microfilm Roll 1905520, <<www.familysearch.org>>, downloaded February 3, 2017, re: Mr. Peter Benner, Philadelphia Cemetery.

[8]Obituary of Peter Benner (the elder), *Philadelphia Public Ledger*, Monday, July 2, 1838, Library of Congress, Newspaper Reading Room, Washington, D.C.

[9]Philadelphia, Pennsylvania, City Registration of Deaths, 1803-1903, FHL Microfilm Roll 1905620, <<www.familysearch.org>>, downloaded February 3, 2017, re: Susan (sic) Benner, Philadelphia Cemetery, who died June 1, 1840.

                                    Appendix D

further notice.[10]

They were both buried in the Vault of Peter Benner (the elder) at Ronaldson's Cemetery also known as Philadelphia Cemetery.[11] The cemetery was located at Shippen (now Bainbridge), 9th and Fitzwater St. It was established by a deed of trust from James Ronaldson in 1827. The cemetery is now defunct. The burials were removed to Forest Hills Memorial Park, Huntingdon Valley, Montgomery County, Pennsylvania.

Peter Benner (the elder)'s brother, Matthias Benner, lived another seventeen years at the 13th and Spruce Street address. He died on June 22, 1857. His obituary, which appeared in the *Philadelphia Public Ledger*, read as follows:

> On the 19th inst., MATTHIAS BENNER, in the 85th year of his age.
>
> The relatives and friends of the family are invited to attend his funeral, from his late residence in Spruce Street above Thirteenth, this afternoon at 3 o'clock.[12]

His wife, Sarah (Lewis) Benner, died the very next year on August 1, 1858. Her obituary, which appeared in the *Philadelphia Public Ledger*, read as follows:

> On Sunday morning, August 1st, SARAH, wife of the late MATTHIAS BENNER, aged 85 years.
>
> The relatives and friends of the family are respectfully invited to attend the funeral from her late residence 1312 Spruce Street, on Wednesday afternoon, the 4th inst., at 4 o'clock.[13]

Matthias Benner and his wife, Sarah (Lewis) Benner, were both buried in Ronaldson's Cemetery in a plot that belonged to their son-in-law, Samuel Tiller.[14]

------

[10]Obituary of Sarah Benner, *Philadelphia Public Ledger*, Thursday, June 4, 1840, Library of Congress, Newspaper Reading Room, Washington, D.C..

[11]Ronaldson's Cemetery Lot Holders Books, Lot # 4E3S (Vault of Peter Benner), Historical Society of Pennsylvania, Philadelphia, Pennsylvania., *incorrectly* states Sarah Benner's name as Susan (sic) Benner.

[12]Obituary for Matthias Benner, *Philadelphia Public Ledger*, Monday, June 22, 1857, Library of Congress, Newspaper Reading Room, Washington, D.C.

[13]Obituary for Sarah Benner, *Philadelphia Public Ledger*, Monday, August 2, 1858, Tuesday, August 3, 1858, and Wednesday, August 3, 1858, Library of Congress, Newspaper Reading Room, Washington, D.C.

[14]Ronaldson's Cemetery Lot Holders Books, Lot # 12E23S (Plot of Samuel Tiller), Historical Society of Pennsylvania, Philadelphia, Pennsylvania.

CHILDREN OF PETER (THE ELDER) AND SARAH BENNER. It is believed, but not proven, that Peter Benner (the elder) and his wife, Sarah, had the following children:

1. JOHN BENNER.

2. HENRY BENNER. Henry Benner (the father of Peter Benner) was born about 1794. He is described in greater detail in the next section.

3. SARAH BENNER.

4. MARIA BENNER. Maria Benner was born about 1801.[15] About 1820 she married Peter Bobb, Jr., who operated a brick making establishment at Federal and Gray's Ferry in the Moyamensing District of Philadelphia. The parents of Peter Bobb, Jr., were Peter Bobb, Sr., and his second wife, Abigail Maxfield.[16] They were married on March 31, 1795, at the Third Presbyterian Church.[17] Peter Bobb, Sr., was also in his brickmaking business. He is thought to have been fairly prosperous in that he is known to have employed at least three master carpenters to work on two of his buildings in 1813.[18]

Maria (Benner) Bobb had at least thirteen children. She and her husband, a master brickmaker, and their large family appear to have lived at the Benner family home at 13th and Spruce Streets until at least 1860.[19] Exactly what happened after that is not completely clear, but the Bobb family may have moved to 1327 S. Broad Street in South Philadelphia (between

---

[15] 1850 U.S. Census (population), Pennsylvania, Philadelphia County, City of Philadelphia, Lombard Ward, page 249-250, lines 37-11, Household of Peter Bobbe (sic), National Archives Microfilm Publication M432, Roll 812.

[16] E-mail dated April 25, 1998, from Sheila Wood, Gsslr@aol.com regarding the Bobb family.

[17] Pennsylvania Compiled Marriage Records, 1700-1821, *Pennsylvania Archives, Second Series, Volume 6,* "Early Marriages in Pennsylvania Churches, Third Presbyterian Church," (Harrisburg, Pennsylvania: State Printer, 1876), p. 517, <<www.ancestry.com>>, downloaded February 11, 2017, says: 1795, March 31 Bob (sic), Peter and Abigail Maxfield.

[18] Donna J. Rilling, *Making Houses, Crafting Capitalism - Builders in Philadelphia 1790-1850,* (Philadelphia, Pennsylvania: University of Pennsylvania Press, 2001), p. 148.

[19] 1860 U.S. Census (population), Pennsylvania, Philadelphia County, City of Philadelphia, Ward 7, page 527, lines 2-13, Household of Peter Bobb, National Archives Microfilm Publication M653, Roll 1157.

Federal and Wharton). Peter Bobb died there on August 12, 1867, from Disease of the Brain.[20]
His obituary, which appeared in the *Philadelphia Public Ledger*, read as follows:

> BOBB - On the 12th inst., PETER BOBB, aged 70 years.
>
> His male friends are respectfully invited to the funeral, from his late residence 1327 South
> Broad Street, on Tuesday morning, 20th inst., at 10 o'clock.[21]

Peter Bobb was buried in the Vault of Peter Benner (the elder), his father-in-law, at
Ronaldson's Cemetery.[22] Four of their children (William Bobb, George Bobb, Charles Bobb,
and Henry B. Bobb) and three of their grandchildren (Frank L. Thompson, George A. Bobb, and
Seymour Bobb) were also buried in the Vault of Peter Benner (the elder).[23]

In the 1870 census, Peter Bobb's widow, Maria (Benner) Bobb, and some of her children
were enumerated in South Philadelphia.[24] By 1880, she and some of the children had moved to
1622 Columbia Avenue in North Philadelphia.[25] She died there seven years later on August 9,
1887 at the age of 86.[26] The cause of death was listed in the cemetery records as "old age." No
obituary appeared in the *Philadelphia Public Ledger* to commemorate her passing. She was

---

[20]Ronaldson's Cemetery Lot Holders Books, Lot # 4E3S (Vault of Peter Benner),
Historical Society of Pennsylvania, Philadelphia, Pennsylvania.

[21]Obituary of Peter Bobb, *Philadelphia Public Ledger*, Monday, August 19, 1867, and
Tuesday, August 20, 1867, Library of Congress, Newspaper Reading Room, Washington, D.C.

[22]Ronaldson's Cemetery Lot Holders Books, Lot # 4E3S (Vault of Peter Benner),
Historical Society of Pennsylvania, Philadelphia, Pennsylvania.

[23]Ronaldson's Cemetery Lot Holders Books, Lot # 4E3S (Vault of Peter Benner),
Historical Society of Pennsylvania, Philadelphia, Pennsylvania.

[24]1870 U.S. Census (population), First Enumeration, Pennsylvania, Philadelphia County,
City of Philadelphia, Ward 26, page 217, lines 1-6, Household of Maria Bobb, National Archives
Microfilm Publication M593, Roll 1413.

[25]1880 U.S. Census (population), Pennsylvania, Philadelphia County, City of
Philadelphia, E.D. 616, sheet 85D, lines 43-47, Household of Maria Bobb, National Archives
Microfilm Publication T9, Roll 1188.

[26]Philadelphia, Pennsylvania, City Registration of Deaths, 1803-1903, FHL Microfilm
Roll 2078810, <<www.familysearch.org>>, downloaded February 8, 2017, re: Maria Bobb,
August 9, 1887.

buried in the Vault of Peter Benner (the elder), her father, at Ronaldson's Cemetery.[27]

HENRY AND MARY (BUSER) BENNER
(Peter Benner's Parents)

Henry Benner, the father of Peter Benner, was born about 1794. He married Mary Buser (sic) on November 9, 1817, at the First Reformed Church.[28] They lived at 220 Vaughan Street just a short distance from Henry Benner's father, Peter (the elder), and his uncle, Matthias, who owned two adjacent lots at 13th and Spruce Streets.[29,30,31] Per the city directories, Henry Benner's occupation was that of a brickmaker and, later, a carter.[32,33]

Henry Benner died on May 5, 1852, at the age of 58 from gastritis.[34] He was buried in the

---

[27]Ronaldson's Cemetery Lot Holders Books, Lot # 4E3S (Vault of Peter Benner), Historical Society of Pennsylvania, Philadelphia, Pennsylvania.

[28]Church Records of First Reformed Church, Philadelphia, Pennsylvania, v. 1-4, 1748-1831, FHL Microfilm Roll 20352, Item 8, <<www.familysearch.org>>, downloaded December 6, 2016.

[29]Obituary of Henry Benner, *Philadelphia Public Ledger*, Friday, May 7, 1852, Library of Congress, Newspaper Reading Room, Washington, D.C., states his residence was Vaughn (sic) Street between Locust and Walnut and Schuylkill Seventh and Eighth.

[30]Obituary of Mary Benner, *Philadelphia Public Ledger*, Friday, January 25, 1861, Library of Congress, Newspaper Reading Room, Washington, D.C., states her residence was No. 229 Vaughn (sic).

[31]*Genealogies of Pennsylvania Families From the Pennsylvania Genealogical Magazine*, (Baltimore, Maryland: Genealogical Publishing Company, 1982), Volume I (Arnold - Hertzel), p. 354-355 (also see fn 42 re: Deed Book, D-59, 229, 233: 28 July 1796, Elizabeth Cornman *et al* to Mathias (sic) Benner and Peter Benner), <<www.ancestry.com>>, downloaded February 11, 2017.

[32]1829-1837 Philadelphia city directories lists Henry Benner, brickmaker, Knoodle n W Walnut. Knoodle Street was officially renamed Vaughan Street in 1840.

[33]1838 Philadelphia city directory lists Henry Benner, carter, Knoodle ab Walnut.

[34]Pennsylvania, Philadelphia City Death Certificates, 1803-1915, FHL Microfilm Roll 1940065, <<www.familysearch.org>>, downloaded February 9, 2017, re: Henry Benner, Philadelphia Cemetery.

The [subscriber] has attended Henry Benner aged 58 years residing in Vaughan st who

                                                          Appendix D

Vault of Peter Benner (the elder), his father, at Ronaldson's Cemetery.[35] His obituary read as follows:

On the 5th inst., Mr. Henry Benner in the 58th year of his age. The relatives and friends of the family are respectfully invited to attend the funeral on Sunday afternoon next at 4 o'clock from his late residence Vaughn (sic) st between Locust and Walnut and Schuylkill Seventh and Eighth.[36]

He left a will dated May 3, 1852, that named his dear wife, Mary, and his children, but not individually, by name.[37]

Mary (Buser) Benner seems to have been the matriarch of a close knit family. Eight years of the death of her husband, she was enumerated as follows at 220 Vaughan Street:

Mary Benner	58 F		b. in Penna.
Mary Benner	7 F (sic)		b. in Penna.
Mary Schutz (sic)	14 F		b. in Penna.
Sam Benner	13 M		b. in Penna.
Henry Benner	10 M		b. in Penna.
Mary Benner	9 F		b. in Penna.
Peter Benner	6 M		b. in Penna.
Jno. Schutz (sic)	13 M		b. in Penna.
Geo. Benner	22 M	laborer	b. in Penna.
Wm Schutz (sic)	17 M		b. in Penna.[38]

The enumeration encompasses three generations of the Benner family. That is, Mary (Buser) Benner is enumerated with her youngest child, George Benner, and eight grandchildren including the four children of her son, Peter Benner and the three children of her daughter, Maria (Benner) Shultz. The identity of the second child named Mary Benner, aged 7 (sic), has not been positively ascertained, but she is believed to be the daughter of Mary (Buser) Benner's son, Charles Benner.

---

died on the 5th inst. of chronic gastritis. May 7 1852   [Jos Getanunde]

[35]Ronaldson's Cemetery Lot Holders Books, Lot # 4E3S (Vault of Peter Benner), Historical Society of Pennsylvania, Philadelphia, Pennsylvania.

[36]Obituary of Henry Benner, *Philadelphia Public Ledger*, Friday, May 7, 1852, Library of Congress, Newspaper Reading Room, Washington, D.C.

[37]Estate of Henry Benner, June 15, 1852, Will No. 188, 1852, Book 29, p 415, Philadelphia, Pennsylvania, <<www.ancestry.com>>, downloaded 23 May 2017.

[38]1860 U.S. Census (population), Pennsylvania, Philadelphia County, City of Philadelphia, Ward 8, page 560, lines 16-25, Household of Mary Benner, National Archives Microfilm Publication M653, Roll 1158.

She was still living at 220 Vaughan Street when she died, suddenly, on January 24, 1861.[39] The cause of her sudden death at the age of 65 was burns from a flammable fluid.[40] She was mourned deeply by her children. Their anguish at her passing is clearly described in the following poem that appeared in the *Philadelphia Public Ledger* along with her obituary:

> *A mother once so kind we had*
> *Who dwelt with us on earth*
> *She now is dead. Her smile no more*
> *Will cheer our fireside hearth*[41]

She, too, was buried in the Vault of Peter Benner (the elder), her father-in-law, at Ronaldson's Cemetery.[42]

CHILDREN OF HENRY AND MARY (BUSER) BENNER). Henry and Mary (Buser) Benner, the parents of Peter Benner, appear to have had the following seven children: Maria, Peter, Margaret, Sarah, John, Charles, and George.

1. MARIA BENNER. Maria Benner was born about 1819. She married Jacob S. Shultz. Altogether, they appear to have had at least five children.

In 1840, they were enumerated with a male child under 5 years old, probably their son Henry. They were then living immediately beside Maria (Benner) Shultz's father, Henry

---

[39]1861 Philadelphia city directory lists Mary Benner, widow Henry, 220 Vaugh (sic).

[40]Pennsylvania, Philadelphia City Death Certificates, 1803-1915, FHL Microfilm Roll 1977525, <<www.familysearch.org>>, downloaded May 24, 2017, re: Mary Benner, widowed, d. January 24, 1861, Ronaldson's Cemetery.

[41]Obituary of Mary Benner, *Philadelphia Public Ledger*, Friday, January 25, 1861, Library of Congress, Newspaper Reading Room, Washington, D.C.

> Benner - Suddenly on the 24th of June, Mrs. Mary, wife of the late Henry Benner, in the 64th year of her age. [POEM INSERT] The relatives and friends of the family are respectfully invited to attend her funeral from her late residence No. 220 Vaughn (sic) street on Sunday afternoon at 2 o'clock.

[42]Ronaldson's Cemetery Lot Holders Books, Lot # 4E3S (Vault of Peter Benner), Historical Society of Pennsylvania, Philadelphia, Pennsylvania.

Benner.[43] Unfortunately, their son died of cholera infantum on September 9, 1841.[44] His obituary read as follows:

He was buried on September 10, 1841, at Ronaldson's Cemetery in the Vault of Peter Benner (the elder).[46] Another child, an unnamed son, was stillborn on September 15, 1850. He was buried the next day at Monument Cemetery.[47]

In 1860, their three surviving children (William, John, and Mary) were living with their maternal grandmother, Mary (Buser) Benner.[48] The whereabout of Jacob and Mary (Benner) Shultz are unknown.

Maria (Benner) Shultz, widow (sic), died on October 23, 1861, at the age of 43 (sic) from cancer of the uterus.[49] She was buried in the Vault of Peter Benner (the elder), her grandfather, at

---

[43] 1840 U.S. Census (population), Pennsylvania, Philadelphia County, City of Philadelphia, Locust Ward, page 87, line 24, Household of Jacob Shultz, National Archives Microfilm Publication M704, Roll 483.

[44] Pennsylvania, Philadelphia City Death Certificates, 1803-1915, FHL Microfilm Roll 1905884, <<www.familysearch.org>>, downloaded March 15, 2017, re: Henry Shultz, 17 months, September 9, 1841, Philadelphia (aka Ronaldson's) Cemetery.

[45] Obituary of Henry Shultz, *Philadelphia Public Ledger*, Friday, September 10, 1841,<<www.genealogybank.com>>, downloaded March 14, 2017.

[46] Ronaldson's Cemetery Lot Holders Books, Lot # 4E3S (Vault of Peter Benner), Historical Society of Pennsylvania, Philadelphia, Pennsylvania.

[47] Pennsylvania, Philadelphia City Death Certificates, 1803-1915, FHL Microfilm Roll 1939736, <<www.familysearch.org>>, downloaded March 14, 2017, re: Shultz, male child, stillborn, September 16, 1850, Monument Cemetery.

[48] 1860 U.S. Census (population), Pennsylvania, Philadelphia County, City of Philadelphia, Ward 8, page 560, lines 16-25, Household of Mary Benner, National Archives Microfilm Publication M653, Roll 1158.

[49] Pennsylvania, Philadelphia City Death Certificates, 1803-1915, FHL Microfilm Roll 1986426, <<www.familysearch.org>>, downloaded February 11, 2017, re: Maria Shultz, widow (sic), 43 (sic) years, October 23, 1861, Ronaldson's Cemetery.

                                        Appendix D

Ronaldson's Cemetery.[50] Her obituary read as follows:

> SHULTZ - On the 23rd (sic) inst., Maria Shultz aged 42 years, daughter of Henry Benner (late). The relatives and friends of the family are invited to attend the funeral from the residence of her brother-in-law, Robert M. Shields, No. 232 Dean Street on Sunday the 27th inst., at 3 o'clock P.M.[51]

Her son, John Shultz, died on March 15, 1864, suddenly and unexpectedly. He was buried at Philanthropic Cemetery.[52] His obituary read as follows:

> SHULTZ - Suddenly, on the 15th, JOHN, son of Jacob and the late Maria Shultz, in the 17th year of his age. The relatives and friends of the family are respectfully invited to attend the funeral from the residence of his uncle, John Benner, No 117 Selfridge street, below Shippen, on Sunday afternoon at 3 o'clock.[53,54]

Even though Maria (Benner) Shultz was listed as a widow in her death certificate, her husband, Jacob S. Shultz, appears to have been living on March 15, 1864 when their son, John, died. Nothing is known about the death date or place of Jacob S. Shultz.

2. PETER BENNER. Peter Benner was born October 28, 1824. He was baptized on August 10, 1825 at the First Reformed Church in the City of Philadelphia.[55] He was married at least four times. His first wife was Rosanna. His second wife was Mary (–?–) Tryon, his third wife was Isabella Bartles, and his fourth wife was Lucy (Devlin) Reitze. He is described at greater length in the next section.

3. MARGARET BENNER. Margaret Benner was born on November 11, 1827. She was

---

[50]Ronaldson's Cemetery Lot Holders Books, Lot # 4E3S (Vault of Peter Benner), Historical Society of Pennsylvania, Philadelphia, Pennsylvania.

[51]Obituary of Maria Shultz, *Philadelphia Public Ledger*, Friday, October 25, 1861, and Saturday, October 26, 1861, Library of Congress, Newspaper Reading Room, Washington, D.C.

[52]Pennsylvania, Philadelphia City Death Certificates, 1803-1915, FHL Microfilm Roll 1986425, <<www.familysearch.org>>, downloaded March 15, 2017, re: John Shultz, 17 years, March 16 (sic), 1864, Philanthropic Cemetery.

[53]Obituary of John Shultz, *Philadelphia Public Ledger*, Saturday, March 19, 1864, <<www.genealogybank.com>>, downloaded March 15, 2017.

[54]Obituary of John Shultz, *Philadelphia Inquirer*, Saturday, March 19, 1864, <<www.genealogybank.com>>, downloaded March 15, 2017.

[55]First Reformed Church, Item 1, Baptisms 1805-1831; Confirmations 1813, Philadelphia, Philadelphia County, Pennsylvania, FHL Microfilm Roll 1905896.

baptized on October 8, 1829 at the First Reformed Church in the City of Philadelphia.[56] She married William E. Esher.

In 1860, William E. Esher, his wife, Margaret (Benner) Esher, and their two children, Ellen and Kate, were enumerated with his mother, Mary B. Esher.[57] In 1870, William E. Esher and his wife, Margaret (Benner) Esher, were enumerated together with all six of their children, Ellen, Kate, William, Harry, Alfred, and Laura. William Esher was working as a carpenter.[58]

William E. Esher, died from consumption on April 22, 1880.[59] At the time of his death he was working as a warf builder. He was buried at Monument Cemetery. His obituary read as follows:

> ESHER - On the 22nd inst., WILLIAM E., the son of Mary B. and the late William I. Esher, aged 49 years. Funeral on Sunday afternoon at 1 o'clock, from No. 1204 N. Nineteenth street.[60]

In 1880, Margaret (Benner) Esher, widow, was enumerated at 1204 N. 19th Street with three of her children, William, Henry, and Laura, and her youngest brother, George Benner, who was then working as a car driver.[61]

According to the Philadelphia city directories, Margaret (Benner) Esher continued living at 1204 N. 19th Street until at least 1900. In 1900, she was enumerated at that location with her

---

[56]First Reformed Church, Item 1, Baptisms 1805-1831; Confirmations 1813, Philadelphia, Philadelphia County, Pennsylvania, FHL Microfilm Roll 1905896.

[57]1860 U.S. Census (population), Pennsylvania, Philadelphia County, City of Philadelphia, Ward 20, Division 1, page 459, lines 31-35, Household of Mary B. Esher, National Archives Microfilm Publication M653, Roll 1171.

[58]1870 U.S. Census (population), First Enumeration, Pennsylvania, Philadelphia County, City of Philadelphia, Ward 20, page District 63, lines 8-15, Household of William Esher, National Archives Microfilm Publication M593, Roll 1406.

[59]Pennsylvania, Philadelphia City Death Certificates, 1803-1915, FHL Microfilm Roll 2032260, <<www.familysearch.org>>, downloaded February 25, 2017, re: William E. Esher, 49 years, April 25, 1880, Monument Cemetery.

[60]Obituary of William E. Esher, *Philadelphia Inquirer*, Saturday, April 24, 1880, <<www.genealogybank.com>>, downloaded February 25, 2017.

[61]1880 U.S. Census (population), Pennsylvania, Philadelphia County, City of Philadelphia, E.D. 624, Ward 29, page 172D, lines 39-44, Household of Margaret Esher, National Archives Microfilm Publication T9, Roll 1188.

daughter, Laura Esher, and two grandsons, Clarence Snyder and Charles Carter.[62]

Margaret (Benner) Esher died in West Rockhill Township, Bucks County, Pennsylvania, on January 21, 1908, from chronic bright's disease.[63] She was buried in Monument Cemetery in the same plot with her husband and other family members.[64] Her obituary read as follows:

> ESHER - On the 21st inst., MARGARET ESHER, widow of William Esher. Services on Saturday at 2 PM at her son's residence, Harry Esher, 909 N. 20th st. Interment private.[65]

4. SARAH BENNER. Sarah Benner was born on September 20, 1829. She was baptized on October 8, 1829 at the First Reformed Church in the City of Philadelphia.[66] She married Robert Morris Shields.[67] He was a painter.

Robert Morris Shields and Sarah (Benner) Shields had at least seven children, Howard Malcolm, Mary Julia, Robert Morris (Jr.), Harry, Elizabeth L.P., Sallie, and Thomas. Their daughter, Mary Julia, died on March 26, 1856, at the age of 5 years. Their sorrow over the loss of their young daughter is described in the following poem which accompanied her obituary:

------

[62]1900 U.S. Census (population), Pennsylvania, Philadelphia County, City of Philadelphia, E.D. 0717, Ward 29, page 5B, lines 80-83, Household of Margaret Esher, National Archives Microfilm Publication T623, Roll 1471.

[63]Pennsylvania, Death Certificates, 1906-1964, Pennsylvania Historic and Museum Commission, Harrisburg, Pennsylvania, re: Margaret Esher, January 21, 1908, West Rockville Township, Bucks County, Pennsylvania, <<www.ancestry.com>>, downloaded February 25, 2017.

[64]Mary B. Esher Family Plot, B-162, Monument Cemetery, Philadelphia, Philadelphia County, Pennsylvania, Plot Removed to Lawnview Cemetery, Rockledge, Montgomery County, Pennsylvania, on July 23, 1956, Pennsylvania and New Jersey, Church and Town Records, 1708-1985, <<www.ancestry.com>>, downloaded February 25, 2017.

[65]Obituary of Margaret Esher, *Philadelphia Inquirer*, Thursday, January 23, 1908, Friday, January 24, 1908, and Saturday, January 25, 1908, <<www.genealogybank.com>>, downloaded February 25, 2017.

[66]First Reformed Church, Item 1, Baptisms 1805-1831; Confirmations 1813, Philadelphia, Philadelphia County, Pennsylvania, FHL Microfilm Roll 1905896.

[67]Obituary of Maria Shultz, *Philadelphia Public Ledger*, Friday, October 25, 1861, and Saturday, October 26, 1861, Library of Congress, Newspaper Reading Room, Washington, D.C., says Maria Shultz, the daughter of the late Henry Benner, died at the residence of her brother-in-law, Robert M. Shields, 232 Dean Street.

On the 26th inst., MARY J., only daughter of Robt. M. and Sarah Shields, in the 5th year of her age.

Sweet bud of promise, thou are gone
Unto a happier clime -
Angel's harp in endless song
Shall be forever thine,
I take the little lamb said He,
and fold it in my breast;
Protection it shall find in Me,
and be forever blest.

The relatives and the friends of the family are respectfully invited to attend the funeral, from the residence of her parents, No. 16 Dean Street, on Saturday afternoon at 4 o'clock.[68]

Their son, Robert Morris (Jr.), died on February 1, 1863 at the age of 9½ years.[69] His obituary read as follow:

SHIELDS - Suddenly, on the 1st, ROBERT M. SHIELDS, JR., son of Robert and Sarah Shields, aged 9 years, 5 months, and 9 days. The relatives and friends of the family are respectfully invited to attend the funeral, from the residence of his father, 232 Dean Street, bel Locust, on Sunday afternoon at 2 o'clock.[70]

Robert Morris (Jr.) and his sister, Mary Julia, were both buried in the Vault of Robert Shields (likely their paternal grandfather) at Ronaldson's Cemetery.[71]

In 1850, Robert Morris and Sarah (Benner) Shields were enumerated together in a boarding house with their son, Howard Malcolm, and several others including a man named

---

[68]Obituary of Mary J. Shields, *Philadelphia Public Ledger*, Friday, March 28, 1856, Library of Congress, Newspaper Reading Room, Washington, D.C..

[69]Pennsylvania, Philadelphia City Death Certificates, 1803-1915, FHL Microfilm Roll 1977921, <<www.familysearch.org>>, downloaded February 12, 2017, re: Robert Morris Shields, 10 years, February 1, 1863, Ronaldson's Cemetery.

[70]Obituary of Robert M. Shields, Jr., *Philadelphia Public Ledger*, Friday, February 6, 1863, and Saturday, February 7, 1863, Library of Congress, Newspaper Reading Room, Washington, D.C.

[71]Ronaldson's Cemetery Lot Holders Books, Lot # 1W10S (Vault of Robert Shields), Historical Society of Pennsylvania, Philadelphia, Pennsylvania.

William Shields who may have been the brother of Robert Morris Shields.[72]

In 1860, Robert Morris and Sarah (Benner) Shields were enumerated together in their own home with their daughter, Elizabeth. The whereabouts of their two sons, Howard Malcolm and Harry, are unknown.[73]

In 1870, the Shields family was enumerated at 232 Dean Street.[74,75,76] George Benner, the younger brother of Sarah (Benner) Shields, was living with them. He was then working as a teamster. Also living with them in 1870 was a young man named Morris Shields (aged 14 in the first enumeration and 16 in the second enumeration) whose identity in unclear given that their son, Robert Morris Shields, Jr., died in 1863 at the age of 9½ years.

In 1880, Robert Morris Shields was still living at 232 Dean Street with three of his children, Henry, Sallie, and his married daughter, Elizabeth (Shields) Rawlings, her husband, William Rawlings, and their 2 month old son, Robert Rawlings.[77] His wife, Sarah (Benner) Shields, could not be located in the 1880 census.

---

[72]1850 U.S. Census (population), Pennsylvania, Philadelphia County, City of Philadelphia, Locust Ward, page 158A, lines 3-6, Household of Matilda Burlett, National Archives Microfilm Publication M432, Roll 814.

[73]1860 U.S. Census (population), Pennsylvania, Philadelphia County, City of Philadelphia, Ward 8, page 193, lines 1-3, Household of Robt. M. Shields, National Archives Microfilm Publication M653, Roll 1158.

[74]1870 U.S. Census (population), First Enumeration, Pennsylvania, Philadelphia County, City of Philadelphia, Ward 8, page 27A, lines 22-31, Household of Robert M. Shields, National Archives Microfilm Publication M593, Roll 1393.

[75]1870 U.S. Census (population), Second Enumeration, Pennsylvania, Philadelphia County, City of Philadelphia, Ward 8, page 274B, lines 5-14, Household of Robt. Shields, National Archives Microfilm Publication M593, Roll 1421.

[76]Dean Street ran from Locust to Spruce between 12th and 13th Streets, just a block and a half away from the Benner family home at 13th and Spruce Streets. According to Philadelphia City directories, Robert M. Shields lived at 232 Dean Street from 1861 to 1884. John Benner lived there in 1862. George Benner lived there from 1868 to 1874. According to her obituary, Maria (Benner) Shultz was buried from 232 Dean Street in 1861.

[77]1880 U.S. Census (population), Pennsylvania, Philadelphia County, City of Philadelphia, E.D. 147, Ward 8, page 452C, lines 27-32, Household of Robt. Shields, National Archives Microfilm Publication T9, Roll 1171.

                                          Appendix D

In 1890, Robert M. Shields was enumerated at 2443 Ingersoll Street.[78] According to the enumeration, he served during the Civil War as a private in Company G of the 22nd Pennsylvania Infantry from April 18 (sic), 1861 to August 7, 1861. Later, he served as a private in Company G of the 29th Pennsylvania Infantry from September 23, 1862 to May 4, 1865. He appears to have initially filed for a pension on January 19, 1891. He appears to have filed again on February 25, 1907 (29th PA) and on October 25, 1907 (22nd PA). He received a pension for his service.[79]

Sarah (Benner) Shields, died on February 19, 1896, of gastritis at about the age of 65.[80] Her obituary, which appeared in the *Philadelphia Inquirer* on February 22, 1896, read as follows:

> SHIELDS - On February 19, 1896, Sarah B. Shields. The relatives and friends
> of the family are respectfully invited to attend the funeral, on Sunday afternoon,
> at 1 o'clock, from her late residence, 2127 Nicholas street. Interment at
> Ronaldson's Cemetery.[81]

She was buried in the Vault of Peter Benner (her grandfather) at Ronaldson's Cemetery.[82] Her death certificate and two city directories say she was a widow.[83] To the contrary, the evidence reveals that Robert Morris Shields was remarried in 1891 to Josephine (Hance) Shinkel.[84] After her death on September 28, 1895, he removed to 1636 N. Dover Street to live

---

[78]1890 U.S. Special Schedule (Union veterans & widows), Pennsylvania, Philadelphia County, City of Philadelphia, E.D. 691, Ward 29, page 1, line 11, Robert M. Shields, National Archives Microfilm Publication M123, Roll 80.

[79]Robert M. Shields, Civil War Pension Application, SO 980680, SC 781526, Records of the Veterans Administration, Records Group 15, National Archives, Washington, D.C.

[80]Pennsylvania, Philadelphia City Death Certificates, 1803-1915, FHL Microfilm Roll 1863482, <<www.familysearch.org>>, downloaded February 12, 2017, re: Sarah Shields, widow, d. February 19, 1896, Ronaldson's Cemetery.

[81]Obituary of Sarah B. Shields, *Philadelphia Inquirer*, Saturday, February 22, 1896, and Sunday, February 23, 1896, Library of Congress, Newspaper Reading Room, Washington, D.C.

[82]Ronaldson's Cemetery Lot Holders Books, Lot # 4E3S (Vault of Peter Benner), Historical Society of Pennsylvania, Philadelphia, Pennsylvania.

[83]1891, 1892 Philadelphia city directories says: Sarah Shields, widow, Robert, 2127 Nicholas Street and Harry B. Shields, 2127 Nicholas Street.

[84]Philadelphia Marriage Index, 1885-1951, Philadelphia, Pennsylvania, <<www.ancestry.com>>, downloaded July 4, 2017, re: Robert Morris Shields to Josephine Shinkel, 1891, Certificate # 42989.

　　　　　　　　　　　　Appendix D

with his daughter Elizabeth (Shields) Rawlings and her family.[85,86,87] He died at that address on February 18, 1910, from apoplexy (i.e., stroke).[88] He and his second wife, Josephine (Hance) Shinkel Shields, were buried in Mount Peace Cemetery.

    5. JOHN BENNER. John Benner was born about 1834. He married Maria Ward on August 19, 1860 at the First Independent [Christian] Church in the City of Philadelphia.[89]

    In 1860, John Benner and his wife, Maria (Ward) Benner, were enumerated in the same household with his brother, Peter Benner.[90] Maria (Ward) Benner was also enumerated with her parents, James and Maria Ward, in the 1860 census.[91]

    In 1862, John Benner appears in the Philadelphia city directory at 232 Dean Street, the home of his brother-in-law, Robert M. Shields.[92] John Benner may have been living with his sister, Sarah (Benner) Shields, and her family while Robert M. Shields was away serving as a

---

[85]Pennsylvania, Philadelphia City Death Certificates, 1803-1915, FHL Microfilm Roll 1863235, <<www.familysearch.org>>, downloaded July 7, 2017, re: Josephine Shields, 41 y, married, d. September 28, 1895, typhoid fever, Mount Peace Cemetery.

[86]Obituary of Josephine Shields, *Philadelphia Inquirer*, Tuesday, October 1, 1895, <<www.genealogybank.com>>, downloaded July 4, 2017, states: wife of Robert M. Shields, daughter of Elizabeth and the late John Hance, residence 2730 Master street.

[87]1900 U.S. Census (population), Pennsylvania, Philadelphia County, City of Philadelphia, E.D. 0750, Ward 29, page 11B, lines 64-68, Household of Elizabeth Rawlings, National Archives Microfilm Publication T623, Roll 1472.

[88]Pennsylvania, Philadelphia City Death Certificates, 1803-1915, FHL Microfilm Roll 1405125, <<www.familysearch.org>>, downloaded February 26, 2017, re: Robert Morris Shields, widowed, d. February 18, 1910, Mount Peace Cemetery.

[89]Marriage of John Binner (sic) to Maria L. Ward, First Independent Church, Philadelphia, Pennsylvania, Pennsylvania and New Jersey, Church and Town Records, 1708-1985, <<www.ancestry.com>>, downloaded February 3, 2017.

[90]1860 U.S. Census (population), Pennsylvania, Philadelphia County, City of Philadelphia, Ward 9, page 130, lines 8-14. Household of Peter Benna (sic), National Archives Microfilm Publication M653, Roll 1159.

[91]1860 U.S. Census (population), Pennsylvania, Philadelphia County, City of Philadelphia, Ward 9, page 84, lines 24-31. Household of James Ward, National Archives Microfilm Publication M653, Roll 1159.

[92]1862 Philadelphia city directory.

private in Company G of the 29th Pennsylvania Infantry during the Civil War.

In 1870, John and Maria (Ward) Benner appear in the first enumeration with various members of their extended family at 1832 Montrose Street. The enumeration was as follows:

Benner, John	26 (sic)	bartender	HEAD
Benner Maria	33		Wife of HEAD
Tryon, Harrison	28	conductor	Step-son of Peter Benner
Tryon, Emeline	22		SIL of HEAD
Ward, Maria	58	keeping house	MIL of HEAD
Ward, Harriet	14		SIL of HEAD
Ward, James	19		BIL of HEAD
Benner, Peter	48	driver	Brother of HEAD
Benner, Henry	19	laborer	Nephew of HEAD
Tryon, Mary	2		Niece of HEAD
Fisher, Charles	16	musician	Possibly a boarder[93]

In the second enumeration of the 1870 census they were again enumerated with extended family members. The enumeration was as follows:

Benner, John	36	HEAD
Benner, Maria	33	Wife of HEAD
Tryon, Harrison	29	Step-son of Peter Benner
Tryon, Emelyne	23	SIL of HEAD
Tryon, Mary J.	2	Niece of HEAD
Benner, Charles	36	Brother of HEAD
Benner, Isabella	31	SIL of HEAD
Benner, George	11	Nephew of HEAD
Benner, Charles	5	Nephew of HEAD
Benner, Peter	40	Brother of HEAD
Benner, Henry	19	Nephew of HEAD
Ward, Maria	51	MIL of HEAD
Ward, Harriet	15	SIL of HEAD[94]

---

[93] 1870 U.S. Census (population), First Enumeration, Pennsylvania, Philadelphia County, City of Philadelphia, Ward 26, page 351B, lines 23-33, Household of John Benner, National Archives Microfilm Publication M593, Roll 1414.

[94] 1870 U.S. Census (population), Second Enumeration, Pennsylvania, Philadelphia County, City of Philadelphia, Ward 26, page 159, lines 26-38, Household of John Benner, National Archives Microfilm Publication M593, Roll 1441.

 Appendix D

During those years, John Benner was usually listed in the city directories as a bartender.[95] In 1880, John and Maria (Ward) Benner were enumerated as boarders at 3415 Warren Street. John Benner was then working as a hack driver[96]

Maria (Ward) Benner died from an ovarian cystic tumor on February 12, 1888.[97,98,99] Her obituary read as follows:

> BENNER - On the 12th inst., MARIAH E., wife of John Benner, in the 51st year of her age. The relatives and friends of the family, also Industrial Division, No. 62, Sons of Temperance, are respectfully invited to attend the funeral, this Thursday morning, at 9:30 o'clock, from her brother-in-law's [Harrison Tryon per 1888 city directory] residence, No. 2326 Vine Street. Services at St. Clement's Church, Twentieth and Cherry streets, at 10:30 o'clock.[100] To proceed to Odd Fellows cemetery.[101]

The death date and place of John Benner is unknown. It is possible that he and his wife, Maria (Ward) Benner, never had any children.

---

[95]1870, 1872, 1873 Philadelphia city directories list John L. Benner, bartender, h 1832 Montrose.

[96]1880 U.S. Census (population), Pennsylvania, Philadelphia County, City of Philadelphia, E.D. 485, Ward 24, page 34D, lines 1-8, Household of Michael Sheean, National Archives Microfilm Publication T9, Roll 1182.

[97]Pennsylvania, Philadelphia City Death Certificates, 1803-1915, FHL Microfilm Roll 2079026, <<www.familysearch.org>>, downloaded March 5, 2017, re: Maria E. Benner, d. February 12, 1888 at 2326 Vine Street, Ward 10, Odd Fellows Cemetery.

[98]James O. Ward Family Plot, Lot A-292, Odd Fellows Cemetery, Philadelphia, Philadelphia County, Pennsylvania, Plot Removed to Lawnview Cemetery, Rockledge, Montgomery County, Pennsylvania, on July 14, 1951, Pennsylvania and New Jersey, Church and Town Records, 1708-1985, <<www.ancestry.com>>, downloaded March 6, 2017.

[99]Odd Fellows Cemetery Register of Interments (1888), Philadelphia, Philadelphia County, Pennsylvania,, Pennsylvania and New Jersey, Church and Town Records, 1708-1985, <<www.ancestry.com>>, downloaded March 6, 2017.

[100]1888 Philadelphia city directory says: Tryon, Harrison J., switchman, 2326 Vine.

[101]Obituary of Mariah (sic) E. Benner, *Philadelphia Inquirer*, Thursday, February 16, 1888, <<www.genealogybank.com>>, downloaded March 6, 2017.

6. CHARLES BENNER. Charles Benner was born August 11, 1836.[102] His wife was named Isabella Russell.   Charles and Isabella (Russell) Benner had at least five children, Mary, George, Sarah, Charles, and Minerva. Their five-month-old daughter, Sarah S. Benner, died from cholera infantum on July 13, 1863.[103]   She was buried in the Vault of Peter Benner (the elder), her great-grandfather, at Ronaldson's Cemetery.[104]

In 1870, Charles Benner, his wife, Isabella (Russell) Benner, and their two sons, George and Charles, were enumerated in the household of his brother, John Benner, at 1832 Montrose Street.[105] The whereabouts of their oldest surviving daughter, Mary E. Benner, are unknown.

Two years later, on April 25, 1872, their oldest son, George W. Benner, died from injuries due to a tragic accident on the railroad.[106,107] He was buried in the Vault of Peter Benner (the elder), his great-grandfather, at Ronaldson's Cemetery.[108] His obituary read as follows:

---

[102]Pennsylvania, Death Certificates, 1906-1964, Pennsylvania Historic and Museum Commission, Harrisburg, Pennsylvania, re: Charles B. (sic) Benner, April 30, 1907, Pennsylvania Soldiers & Sailors Home, Erie, Erie County, Pennsylvania, <<www.ancestry.com>>, downloaded March 17, 2017.

[103]Pennsylvania, Philadelphia City Death Certificates, 1803-1915, FHL Microfilm Roll 1985763, <<www.familysearch.org>>, downloaded February 26, 2017, re: Sarah S. Bennar (sic), daughter of Chas. B. and Isabella F. Benner, d. July 13, 1863 at 507 S 21st Street; Ronaldson's Cemetery.

[104]Ronaldson's Cemetery Lot Holders Books, Lot # 4E3S (Vault of Peter Benner), Historical Society of Pennsylvania, Philadelphia, Pennsylvania, says: July 13, 1863, Sarah Benner, 5 months, Chol. Infantum.

[105]1870 U.S. Census (population), Second Enumeration, Pennsylvania, Philadelphia County, City of Philadelphia, Ward 26, page 159, lines 26-38, Household of John Benner, National Archives Microfilm Publication M593, Roll 1441.

[106]Pennsylvania, Philadelphia City Death Certificates, 1803-1915, FHL Microfilm Roll 2021141, <<www.familysearch.org>>, downloaded March 6, 2017, re: Geo. Benner, son of Charles Benner, d. April 25, 1872, Ronaldson's Cemetery.

[107]Pennsylvania, Philadelphia City Death Register, 1872, FHL Microfilm Roll 1003699, <<www.familysearch.org>>, downloaded March 6, 2017, re: George Benner, d. April 25, 1872, Ronaldson's Cemetery.

[108]Ronaldson's Cemetery Lot Holders Books, Lot # 4E3S (Vault of Peter Benner), Historical Society of Pennsylvania, Philadelphia, Pennsylvania, *incorrectly* states the child's name and age as follows: Charles (sic) Benner, 13 months (sic), d. April 25, 1872.

> BENNER - On the 25th inst., George W. Benner, eldest son of Charles and
> Isabella Benner in his 13th year. The relatives and friends of the family are
> respectfully invited to attend the funeral from the residence of his parents, 291[8]
> Market Street at 2 o'clock P.M. on Sunday afternoon.[109]

Their youngest child, Minerva Russell Benner, was born on October 22, 1873, while
Charles and Isabella (Russell) Benner were living at Spruce and Aspen Streets.[110] She was
baptized on January 21, 1874, at Saint James Episcopal Church.[111]

Isabella (Russell) Benner died on June 1, 1876, from phthisis pulmonalis. She was buried
at Ronaldson's Cemetery. Her death certificate says she was living at 1340 Pritchard (sic) Street.
This may be a reference to Pritchett Street, later known as Annin Street, which ran west from 13th
Street south of Washington Avenue.[112]   Her obituary read as follows:

> BENNER - On the 1st instant, ISABELLA, wife of Charles Benner, aged 37 years. The
> relatives and friends of the family are respectfully invited to attend the funeral, from the
> residence of Francis Cooper, No. 1340 Pritchard (sic) street this (Monday) afternoon, at 4
> o'clock. To proceed to Ronaldson.[113]

An account of the life of Charles Benner was provided by an anonymous source who
claims direct descent from Charles and Isabella (Russell) Benner. According to the anonymous
source, Charles Benner was badly injured in 1863 at Chancellorsville while serving in the 8th
Pennsylvania Cavalry during the Civil War. After the death of his wife, Charles Benner was
unable to care for his children. His oldest daughter, Mary E. Benner, married William S.

---

[109]Obituary of George Benner, *Philadelphia Public Ledger*, Saturday, April 27, 1872,
Library of Congress, Newspaper Reading Room, Washington, D.C.

[110]1873 Birth Register, City of Philadelphia, page 51, Minerva BENNER, October 22,
1873, Philadelphia City Archives, Philadelphia, Pennsylvania.

[111]Saint James Episcopal Church Baptismal Records, Pennsylvania and New Jersey,
Church and Town Records, 1708-1985, <<www.ancestry.com>>, downloaded March 12, 2017.
Note: This church was built in 1762 as a Swedish Lutheran church named Saint James of
Kingsess. It united with the Episcopal church in 1844. It is now known as Saint James
Episcopal Church of Kingsessing.

[112]Pennsylvania, Philadelphia City Death Certificates, 1803-1915, FHL Microfilm Roll
2027372, <<www.familysearch.org>>, downloaded February 5, 2017, re: Isabella Benner, d.
June 1, 1876, Ronaldson's Cemetery.

[113]Obituary of Isabella Benner, *Philadelphia Public Ledger*, Monday, June 5, 1876,
<<www.genealogybank.com>>, downloaded March 6, 2017.

                                    Appendix D

Taylor.[114] His youngest daughter, Minerva Russell Benner, was adopted by Joseph and Elizabeth Jackson. Her name was changed to Daisy Jackson. In 1885, Charles Benner tried to recover custody of his youngest daughter at the insistence of his oldest daughter, Mary (Benner) Taylor, but his petition was denied by the court.[115] His youngest daughter later married James J. "Jake" Dilks, a vaudeville performer. Minerva Russell Benner, also known as Daisy (Jackson) Dilks, died on June 23, 1949, in Philadelphia and is buried in Oakland Cemetery.[116,117,118]

The only surviving son of Charles Benner, Charles Henry Benner, was placed in a home for motherless children. This appears to be a reference to the House of Refuge where Charles Henry Benner was enumerated in the 1880 census.[119] Charles Henry Benner was baptized as an adult at Saint James Lutheran (sic) Church on November 11, 1906.[120] The witnesses included his

------

[114]1880 U.S. Census (population), Pennsylvania, Philadelphia County, City of Philadelphia, E.D. 568, Ward 27, page 5A, lines 44-46, Household of William Taylor, National Archives Microfilm Publication T9, Roll 1186. The Taylor family was living in the rear of 3133 Ludlow Street and William Taylor was working in a gas office.

[115]News Story, "Denied Possession of An Adopted Child," *Philadelphia Inquirer*, Saturday, January 10, 1885, <<www.genealogybank.com>>, downloaded May 24, 2017.

[116]Brahms Family Tree (private), created by wbrahms66, member since January 28, 2014, <<www.ancestry.com>>, anonymous message exchanged March 17, 2017.

[117]Benner Forum, <<www.genealogy.com>>, anonymous message posted September 3, 2000.

> Charles and Isabelle (sic) Benner - I am looking for any information on Charles Benner and his wife Isabelle. Isabelle may have died about 1876 in Philadelphia. They had a daughter Minerva (born October 22, 1873 in Philadelphia and died June 23, 1949 in Philadelphia). Minerva was adopted by the Jackson family and changed her name to Daisy Jackson before marrying James Jacob Dilks in 1894. She also had a brother Charles Benner. Daisy and "Jake" Dilks were in show business c. 1900. Any info would be appreciated. Thanks.

[118]1880 U.S. Census (population), Pennsylvania, Philadelphia County, City of Philadelphia, E.D. 227, Ward 14, page 383B, lines 7-19, Household of Joseph Jackson, National Archives Microfilm Publication T9, Roll 1174. Joseph Jackson was a painter.

[119]1880 U.S. Census (population), Pennsylvania, Philadelphia County, City of Philadelphia, E.D. 279, Ward 15, page 412D, line 15, Charles Benner, 14, At School, National Archives Microfilm Publication T9, Roll 1175.

[120]Saint James Lutheran (sic) Church, Kingsessing, Philadelphia, Pennsylvania, Baptisms, Charles Henry Benner, November 11, 1906, Pennsylvania and New Jersey, Church and Town Records, 1708-1985, <<www.ancestry.com>>, downloaded March 20, 2017. Note: This church

wife, Mrs. Ella Benner. He died a widower on August 15, 1942, and was buried in Saint James of Kingsessing Churchyard.[121] His wife, Ella O. (Moore) Benner, predeceased him on May 14, 1928. She was also buried at Saint James of Kingsessing Churchyard.[122]

Eventually, Charles Benner was admitted to the Pennsylvania Soldiers and Sailors Home in Erie. According to his Civil War pension index card, he served in Companies C, F, and M of the 8th Pennsylvania Cavalry.[123] According to his death certificate, he accidentally drowned in Erie on April 30, 1907. His body was transported to Philadelphia.[124] According to his obituary, the funeral was held at the home of his son-in-law, William S. Taylor, the husband of Mary Benner, oldest daughter of Charles and Isabella (Russell) Benner.[125,126] His obituary read as follows:

> BENNER - Suddenly, at Erie, Pa on April 30, 1907, CHARLES HENRY BENNER.
> Relatives and friends invited to attend the funeral services, on Friday, at 2:30 P.M.
> precisely at the residence of his son-in-law, Mr. William S. Taylor, 2101 South 68th st.

____

was built in 1762 as a Swedish Lutheran church named Saint James of Kingsess. It united with the Episcopal church in 1844. It is now known as Saint James Episcopal Church of Kingsessing.

[121]Pennsylvania, Death Certificates, 1906-1964, Pennsylvania Historic and Museum Commission, Harrisburg, Pennsylvania, re: Charles Benner, August 15, 1942, Philadelphia, Philadelphia County, Pennsylvania, <<www.ancestry.com>>, downloaded March 20, 2017.

[122]Pennsylvania, Death Certificates, 1906-1964, Pennsylvania Historic and Museum Commission, Harrisburg, Pennsylvania, re: Ella O. Benner, May 14, 1928, Philadelphia, Philadelphia County, Pennsylvania, <<www.ancestry.com>>, downloaded March 20, 2017.

[123]Charles H. Benner, Civil War Pension Application, SO 837395, Records of the Veterans Administration, Records Group 15, National Archives, Washington, D.C. Note: On September 11, 2017, NARA reported that the pension file of Charles H. Benner has been missing or misfiled since July 14, 2004.

[124]Pennsylvania, Death Certificates, 1906-1964, Pennsylvania Historic and Museum Commission, Harrisburg, Pennsylvania, re: Charles B. (sic) Benner, April 30, 1907, Pennsylvania Soldiers & Sailors Home, Erie, Erie County, Pennsylvania, <<www.ancestry.com>>, downloaded March 17, 2017.

[125]Pennsylvania, Death Certificates, 1906-1964, Pennsylvania Historic and Museum Commission, Harrisburg, Pennsylvania, re: Mary E. Taylor, April 10, 1924, Philadelphia, Philadelphia County, Pennsylvania, <<www.ancestry.com>>, downloaded March 19, 2017.

[126]Pennsylvania, Death Certificates, 1906-1964, Pennsylvania Historic and Museum Commission, Harrisburg, Pennsylvania, re: William S. Taylor, May 31, 1913, Philadelphia, Philadelphia County, Pennsylvania, <<www.ancestry.com>>, downloaded March 19, 2017.

The burial of Charles Benner is recorded in the records of both Mount Moriah Cemetery and Saint James of Kingsessing Churchyard.[128,129] As best can be determined from an examination of the Andrew Bair Funeral Home records, he was buried at Mount Moriah Cemetery.[130]

7. GEORGE BENNER. George Benner was the youngest son of Henry and Mary (Buser) Benner. His whereabouts at the time of the censuses was invaluable in tying together the Benner family. That is, in 1860, George Benner appears in the census with his mother, Mary (Buser) Benner, and eight of his nieces and nephews the children of his sister, Maria (Benner) Shultz, his brother, Peter Benner, and probably his brother, Charles Benner.[131] George Benner was then working as a laborer.

In 1870, George Benner was living with his sister and brother-in-law, Robert M. and Sarah (Benner) Shields, at 232 Dean Street which ran from Locust to Spruce between 12th and 13th Streets, just a block and a half away from the Benner family home at 13th and Spruce

---

[127]Obituary of Charles Henry Benner, *Philadelphia Inquirer*, Friday, May 3, 1907, <<www.genealogybank.com>>, downloaded February 24, 2017.

[128]Mount Moriah Cemetery Database, Section 153, Lot 75, Genealogical Society of Pennsylvania, <<https://genpa.org/>>, downloaded April 2, 2017.

4726	BENNER Taylor 1894 OCT 12
4772	BENNER Chas 1907 MAY 3
81503	MORRIS (sbc) 1906 SEP 20
90419	TAYLOR (sbc) 1903 JUN 9

[129]Saint James of Kingsessing Churchyard, Philadelphia, Pennsylvania, Burials, Charles Henry Benner, April 30, 1907, Pennsylvania and New Jersey, Church and Town Records, 1708-1985, <<www.ancestry.com>>, downloaded March 17, 2017.

[130]Andrew Bair Funeral Homes Record Cards, Charles Henry Benner, April 30, 1907, says: Cemetery-Mount Moriah, Pennsylvania and New Jersey, Church and Town Records, 1708-1985, <<www.ancestry.com>>, downloaded February 25, 2017.

[131]1860 U.S. Census (population), Pennsylvania, Philadelphia County, City of Philadelphia, Ward 8, page 560, lines 16-25, Household of Mary Benner, National Archives Microfilm Publication M653, Roll 1158.

Streets.[132,133] George Benner was then working as a teamster. According to the Philadelphia city directories, he lived there from 1868 to 1874.

And, in 1880, George Benner was enumerated with his widowed sister, Margaret (Benner) Esher, at 1204 N. 19th Street. He was then working as a car driver.[134]

George Benner later lived at 2103 Nicholas Avenue. In 1898, he was committed to the Philadelphia Almshouse & Hospital where he died of myocarditis and nephritis on April 13, 1907.[135,136] His obituary read as follows:

> BENNER - On April 13, 1907, GEORGE BENNER, aged 68 years. Relatives and friends are invited to attend the funeral services on Wednesday, at 2 P.M. precisely, at the parlors of Andrew J. Bair & Son, corner Nineteenth and Filbert streets. Interment private.[137]

His burial is recorded in the burial register of Trinity Episcopal Church.[138] He was buried

---

[132]1870 U.S. Census (population), First Enumeration, Pennsylvania, Philadelphia County, City of Philadelphia, Ward 8, page 27A, lines 22-31, Household of Robert M. Shields, National Archives Microfilm Publication M593, Roll 1393.

[133]1870 U.S. Census (population), Second Enumeration, Pennsylvania, Philadelphia County, City of Philadelphia, Ward 8, page 274B, lines 5-14, Household of Robt. Shields, National Archives Microfilm Publication M593, Roll 1421.

[134]1880 U.S. Census (population), Pennsylvania, Philadelphia County, City of Philadelphia, E.D. 624, Ward 29, page 172D, lines 39-44, Household of Margaret Esher, National Archives Microfilm Publication T9, Roll 1188.

[135]1900 U.S. Census (population), Pennsylvania, Philadelphia County, City of Philadelphia, E.D. 0652, Ward 27, page 24B, line 63, George Benner - Inmate, Philadelphia Almshouse & Hospital, National Archives Microfilm Publication T623, Roll 1469.

[136]Pennsylvania, Death Certificates, 1906-1964, Pennsylvania Historic and Museum Commission, Harrisburg, Pennsylvania, re: George Benner, April 13, 1907, Philadelphia Almshouse & Hospital, Ward 27, Philadelphia, Philadelphia County, Pennsylvania, <<www.ancestry.com>>, downloaded February 24, 2017.

[137]Obituary of George Benner, *Philadelphia Inquirer*, Wednesday, April 13, 1907, <<www.genealogybank.com>>, downloaded February 24, 2017.

[138]Trinity Episcopal Church Burial Register, Pennsylvania and New Jersey, Church and Town Records, 1708-1985, <<www.ancestry.com>>, downloaded February 24, 2017.

in Monument Cemetery on April 17, 1907.[139]

PETER BENNER

Peter Benner has been difficult to trace. He appears to have loved poetry, women, and children. He was married at least four times and had at least six children.

Peter Benner's first wife was named Rosanna. They appear to have had at least five children - Henry, Samuel, Henry (2nd), Mary, and Peter.

Peter Benner's son, Henry, died of inflammation of the lungs on September 3, 1850, at the age of two years, three months and seven days while the family was living on Vaughan Street. Henry Benner was buried in the Vault of Peter Benner (the elder), his great-grandfather.[140] Peter and Rosanna Benner's sorrow is described in a poem that accompanied their son's obituary:

> BENNER - On the 3rd inst., Henry Benner, son of Peter and Roseanna (sic)
> Benner, aged 2 years, 3 months, 7 days.
>
> *Weep lovely boy in death's cold arms*
> *No pain afflicts or fear alarms*
> *Your tender spirit now at rest*
> *With angels bright, with [----] the blest*
>
> *We grieve your stay on earth so brief*
> *But in our hearts there is relief*
> *Your fleeting race below is run*
> *Your little work on earth is done*
>
> *Farewell my lovely boy, farewell*
> *In Heaven I hope we'll meet*
> *And there with Holy angels dwell*
> *And rest at Jesus feet*
>
> The friends and family are respectfully invited to attend his funeral this
> (Thursday) afternoon at 1 o'clock from the residence of his father, in Vaughn
> (sic) Street, between Schuylkill Seventh and Eighth. [141]

---

[139] A.J. Bair & Son Funeral Home Plot, C-131, Monument Cemetery, Philadelphia, Philadelphia County, Pennsylvania, Pennsylvania and New Jersey, Church and Town Records, 1708-1985, <<www.ancestry.com>>, downloaded March 4, 2017.

[140] Ronaldson's Cemetery Lot Holders Books, Lot # 4E3S (Vault of Peter Benner), Historical Society of Pennsylvania, Philadelphia, Pennsylvania.

[141] Obituary of Henry Benner, *Philadelphia Public Ledger*, Thursday, September 8, 1850, Library of Congress, Newspaper Reading Room, Washington, D.C.

                    Appendix D

Little is known about Peter Benner and his family immediately after the death of Henry Benner except that Rosanna Benner is presumed to have died before 1860.

Peter Benner remarried on August 19, 1860. His second wife was Mary Ann (–?–) Tryon. The couple was married at the First Independent [Christian] Church in the City of Philadelphia on the same date his brother, John Benner, married Maria Ward.[142,143]

In the 1860 census, Peter Benner was enumerated with his second wife, Mary Ann (–?–) Tryon Benner, who was about 5 years older than Peter Benner and born in England. She is presumed to have been married previously and to have had a son named Harrison Tryon. Also enumerated in the same household were his brother, John Benner, and his wife, Maria (Ward) Benner as well as John and Clara Chambers whose relationship, if any, to the Benner family is unknown and a servant.[144] Peter Benner's four surviving children by his first wife, Rosanna Benner, were enumerated with his mother, Mary (Buser) Benner.[145]

Further complicating the story is the obituary of Coulter Russell who died on July 23, 1861, and is described as Peter Benner's step-son. It has not been possible to determine the identity of his mother. His obituary read as follows:

> RUSSELL - On the 23[d] inst., Coulter Russell, in the 17th year of his age.
>
> *Dear son, thou hast left us;*
> *'Tis thy loss we deeply feel;*
> *It is God that has bereft us,*
> *He can all our sorrows heal.*
>
> The relatives and friends of the family are respectfully invited to attend the funeral, from the residence of his step-father, Peter Benner, No. 220 Vaughn (sic) street, below Walnut,

---

[142]Marriage of Peter Binner (sic) to Mary H. Tryon, First Independent Church, Philadelphia, Pennsylvania, Pennsylvania and New Jersey, Church and Town Records, 1708-1985, <<www.ancestry.com>>, downloaded February 3, 2017.

[143]Marriage of John Binner (sic) to Maria L. Ward, First Independent Church, Philadelphia, Pennsylvania, Pennsylvania and New Jersey, Church and Town Records, 1708-1985, <<www.ancestry.com>>, downloaded February 3, 2017.

[144]1860 U.S. Census (population), Pennsylvania, Philadelphia County, City of Philadelphia, Ward 9, page 130, lines 8-14. Household of Peter Benna (sic), National Archives Microfilm Publication M653, Roll 1159.

[145]1860 U.S. Census (population), Pennsylvania, Philadelphia County, City of Philadelphia, Ward 8, page 560, lines 16-25, Household of Mary Benner, National Archives Microfilm Publication M653, Roll 1158.

between Fifteenth and Sixteenth, this (Friday) afternoon, the 26th inst., at 4 o'clock. To proceed to Odd Fellows Cemetery.[146,147]

Then, on August 19, 1861, a year after his marriage to Mary Ann (–?–) Tryon Benner, Peter Benner enlisted for three years as a private in Company F of the 8th Pennsylvania Cavalry. On October 4, 1861, he was detailed to the regimental quartermaster department as a master wagoner where he consistently performed extra duty. The only absence recorded in his service record was a furlough on April 10, 1863. He was present at the Battle of Gettysburg, July 2-4, 1863. His name is proudly inscribed on the wall of the Pennsylvania Memorial located on Cemetery Ridge at Gettysburg. He was discharged on August 27, 1864, by reason of expiration of his term of service.[148,149]

Apparently, Peter Benner's presumed step-son, Harrison J. Tryon, accompanied his step-father because he too enlisted as a private for three years in Company F of the 8th Pennsylvania Cavalry on the same day (August 19, 1861) as his step-father. Harrison J. Tryon also completed his term of service and was discharged on August 27, 1864.[150]

The whereabouts of Peter Benner's four surviving children during the three year period he was away are unclear. After his mother, Mary (Buser) Benner, died on January 24, 1861, the four children may have moved in with Peter Benner and his second wife, Mary Ann (–?–) Tryon Benner. They may have continued living with their step-mother during the three years their father, Peter Benner, and their step-brother, Harrison J. Tryon, were away during in the Civil War.[151,152]

---

[146]Obituary of Coulter Russell, *Philadelphia Inquirer*, Friday, July 26, 1861, <<www.genealogybank.com>>, downloaded April, 7, 2017.

[147]Obituary of Coulter Russell, *Philadelphia Public Ledger*, Thursday, July 25, 1861 and Friday, July 26, 1861, <<www.genealogybank.com>>, downloaded April, 7, 2017.

[148]Union Compiled Military Service Record for Peter Benner, Co. F, 8th Pennsylvania Volunteer Cavalry, Records of the Adjutant General's Office, Record Group 94, National Archives, Washington, D.C.

[149]Samuel P. Bates, *History of Pennsylvania Volunteers, 1861-1865*, 5 Volumes, (Harrisburg, Pennsylvania: State Printer, 1870), 3:133.

[150]Samuel P. Bates, *History of Pennsylvania Volunteers, 1861-1865*, 5 Volumes, (Harrisburg, Pennsylvania: State Printer, 1870), 3:135

[151]1862 Philadelphia city directory lists Peter Benner, express driver, at 220 Vaughan.

[152]1864 Philadelphia city directory lists Peter Benner, expressman; John Benner, driver; and Harrison Tryon, conductor, all living at 1107 Jefferson. Note: There are two possible

Less than a year after Peter Benner returned home from service during the Civil War, his youngest child, Peter, died of spotted fever (i.e., typhus). The date of his death was May 24, 1865. He was ten years old. His death certificate says his parents' names were Peter and Mary (sic) Benner. The reference to "Mary Benner" is presumed to be an erroneous reference to Peter Benner's second wife, Mary Ann (–?–) Tryon Benner.[153]

According to the obituary, Peter Benner's youngest child was buried from 1913 Christian Street, the residence of "his father."[154] Once again, Peter Benner inserted a poem along with his son's obituary which clearly described a father's sorrow over the loss of his child:

> BENNER - May 24, 1865, Peter Benner in the 10th year of his age.
>
> *Come quick father and mother*
> *I'm lonely for you*
>
> The relatives and friends and those of the family are respectfully invited to attend the funeral from the residence of his father, Peter Benner, No. 1913 Christian St. this Thursday afternoon the 25th inst., at 4 o'clock.[155]

The child was interred in the Vault of Peter Benner (the elder), his great-grandfather.[156]

Then, on July 18, 1866, Mary Ann (–?–) Tryon Benner, the second wife of Peter Benner, died of ascites which is most commonly caused by high blood pressure in the veins that bring

---

locations for this address - Jefferson *Street* was 2 blocks below Vaughan Street and Jefferson *Avenue* was 2 blocks above Vaughan Street.

[153]Pennsylvania, Philadelphia City Death Certificates, 1803-1915, FHL Microfilm Roll 19869516, <<www.familysearch.org>>, downloaded March 8, 2017, re: Peter Benner, d. May 24, 1865, father: Peter Benner; mother: Mary (sic), Ronaldson's Cemetery.

[154]1866 Philadelphia city directory lists Peter Benner, expressman, at 1913 Christian.

[155]Obituary of Peter Benner, *Philadelphia Public Ledger*, Thursday, May 25, 1865, Library of Congress, Newspaper Reading Room, Washington, D.C.

[156]Ronaldson's Cemetery Lot Holders Books, Lot # 4E3S (Vault of Peter Benner), Historical Society of Pennsylvania, Philadelphia, Pennsylvania says the child died on May 23 (sic), 1865.

blood to the liver due to cirrhosis.[157,158] Her obituary read as follows:

> BENNER - On the 18th inst., MARY A. BENNER, wife of Peter Benner, aged 48.
>
> *We saw her suffering, heard her sighs,*
> *With throbbing hearts and weeping eyes;*
> *But now she calmly sleeps at last,*
> *All grief, all pain, all suffering past.*
>
> The relatives and friends of the family are respectfully invited to attend the funeral, from her husband's residence, No. 1913 Christian street, ths (Monday) afternoon, at 1 o'clock. To proceed to Odd Fellows Cemetery.[159]

Two years later, on August 14, 1869, Peter Benner's daughter, Mary, died of paralysis. Her obituary read as follows:

> BENNER - On the 14th inst., MARY, daughter of Peter Benner, in the 16th year of her age.
>
> *Gone home to Jesus.*
>
> The relatives and friends of the family are respectfully invited to attend the funeral, from the residence of her brother in law, Mr. Henry Myers, 1404 North Fifth street this (Monday) afternoon at two o'clock. Interment at Odd Fellows Cemetery.[160]

Exactly how Mary Benner came to be the sister-in-law of Henry Myers is unknown, but she and her brother, Samuel Benner, were both living with the Myers family at the time of her

---

[157]Pennsylvania, Philadelphia City Death Certificates, 1803-1915, FHL Microfilm Roll 1987618, <<www.familysearch.org>>, downloaded March 19, 2017, re: Mary Ann Bennet (sic), d. May 18, 1866, Odd Fellows Cemetery.

[158]Pennsylvania, Philadelphia City Death Register, 1872, FHL Microfilm Roll 1003693, <<www.familysearch.org>>, downloaded March 19, 2017, re: Mary Ann Bennett (sic), d. May 18, 1866, Odd Fellows Cemetery.

[159]Obituary of Mary A. Benner, *Philadelphia Inquirer*, Monday, May 21, 1866, <<www.genealogybank.com>>, downloaded February 24, 2017.

[160]Obituary of Mary Benner, *Philadelphia Public Ledger*, Monday, August 16, 1869, <<www.genealogybank.com>>, downloaded March 15, 2017.

death.[161,162] After the funeral, Mary Benner was laid to rest in the same plot at Odd Fellows Cemetery where Peter Benner's step-son, Coulter Russell and his second wife, Mary Ann (–?–) Tryon Benner were also buried.

One year later, in both the first and second enumerations of the 1870 census, Peter Benner and his son, Henry (2nd) were enumerated at 1832 Montrose Street in the household of his brother, John Benner.[163,164] Various other family members were also enumerated at that location including Peter Benner's brother, Charles Benner and his step-son, Harrison J. Tryon.

Three years later, Peter Benner appears to have married for the third time. The marriage return states that on January 11, 1873, William Neill, alderman, solemnized the marriage of Peter Benner (49) and Isabella Bartles (38). In the marriage return, Peter Benner was stated to be a driver living at 2310 (sic) Lancaster Avenue.[165] The newspaper announcement of their marriage read as follows:

> BENNER-BARTLES - On the 11th instant. by Alderman Wm. Neill, PETER BENNER to ISABELLA BARTLES, all of this city.[166]

Their Christmas gift that year was the birth of a son named Peter Christian Benner born

---

[161]1870 U.S. Mortality Schedule, Pennsylvania, Philadelphia County, City of Philadelphia, Ward 17, page 1, line 15, Mary Benner, National Archives Microfilm Publication M1838, Roll 6, re: Family Number 270.

[162]1870 U.S. Census (population), First Enumeration, Pennsylvania, Philadelphia County, City of Philadelphia, Ward 17, page 104A, lines 4-16, Household of Henry Myers, National Archives Microfilm Publication M593, Roll 1402, re: Family Number 270.

[163]1870 U.S. Census (population), First Enumeration, Pennsylvania, Philadelphia County, City of Philadelphia, Ward 26, page 351B, lines 23-33, Household of John Benner, National Archives Microfilm Publication M593, Roll 1414.

[164]1870 U.S. Census (population), Second Enumeration, Pennsylvania, Philadelphia County, City of Philadelphia, Ward 26, page 159, lines 26-38, Household of John Benner, National Archives Microfilm Publication M593, Roll 1441.

[165]1873 Philadelphia Marriage Returns for Alderman William Neill, No. 1638 N. 2nd Street, First Quarter, Peter Benner (49) to Isabella Bartles (38), January 11, 1873, Philadelphia City Archives, Philadelphia, Pennsylvania, FHL Microfilm Roll 1765164.

[166]Marriage of Peter Benner and Isabella Bartles, *Philadelphia Public Ledger*, Tuesday, January 14, 1873, <<www.genealogybank.com>>, downloaded March 9, 2017.

on December 24, 1873. He was baptized at Methodist Midtown Parish on February 16, 1874.[167]
All went well until mid-summer when the child contracted cholera infantum. Sadly, he died on
July 30, 1874, and was buried in Machpelah Cemetery.[168]

Thereafter, Peter and Isabella (Bartles) Benner lived at the following addresses:

1875	Peter Benner	driver	2459 Hope
1876	Peter Benner	driver	2502 Hope
	Isabella Benner	dressmaking	2502 Hope
1877	Peter Benner	driver	2502 Hope
	Isabella Benner	dressmaker	2502 Hope

Nothing more is known about Isabella (Bartles) Benner.

On July 29, 1879, Peter Benner, teamster, joined GAR Post 118.[169] Then, on November
25, 1879, he married his fourth wife, Lucy (Devlin) Reitze. Although the Benner-Reitze
marriage was recorded in the *Reitze Family Bible*, it has not been found in the Philadelphia
marriage registers or in the New Jersey marriage index.[170,171,172]

How Peter Benner met Lucy (Devlin) Reitze is unclear. According to family legend,
they were childhood sweethearts, but there is no evidence that they knew each other when they

---

[167]Baptism of Peter Christian Benner, Methodist Midtown Parish (also known as
Cohocksink Midtown Parish) Philadelphia, Pennsylvania, Pennsylvania and New Jersey, Church
and Town Records, 1708-1985, <<www.ancestry.com>>, downloaded January 11, 2017.

[168]Pennsylvania, Philadelphia City Death Certificates, 1803-1915, FHL Microfilm Roll
2022203, <<www.familysearch.org>>, downloaded March 11, 2017, re: Peter Christian Benner,
d. July 30, 1874, Machpelah Cemetery.

[169]Grand Army of the Republic Membership Records, 1865-1936, FHL Microfilm Roll
2311108, <<www.familysearch.org>>, downloaded March 8, 2017.

[170]*The Reitze Family Bible - Latin Vulgate Version*. (New York: 35 Gold Street, 1844)
was in the possession of the late Josephine Thompson Marshall, 121 Reillywood Avenue,
Haddonfield, New Jersey 08033-2201.

[171]No Record of Registration # 951628, August 1997, Benner/Reitze Marriage; 1878,
1879, 1880 Marriage Registers, City of Philadelphia, Philadelphia City Archives, Philadelphia,
Pennsylvania.

[172]New Jersey State Marriage Index (1878-1900), New Jersey State Archives, Trenton,
New Jersey.

were young.[173] It seems more likely that Peter Benner met Lucy (Devlin) Reitze after the death of her husband, Christopher Reitze, through mutual friends she and/or her daughter, Lizzie (Reitze) Collins Douglass, had in West Philadelphia.[174]

In the 1880 census, Peter Benner was enumerated with his fourth wife, Lucy (Devlin) Reitze Benner and her four minor children at 32[3]4 St. James Place in West Philadelphia.

The enumeration was as follows:

Peter Benner	54	drives car	PA PA PA
Lucie (sic) Benner	42 wife	keeping house	PA Ire PA
Elizabeth Benner (sic)	16 dau (sic)	works in chemical works	PA PA PA (sic)
Charles Benner (sic)	13 son (sic)	works in wire works	PA PA PA (sic)
John Benner (sic)	10 son (sic)	in school	PA PA PA (sic)
Josephine Benner (sic)	4 dau (sic)		PA PA PA (sic)[175]

The marriage of Peter and Lucy (Devlin) Benner came to a sudden end on January 21, 1881, when Peter Benner was hit and killed by a train.[176,177] They were only married 14 months. His obituary, which appeared in the *Philadelphia Public Ledger*, on Monday, January 24, 1881,

---

[173]Conversation on August 12, 1995, with the late Josephine Thompson Marshall, 121 Reillywood Avenue, Haddonfield, New Jersey 08033-2201.

[174]One possibility is that Peter Benner and Lucy (Devlin) Reitze met through their connections to the Douglass family all of whom resided in West Philadelphia in 1880 within a few blocks of Peter Benner's niece, Mary E. (Benner) Taylor, the oldest daughter of Charles Benner, who resided at 3133 Ludlow Street. (See Appendix D, *The Douglass Family*)

[175]1880 U.S. Census (population), Pennsylvania, Philadelphia County, City of Philadelphia, E.D. 582, Ward 27, page 216C, lines 34-39, Household of Peter Benner, National Archives Microfilm Publication T9, Roll 1186.

[176]News Story, *Philadelphia Public Ledger*, Saturday, January 22, 1881, p. 1, Library of Congress, Newspaper Reading Room, Washington, D.C.

> Killed by a Car - Peter Benner, aged 57, of No. 3214 St. James' place, was last evening run over and killed by a freight car, at the west end of Market street bridge.

[177]News Story, *Philadelphia Inquirer*, Monday, January 24, 1881, <<www.newspapers.com>>, downloaded August 17, 2017.

> Peter Benners (sic) aged forty-five (sic) years, was found dead on Friday evening under a freight car on the west side of Market street bridge. The wheels had passed over his body. Benners (sic) resided at No. 3214 St. James' place and was well-known as a driver of a mule team for Charles Lafferty, hauling freight cars on Market street.

                    Appendix D

read as follows:

> BENNER - Suddenly, in the 21st inst., PETER BENNER, aged 57 years.
>
> The relatives and friends of the family, also members Company F, Eighth Regiment, Penna Cavalry, and Post No. 18, G.A.R., are respectfully invited to attend the funeral, on Tuesday afternoon at 2 o'clock, from his late residence 3214 St. James street, west of Twenty-second, below Walnut, West Phila. To proceed to Ronaldson's Cemetery.[178]

Oddly, his wife, Lucy (Devlin) Reitze Benner, was not mentioned in his obituary. He was buried in the Vault of Peter Benner (the elder), his grandfather, at Ronaldson's Cemetery.[179,180]

---

[178]Obituary of Peter Benner, *Philadelphia Public Ledger*, Monday, January 24, 1881, Library of Congress, Newspaper Reading Room, Washington, D.C.

[179]1881 Death Register, City of Philadelphia, page 37, Peter Benner, January 21, 1881, Philadelphia City Archives, Philadelphia, Pennsylvania.

[180]Ronaldson's Cemetery Lot Holders Books, Lot # 4E3S (Vault of Peter Benner), Historical Society of Pennsylvania, Philadelphia, Pennsylvania.

Appendix D

Descendants of Peter Benner

Generation 1

1.   **PETER[1] BENNER** was born in 1764 in Pennsylvania. He died on 29 Jun 1838 in Philadelphia, Pennsylvania. He married **SARAH "SALOME"**. She was born in 1760 in Pennsylvania. She died on 01 Jun 1840 in Philadelphia, Pennsylvania.

Peter Benner and Sarah "Salome" had the following children:

      i.   JOHN[2] BENNER was born on 04 Apr 1792 in Philadelphia, Pennsylvania.

2.   ii.   HENRY BENNER was born on 01 Jan 1794 in Pennsylvania. He died on 05 May 1852 in Philadelphia, Pennsylvania. He married Mary Buser on 09 Nov 1817 in Philadelphia, Pennsylvania. She was born in 1796 in Pennsylvania. She died on 24 Jan 1861 in Philadelphia, Pennsylvania.

     iii.   SARAH BENNER was born in 1797 in Philadelphia, Pennsylvania. She died on 27 Nov 1832 in Philadelphia, Pennsylvania.

3.   iv.   MARIA BENNER was born in 1801 in Pennsylvania. She died on 09 Aug 1887 in Philadelphia, Pennsylvania. She married Peter Bobb, son of Peter Bobb Sr. and Abigail Maxfield about 1820. He was born about 1797 in Pennsylvania. He died on 12 Aug 1867 in Philadelphia, Pennsylvania.

Generation 2

2.   **HENRY[2] BENNER** (Peter[1]) was born on 01 Jan 1794 in Pennsylvania. He died on 05 May 1852 in Philadelphia, Pennsylvania. He married Mary Buser on 09 Nov 1817 in Philadelphia, Pennsylvania. She was born in 1796 in Pennsylvania. She died on 24 Jan 1861 in Philadelphia, Pennsylvania.

Henry Benner and Mary Buser had the following children:

4.   i.   MARIA "MARY"[3] BENNER was born in 1819 in Philadelphia, Pennsylvania. She died on 23 Oct 1861 in Philadelphia, Pennsylvania. She married Jacob S. Shultz about 1839. He was born about 1815. He died after 1864.

5.   ii.   PETER BENNER was born on 28 Oct 1824 in Philadelphia, Pennsylvania. He died on 21 Jan 1881 in Philadelphia, Pennsylvania. He married (1) ROSANNA about 1845. He married (2) MARY ANN on 19 Aug 1860 in Philadelphia, Pennsylvania. She was born in 1818 in England. She died on 18 May 1866 in Philadelphia, Pennsylvania. He married (3) ISABELLA BARTLES on 11 Jan 1873 in Philadelphia, Pennsylvania. She was born in 1835. She died before 1879. He married (4) LUCY S. DEVLIN, daughter of Peter Devlin and Susan Kennedy on 25 Nov 1879. She was born on 12 Jun 1836 in Philadelphia, Pennsylvania. She died on 07 May 1909 in Gloucester City,Camden County, New Jersey.

6.   iii.   MARGARET BENNER was born on 11 Nov 1827 in Philadelphia, Pennsylvania. She died on 21 Jan 1908 in West Rockhill, Bucks County, Pennslyvania. She married WILLIAM E. ESHER. He was born in 1831 in Pennsykvania. He died on 22 Apr 1880 in Philadelphia, Pennsylvania.

7.   iv.   SARAH BENNER was born on 20 Sep 1829 in Philadelphia, Pennsylvania. She died

Appendix E

on 19 Feb 1896 in Philadelphia, Pennsylvania. She married ROBERT MORRIS SHIELDS. He was born between 1832-1835 in Philadelphia, Pennsylvania. He died on 18 Feb 1910 in Philadelphia, Pennsylvania.

    v.   JOHN BENNER was born in 1834 in Philadelphia, Pennsylvania. He died after 1888. He married Maria L. Ward, daughter of James Ward and Maria on 19 Aug 1860 in Philadelphia, Pennsylvania. She was born in 1837 in Pennsylvania. She died on 12 Feb 1888 in Philadelphia, Pennsylvania.

8.   vi.   CHARLES HENRY BENNER was born on 11 Aug 1836 in Philadelphia, Pennsylvania. He died on 30 Apr 1907 in Erie, Erie County, Pennsylvania. He married ISABELLA RUSSELL. She was born about 1837. She died on 01 Jun 1876 in Philadelphia, Pennsylvania.

    vii.   GEORGE BENNER was born in 1839 in Philadelphia, Pennsylvania. He died on 13 Apr 1907 in Philadelphia, Pennsylvania.

3.   MARIA[2] BENNER (Peter[1]) was born in 1801 in Pennsylvania. She died on 09 Aug 1887 in Philadelphia, Pennsylvania. She married Peter Bobb, son of Peter Bobb Sr. and Abigail Maxfield about 1820. He was born about 1797 in Pennsylvania. He died on 12 Aug 1867 in Philadelphia, Pennsylvania.

Peter Bobb and Maria Benner had the following children:

    i.   SARAH[3] BOBB was born on 01 Oct 1823 in Philadelphia, Pennsylvania. She died on 12 Jul 1908 in New Orleans, Orleans Parish, Louisiana.

9.   ii.   CHARLOTTE BOBB was born on 24 Mar 1825 in Philadelphia, Pennsylvania. She died on 16 Jan 1909 in New Orleans, Orleans Parish, Louisiana. She married James P. Thompson, son of William C. Thompson and Catherine Bobb on 11 Nov 1858 in Warren County, Mississippi. He was born in Sep 1821 in Hopkinsville, Christian County, Kentucky. He died on 22 Jul 1897 in Harvey, Jefferson Parish, Louisiana.

10.   iii.   HENRY BOBB was born in 1828 in Pennsylvania. He died on 14 Nov 1872 in Philadelphia, Pennsylvania. He married (1) MARY SMITH about 1848. She died before 1870. He married (2) LOUISA SHINN after 1848. She was born about 1845 in Pennsylvania. She died on 20 Jan 1907 in Pennsylvania.

    iv.   WILLIAM BOBB was born in 1829. He died on 27 May 1836 in Philadelphia, Pennsylvania.

11.   v.   PETER BOBB was born on 28 Sep 1830 in Pennsylvania. He died on 14 Nov 1907 in Philadelphia, Pennsylvania. He married (1) MARY NEELY about 1851. She was born in 1832. She died on 08 Oct 1880. He married (2) KATHERINE GREAR, daughter of Jacob F Grear and Anna M Lowry after 1851. She was born in Nov 1843 in Pennsylvania. She died on 17 May 1919 in Camden, Camden County, New Jersey.

12.   vi.   ANNA BOBB was born in 1832 in Pennsylvania. She died on 15 Aug 1911 in Philadelphia, Pennsylvania. She married SAMUEL DAVIS HAWLEY. He was born on

08 May 1820 in Ohio. He died on 18 Apr 1916 in Philadelpha, Pennsylvania.

13.   vii.   ALEXANDER BOBB was born on 18 Feb 1834 in Philadelphia, Pennsylvania. He died on 17 Feb 1917 in Philadelphia, Pennsylvania.

    viii.   GEORGE BOBB was born in 1836 in Pennsylvania. He died on 04 Apr 1864 in Philadelphia, Pennsylvania. He married MARY CHRISTY.

    ix.   CHARLES BOBB was born in 1839. He died on 29 Sep 1876 in Philadelphia, Pennsylvania.

14.   x.   KATE BOBB was born on 27 Oct 1840 in Philadelphia, Pennsylvania. She died on 01 Dec 1922 in Philadelphia, Pennsylvania. She married MOSES STARR. He was born in 1838 in Pennsylvania. He died on 27 Dec 1904 in Philadelphia, Pennsylvania.

15.   xi.   WILLIAM BOBB was born in 1843. He died on 07 Jun 1900 in Philadelphia, Pennsylvania. He married MARY ANN BRENDEN.

    xii.   JAMES BOBB was born on 22 Jan 1846 in Pennsylvania. He died on 27 Dec 1920 in Philadelphia, Pennsylvania. He married MARGARET TAYLOR. She was born in Jun 1871 in Maryland.

    xiii.   FRANK BOBB was born in Feb 1848 in Pennsylvania. He died on 09 Dec 1933 in Litchfield County, Connecticut. He married ANNIE O. ARMSTRONG. She was born in Nov 1851 in Pennsylvania. She died about 08 Feb 1927 in Winsted, Litchfield, Connecticut.

Generation 3

4.   **MARIA "MARY"³ BENNER** (Henry², Peter¹) was born in 1819 in Philadelphia, Pennsylvania. She died on 23 Oct 1861 in Philadelphia, Pennsylvania. She married Jacob S. Shultz about 1839. He was born about 1815. He died after 1864.

Jacob S. Shultz and Maria "Mary" Benner had the following children:

    i.   HENRY B.⁴ SHULTZ was born in Apr 1840 in Philadelphia, Pennsylvania. He died on 09 Sep 1841 in Philadelphia, Pennsylvania.

    ii.   WILLIAM WELSH SHULTZ was born on 05 Mar 1843 in Philadelphia, Pennsylvania. He died on 03 Oct 1929 in Philadelphia, Pennsylvania. He married BELLA.

    iii.   MARY SHULTZ was born on 10 Jun 1847 in Philadelphia, Pennsylvania. She died on 18 Dec 1920 in Philadelphia, Pennsylvania. She married DANIEL MCCLURE.

    iv.   JOHN SHULTZ was born in 1848 in Philadelphia, Pennsylvania. He died on 15 Mar 1864 in Philadelphia, Pennsylvania.

    v.   BABY BOY SHULTZ was born on 15 Sep 1850 in Philadelphia, Pennsylvania. He died on 16 Sep 1850 in Philadelphia, Pennsylvania.

5. **PETER**[3] **BENNER** (Henry[2], Peter[1]) was born on 28 Oct 1824 in Philadelphia, Pennsylvania. He died on 21 Jan 1881 in Philadelphia, Pennsylvania. He married (1) **ROSANNA** about 1845. He married (2) **MARY ANN** on 19 Aug 1860 in Philadelphia, Pennsylvania. She was born in 1818 in England. She died on 18 May 1866 in Philadelphia, Pennsylvania. He married (3) **ISABELLA BARTLES** on 11 Jan 1873 in Philadelphia, Pennsylvania. She was born in 1835. She died before 1879. He married (4) **LUCY S. DEVLIN**, daughter of Peter Devlin and Susan Kennedy on 25 Nov 1879. She was born on 12 Jun 1836 in Philadelphia, Pennsylvania. She died on 07 May 1909 in Gloucester City,Camden County, New Jersey.

Peter Benner and Rosanna had the following children:

    i.   HENRY[4] BENNER was born in May 1848 in Philadelphia, Pennsylvania. He died on 03 Sep 1850 in Philadelphia, Pennsylvania.

    ii.   SAMUEL BENNER was born on 11 Jan 1849 in Philadelphia, Pennsylvania. He died on 11 Jan 1915 in Philadelphia, Pennsylvania. He married OLIVIA NIXON. She was born on 28 May 1851 in Philadelphia, Pennsylvania. She died on 28 Jan 1927 in Philadelphia, Pennsylvania.

    iii.   HENRY BENNER was born in 1851 in Pennsylvania. He died on 26 Nov 1884 in Philadelphia, Pennsylvania. He married Matilda "Tillie" Dunhour, daughter of Charles Dunhour and Elizabeth Smith on 01 Jan 1878 in Philadelphia, Pennsylvania. She was born on 24 Jun 1858 in Pennsylvania. She died on 03 Oct 1936 in Philadelphia, Pennsylvania.

    iv.   MARY BENNER was born in 1853 in Pennsylvania. She died on 16 Aug 1869 in Philadelphia, Pennsylvania.

    v.   PETER BENNER was born in 1855 in Philadelphia, Pennsylvania. He died on 24 May 1865 in Philadelphia, Pennsylvania.

Peter Benner and Isabella Bartles had the following child:

    vi.   PETER CHRISTIAN BENNER was born on 24 Dec 1873 in Philadelphia, Pennsylvania. He died on 01 Aug 1874 in Philadelphia, Pennsylvania.

6. **MARGARET**[3] **BENNER** (Henry[2], Peter[1]) was born on 11 Nov 1827 in Philadelphia, Pennsylvania. She died on 21 Jan 1908 in West Rockhill, Bucks County, Pennslyvania. She married **WILLIAM E. ESHER**. He was born in 1831 in Pennsykvania. He died on 22 Apr 1880 in Philadelphia, Pennsylvania.

William E. Esher and Margaret Benner had the following children:

    i.   ELLEN ELLA[4] ESHER was born in Nov 1849 in Philadelphia, Pennsylvania. She died on 07 Mar 1934 in Philadelphia, Pennsylvania. She married FRANK HAMILTON SMITH. He was born in 1849 in Pennsylvania. He died on 10 Nov 1917 in Philadelphia, Pennsylvania.

        Appendix E

ii.   KATE R. ESHER was born in Sep 1859 in Philadelphia, Pennsylvania. She died on 25 Jan 1894 in Philadelphia, Pennsylvania. She married DANIEL SNYDER. She married HUSBAND CARTER.

iii.   WILLIAM E. ESHER was born on 19 Sep 1861 in Philadelphia, Pennsylvania. He died on 09 Oct 1928 in Philadelphia, Pennsylvania. He married MARY E. MALLOY. She was born in Dec 1874 in Pennsylvania.

iv.   HENRY L. ESHER was born on 03 Feb 1865 in Philadelphia, Pennsylvania. He died on 14 Jan 1922 in Philadelphia, Pennsylvania. He married Katie S on 18 Apr 1898. She was born on 27 Sep 1855 in Pennsylvania. She died on 11 Sep 1930.

v.   ALFRED H. ESHER was born in 1866 in Philadelphia, Pennsylvania. He died on 30 Jan 1878 in Philadelphia, Pennsylvania.

vi.   LAURA ESHER was born in Jul 1870 in Philadelphia, Pennsylvania. She died on 01 Apr 1963 in Philadelphia, Pennsylvania. She married George A. Luthringer in 1906 in Philadelphia, Pennsylvania. He was born in 1885 in Pennsylvania. He died after 1963.

7.   **SARAH**[3] **BENNER** (Henry[2], Peter[1]) was born on 20 Sep 1829 in Philadelphia, Pennsylvania. She died on 19 Feb 1896 in Philadelphia, Pennsylvania. She married **ROBERT MORRIS SHIELDS**. He was born between 1832-1835 in Philadelphia, Pennsylvania. He died on 18 Feb 1910 in Philadelphia, Pennsylvania.

Robert Morris Shields and Sarah Benner had the following children:

i.   HOWARD MALCOLM[4] SHIELDS was born in 1850 in Philadelphia, Pennsylvania. He died on 10 Feb 1929 in Philadelphia, Pennsylvania. He married MAGGIE. She was born in 1852.

ii.   MARY JULIA SHIELDS was born in 1851 in Philadelphia, Pennsylvania. She died on 26 Mar 1856 in Philadelphia, Pennsylvania.

iii.   ROBERT MORRIS SHIELDS was born in 1853 in Philadelphia, Pennsylvania. He died on 01 Feb 1863 in Philadelphia, Pennsylvania.

iv.   HENRY SHIELDS was born on 04 Dec 1857 in Philadelphia, Pennsylvania. He died on 06 Dec 1939 in Philadelphia, Pennsylvania. He married ROSE.

v.   ELIZABETH J. SHIELDS was born on 31 May 1860 in Philadelphia, Pennsylvania. She died on 07 Dec 1936 in Philadelphia, Pennsylvania. She married William S. Rawlings in 1880. He was born in Philadelphia, Pennsylvania. He died after 1930.

vi.   SARAH ROSALIE "SALLIE" SHIELDS was born on 13 Jun 1862 in Philadelphia, Pennsylvania. She died on 01 Mar 1946 in Philadelphia, Pennsylvania. She married WILLIAM T. WALKER.

    vii.   THOMAS SHIELDS was born on 01 Jan 1864 in Philadelphia, Pennsylvania. He died on 20 Nov 1949 in Philadelphia, Pennsylvania. He married ANNA E.

8.   **CHARLES HENRY³ BENNER** (Henry², Peter¹) was born on 11 Aug 1836 in Philadelphia, Pennsylvania. He died on 30 Apr 1907 in Erie, Erie County, Pennsylvania. He married **ISABELLA RUSSELL**. She was born about 1837. She died on 01 Jun 1876 in Philadelphia, Pennsylvania.

Charles Henry Benner and Isabella Russell had the following children:

    i.   MARY E.⁴ BENNER was born on 20 Nov 1859 in Philadelphia, Pennsylvania. She died on 10 Apr 1924 in Philadelphia, Pennsylvania. She married WILLIAM S. TAYLOR. He was born on 12 Mar 1853 in Philadelphia, Pennsylvania. He died on 31 May 1913 in Philadelphia, Pennsylvania.

    ii.   GEORGE W. BENNER was born in 1859 in Pennsylvania. He died on 25 Apr 1872 in Philadelphia, Pennsylvania.

    iii.   SARAH BENNER was born in Feb 1863 in Pennsylvania. She died on 13 Jul 1863 in Philadelphia, Pennsylvania.

    iv.   CHARLES HENRY BENNER was born on 14 Jun 1867 in Philadelphia, Pennsylvnia. He died on 15 Aug 1942 in Philadelphia, Pennsylvania. He married ELLA O. MOORE. She was born on 06 Feb 1870 in Pennsyvania. She died on 14 May 1928 in Philadelphia, Pennsylvania.

    v.   MINERVA RUSSELL BENNER was born on 22 Oct 1873 in Philadelphia, Pennsylvania. She died on 23 Jun 1949 in Philadelphia, Pennsylvania. She married James Jacob Dilks in 1893. He was born on 15 Apr 1861 in Philadelphia, Pennsylvania. He died on 01 Dec 1935 in Philadelphia, Pennsylvania.

9.   **CHARLOTTE³ BOBB** (Maria² Benner, Peter¹ Benner) was born on 24 Mar 1825 in Philadelphia, Pennsylvania. She died on 16 Jan 1909 in New Orleans, Orleans Parish, Louisiana. She married James P. Thompson, son of William C. Thompson and Catherine Bobb on 11 Nov 1858 in Warren County, Mississippi. He was born in Sep 1821 in Hopkinsville, Christian County, Kentucky. He died on 22 Jul 1897 in Harvey, Jefferson Parish, Louisiana.

James P. Thompson and Charlotte Bobb had the following children:

    i.   WALTER MATTINGLY⁴ THOMPSON was born in 1860 in Louisiana. He died on 18 Apr 1944 in Gretna, Jefferson Parish, Louisiana. He married Mary Ida Faecher on 02 Jan 1912 in Gretna, Jefferson Parish, Louisiana. She was born in 1876 in Louisiana. She died on 02 Mar 1958 in Orleans Parish, Louisiana.

    ii.   FRANK .L. THOMPSON was born about 1861. He died on 11 Oct 1864 in Philadelphia, Pennsylvania.

    iii.   GEORGE D. THOMPSON was born in May 1865 in New Orleans, Orleans Parish, Louisiana. He died on 01 Oct 1893 in Grand Isle, Jefferson Parish, Louisiana.

    iv.   UNKNOWN THOMPSON.

10.   HENRY[3] BOBB (Maria[2] Benner, Peter[1] Benner) was born in 1828 in Pennsylvania. He died on 14 Nov 1872 in Philadelphia, Pennsylvania. He married (1) MARY SMITH about 1848. She died before 1870. He married (2) LOUISA SHINN after 1848. She was born about 1845 in Pennsylvania. She died on 20 Jan 1907 in Pennsylvania.

Henry Bobb and Mary Smith had the following child:
    i.   HENRY[4] BOBB JR was born on 24 Nov 1865 in Philadelphia, Pennsylvania. He died on 02 Dec 1865 in Philadelphia, Pennsylvania.

Henry Bobb and Louisa Shinn had the following child:
    ii.   MARY BOBB was born in Dec 1867 in Philadelphia, Pennsylvania. She died on 18 Dec 1867 in Philadelphia, Pennsylvania.

11.   PETER[3] BOBB (Maria[2] Benner, Peter[1] Benner) was born on 28 Sep 1830 in Pennsylvania. He died on 14 Nov 1907 in Philadelphia, Pennsylvania. He married (1) MARY NEELY about 1851. She was born in 1832. She died on 08 Oct 1880. He married (2) KATHERINE GREAR, daughter of Jacob F Grear and Anna M Lowry after 1851. She was born in Nov 1843 in Pennsylvania. She died on 17 May 1919 in Camden, Camden County, New Jersey.

Peter Bobb and Mary Neely had the following child:
    i.   JAMES K.[4] BOBB was born in 1861 in Pennsylvania.

Peter Bobb and Katherine Grear had the following child:
    ii.   FEMALE BOBB was born on 17 Jul 1886 in Philadelphia, Pennsylvania. She died on 17 Jul 1886 in Philadelphia, Pennsylvania.

12.   ANNA[3] BOBB (Maria[2] Benner, Peter[1] Benner) was born in 1832 in Pennsylvania. She died on 15 Aug 1911 in Philadelphia, Pennsylvania. She married SAMUEL DAVIS HAWLEY. He was born on 08 May 1820 in Ohio. He died on 18 Apr 1916 in Philadelpha, Pennsylvania.

Samuel Davis Hawley and Anna Bobb had the following child:
    i.   EDGAR W.[4] HAWLEY was born in May 1878 in Philadelphia, Pennsylvania.

13.   ALEXANDER[3] BOBB (Maria[2] Benner, Peter[1] Benner) was born on 18 Feb 1834 in Philadelphia, Pennsylvania. He died on 17 Feb 1917 in Philadelphia, Pennsylvania.

Alexander Bobb had the following child:
    i.   SEYMOUR[4] BOBB was born in 1859. He died on 18 Jan 1873 in Philadelphia, Pennsylvania.

14.   KATE[3] BOBB (Maria[2] Benner, Peter[1] Benner) was born on 27 Oct 1840 in Philadelphia, Pennsylvania. She died on 01 Dec 1922 in Philadelphia, Pennsylvania. She married MOSES STARR. He was born in 1838 in Pennsylvania. He died on 27 Dec 1904 in Philadelphia, Pennsylvania.

Moses Starr and Kate Bobb had the following children:

    i.   FRANK C.⁴ STARR was born on 07 Nov 1866. He died on 24 Mar 1941.

    ii.   WILLIAM C. STARR was born on 02 Feb 1868 in Pennsylvania. He died on 28 Jun 1927 in Philadelphia, Pennsylvania.

    iii.   CHARLES TURNER STARR was born in 1869 in Philadelphia, Pennsylvania. He died on 27 Oct 1885 in Philadelphia, Pennsylvania.

    iv.   KATE L. STARR was born in 1872 in Philadelphia, Pennsylvania. She died on 09 Jan 1873 in Philadelphia, Pennsylvania.

15.   **WILLIAM³ BOBB** (Maria² Benner, Peter¹ Benner) was born in 1843. He died on 07 Jun 1900 in Philadelphia, Pennsylvania. He married **MARY ANN BRENDEN**.

William Bobb and Mary Ann Brenden had the following child:

    i.   GEORGE ALEXANDER⁴ BOBB was born in 1870. He died on 13 Aug 1876 in Philadelphia, Pennsylvania.

THE DOUGLASS FAMILY

by Kathryn C. Torpey

Elizabeth M. Reitze married Henry Grafe Douglass as her second husband on April 25, 1892. Tracing Henry Grafe Douglass and his siblings was determined to be important because of their said relationship to Collins and Kennedy families living in Philadelphia.

The analysis and correlation of evidence in original and derivative sources led to the conclusion that Henry Grafe Douglass was the son of Henry G. Douglass (Sr.); the grandson of Joseph Douglass; and the great-grandson of John Douglass who served in the Continental Line during the Revolutionary War.[1,2] The evidence further revealed that Henry G. Douglass (Sr.), the father of Henry Grafe Douglass, was married twice and had five children.

The first wife of Henry G. Douglass (Sr.) was Margaret Trout with whom he has 3 sons - George, Charles and Joseph.[3] Margaret (Trout) Douglass died on June 9, 1845 and was buried in

---

[1]Notice, *Daily Pennsylvanian*, May 31, 1843, Wednesday, Philadelphia, Pennsylvania, <<www.genealogybank.com>>, downloaded December 31, 2016, says:

> NOTICE. At an Orphans' Court for the City and County of Philadelphia, held at Philadelphia, on the 6th day of May, A.D. 1843. In the matter of the Estate of JOHN DOUGLASS, deceased, ss. ... the heirs of Joseph Douglass, a son who deceased before the said intestate, viz: S. Carver Douglass, Charles Douglass, Catharine Kennedy, late Douglass, wife of Charles Kennedy, Henry Douglass, Ellen Carpenter, late Douglass, wife of George W. Carpenter; ... Witness Edward King Esq., at Philadelphia this eighth day of May, A.D. 1843 JACOB LEWIS, Clerk of the O.C.

[2]Virgil D. White, *Genealogical Abstracts of Revolutionary War Pension Files*, (n.p. National Historical Publishing Company, 1993), p. 1012.

> Douglass, John S2180, Cont Line (PA), appl 6 Oct 1832, Philadelphia PA, sol d 8 Jul 1840 aged 80, sol's son John Douglass, Jr. lived at Philadelphia PA in 1840, in 1857 the only surviving children were; Elizabeth Ottinger aged 84 a wid of Christopher Ottinger, Ann Stevenson aged 74 & Samuel L. Douglass aged 65, after the Rev War sol was app'td Alderman of Philadelphia PA and was later Sheriff of Phila.

[3]Marriage of Henry Douglass to Margaret Trout, March 29, 1835, Eleventh Presbyterian Church, Philadelphia, Philadelphia County, Pennsylvania, Pennsylvania and New Jersey, Church and Town Records, 1708-1985, <<www.ancestry.com>>, downloaded December 31, 2016.

                                             Appendix F

Monument Cemetery.[4]

The second wife of Henry G. Douglass (Sr.) was Sarah Ashton with whom he had two children - Catharine and Henry. Their son, Henry, married Elizabeth M. Reitze on April 25, 1892, in Philadelphia.[5] This couple was known as Aunt Lizzie and Uncle Harry

In the 1850 census, the Douglass family was enumerated together in West Philadelphia where Henry G. Douglass (Sr.) operated an inn:

Henry G. Douglass	30	Inn Keeper	b in Penna.
Sarah	33		b in Penna. (sic)
George W.	[12]		b in Penna.
Charles	9		b in Penna.
Joseph [T.]	7		b in Penna.
Catharine	3		b in Penna.[6]

Eventually, Henry G. Douglass (Sr.) went West to seek his fortune. He died there of marasmus on November 25, 1858, and was buried in the Stockton State Hospital Cemetery.[7] It is unclear when his wife and children found out he was dead.

---

[4]Obituary of Margaret Douglass, *Philadelphia Public Ledger*, June 10, 1845, Tuesday, Philadelphia, Pennsylvania, <<www.genealogybank.com>>, downloaded December 31, 2016.

> On Monday, the 9th inst., Mrs. MARGARET, wife of Henry G. Douglass, in the 29th year of her age. The friends of the family are particularly requested to attend her funeral, from the residence of her husband, at the Northwest corner of Ridge Road and Wood street, to-morrow afternoon, the 11th inst., at 4 o'clock, without further notice - funeral to proceed to Monument Cemetery.

[5]Marriage of Henry G. Douglass to Sarah Ashton, February 19, 1846, First Universalist Church, Philadelphia, Philadelphia County, Pennsylvania, Pennsylvania and New Jersey, Church and Town Records, 1708-1985, <<www.ancestry.com>>, downloaded December 31, 2016.

[6]1850 U.S. Census (population), Pennsylvania, Philadelphia County, West Philadelphia, page 501, National Archives Microfilm Publication M432, Roll 823.

[7]Death of Henry Douglass, November 25, 1858, Stockton, San Joaquin County, California. Henry Douglass, Stockton State Hospital Commitment Register 1852-1862, p. 346, California State Hospital Records, 1856-1923, <<www.ancestry.com>>, downloaded January 2, 2017.

> Henry Douglass - Committed by M. C. Blake Co. Judge of San Francisco. Is a native of Penn. 42 yrs of age, says that he is married. Has been insane two weeks, cause of insanity unknown. Has no property. Admitted June 2d 1858. Died Nov 25th of marasmus. Grave No. 22. New G. Yd.

Appendix F

On the eve of the Civil War, the Douglass family was enumerated as follows in the 1860 census in West Philadelphia where Sarah (Ashton) Douglass ran a boarding house.

Sarah Douglass	35 (sic)	Boardinghouse Keeper	b in New Jersey
Catharine	14		b in Penna.
Henry	7		b in Penna.
Joseph	15		b in Penna.
Charles	20		b in Penna.
George	23	Mariner	b in Penna.
Mary Ashton	45		b in New Jersey[8]

The boarding house may have been located on Chestnut Street above 34th Street.[9] The income earned by Sarah (Ashton) Douglass from running the boarding house was probably supplemented by her step-sons, George and Charles Douglass, both of whom served in the United States Navy during the Civil War.

Sarah (Ashton) Douglass died on July 20, 1871, and was buried in Mount Moriah Cemetery.[10] The five Douglass children all married, but left no descendants. Their relationship to the Collins and Kennedy families was clarified, but appears to be immaterial to any ancestral connection to the Reitze family. A brief account of the lives of the five Douglass children is as follows:

GEORGE W. DOUGLASS

The oldest child of Henry G. Douglass (Sr.) was George W. Douglass.

SERVICE IN THE CIVIL WAR. The 1860 census states that George W. Douglass, was a "mariner." According to his Civil War Pension Application File, he enlisted in the United States

---

[8]1860 U.S. Census (population), Pennsylvania, Philadelphia County, City of Philadelphia, Ward 24, page 999, National Archives Microfilm Publication M635, Roll 1175.

[9]1861 Philadelphia city directory states:

Douglass, Sarah, wid Henry, Chestnut ab Moore [now 34th street].

[10]Obituary of Sarah Douglass, Philadelphia Public Ledger, Friday, July 21, 1871, Philadelphia, Pennsylvania, <<www.genealogybank.com>>, downloaded January 1, 2017.

On the [20th] inst., Mrs. Sarah Douglass, wife of the late Henry G. Douglass in the 53rd year of her age.

The relatives and friends of the family and also the [Siloam] Lodge No. 11 [N of L] are respectfully invited to attend the funeral from her late residence, No. 7 Steinmetz Place, West Phila., on Sunday at one o'clock. To proceed to Mount Moriah Cemetery.

                    Appendix F

Navy on March 20, 1860, and served as a coal heaver aboard the U.S.S. Princeton, the U.S.S. Pawnee, the U.S.S. Powhatan, and the U.S.S. North Carolina.[11] He was discharged from the U.S.S. Clifton on April 5, 1863. He reenlisted on September 3, 1864, as a Second Class Fireman and served on the U.S.S. Princeton and the U.S.S. New Hampshire.[12] He was discharged from the U.S.S. Montauk on June 6, 1865 at Washington, D.C.

MARRIAGE TO SARAH COLLINS. After the Civil War, George W. Douglass married Sarah Collins.[13] Their marriage took place on March 31, 1865, in Philadelphia. The ceremony was performed by Alderman Samuel D. Jones, Jr., whose office was located at 1303 Market Street. George W. Douglass' occupation was listed as an augermaker.

OCCUPATION. As shown below, George W. Douglass' occupation was usually listed in the Philadelphia city directories as a fireman:

1864	USA (sic), Ludlow n 31st
1874	fireman, h 9 Steinmetz, W.P.
1875	fireman, h 3627 Ludlow
1877	fireman, h 121 Chestnut Place, W.P.
1878	fireman, h 3411 Woodland av, W.P.
1879	fireman, h 3645 Ludlow
1880	fireman, h 3639 Ludlow
1881	fireman, h 3639 Ludlow
1882	fireman, h 3639 Ludlow
1883	laborer, h 3639 Ludlow
1884	fireman, h 3639 Ludlow
1885	fireman, h 3639 Ludlow
1886	stoker, h 13 Steinmetz pl
1887	fireman, h 13 Steinmetz pl, W.P.
1888	laborer, h 13 Steinmetz pl
1889	fireman, h 13 Steinmetz pl
1894	fireman, 3339 Filbert
1895	fireman, 3339 Filbert
1897	fireman, h 3411 Ludlow
1898	fireman, h 3411 Ludlow

-----

[11]George W. Douglass, Civil War Pension Application File, Navy SO 33012, Navy SC 19429, Records of the Veterans Administration, Record Group 15, National Archives, Washington, D.C.

[12]A fireman is defined as an enlisted man whose general duties are concerned with the ship's engines.

[13]1865 Philadelphia Marriage Returns for Samuel D. Jones, Jr., Alderman, 1303 Market Street, Office # 3, First Quarter, George W. Douglass (28) to Sarah Collins (23), March 31, 1865, Philadelphia City Archives, Philadelphia, Pennsylvania.

Given that he was a coal heaver and a Second Class Fireman in the United States Navy during the Civil War and that his occupation was listed in the 1886 city directory as a stoker, it is thought that George W. Douglass probably tended a fire in a furnace (such as in a blacksmith's shop) as opposed to someone who fought fires as a member of a fire department.

LIFE IN WEST PHILADELPHIA. Other than the time he spent in the United States Navy, George W. Douglass seems to have spent his entire life in West Philadelphia within a few blocks of 33rd and Ludlow Streets.

In the first enumeration of the 1870 census, he and his wife are enumerated as follows:

Douglass, Geo. W.	32 M W	Blacksmith	b. in Penna.
-, Sarah	29 F W	Keeping House	b. in Penna.[14]

Based on information contained in the second enumeration of the 1870 census, their street address appears to have been 3431 Ludlow Street.[15] In the 1880 census, they were enumerated with Sarah (Collins) Douglass' said brothers, Edward Collins and Charles Collins.

3639 LUDLOW STREET:

Douglass, George	W M 42	Fireman	b. in Penna.
-, Sarah	W F 38 wife	Keeping House	b. in Penna.
Collins, Edward	W M 21 BIL (sic)	Shipping Clerk	b. in Penna.[16]
-, Charles	W M 40 BIL	Typecaster	b. in Penna.[17]

---

[14]1870 U.S. Census (population), First Enumeration, Pennsylvania, Philadelphia County, City of Philadelphia, Ward 27, page 65, National Archives Microfilm Publication M593, Roll 1445.

[15]1870 U.S. Census (population), Second Enumeration, Pennsylvania, Philadelphia County, City of Philadelphia, Ward 27, page 219B, National Archives Microfilm Publication M593, Roll 1443.

[16]The exact relationship of Edward Collins to Sarah C. (Collins) Douglass is unclear. If they were siblings, their mother, Rose Collins, would have been 57 years old when he was born. He appears to have lived sporadically with George W. and Sarah C. (Collins) Douglass from 1880 to 1893. On November 7, 1882, he became the first husband of Aunt Lizzie Reitze. They separated in 1887 and their marriage was legally dissolved by divorce on October 3, 1891. On April 25, 1892, Aunt Lizzie married Uncle Harry, the half-brother of George W. Douglass. Edward Collins died on June 23, 1893, at 3339 Filbert Street. He was buried in New Cathedral Cemetery. George W. and Sarah C. (Collins) Douglass are buried in the same plot (Section F, Range 5, Plot 21).

[17]1880 U.S. Census (population), Pennsylvania, Philadelphia County, City of Philadelphia, Ward 27, E.D. 570, page 45D, sheet 6, line 28, National Archives Microfilm

                    Appendix F

In the 1890 veterans schedule, George W. Douglass was enumerated at 3419 Ludlow Street. He was listed as a United States Navy veteran having served 3 years, 1 month, and 23 days.[18]

CIVIL WAR PENSIONER. George W. Douglass received a Civil War Pension Certificate dated February 2, 1893, for his service in the United States Navy during the Civil War.[19] The pension was retroactive to March 26, 1892, at a rate of $6.00 per month payable quarterly. The pension file contains very little information about him of a personal nature other than his wife, Sarah, was alive on May 11, 1892, when he completed the questionnaire for the Bureau of Pensions. Further, in answer to a question in the questionnaire about whether the pensioner had any children living, George W. Douglass answered: "no children living."[20]

DEATH OF SARAH (COLLINS) DOUGLASS. Sarah (Collins) Douglass died of locomotor ataxia on October 23, 1898, at 3411 Ludlow Street.[21] She was buried in New Cathedral Cemetery, Section F, Range 5, Plot 21.[22] To date, no obituary has been found for her in the *Philadelphia Public Ledger* or the *Philadelphia Inquirer*.

DEATH OF GEORGE W. DOUGLASS. On June 5, 1900, George W. Douglass was enumerated as a widower living with the family of Henry and Emma Carey at 3346 Ludlow

---

Publication T9, Roll 1186.

[18]1890 U.S. Census, (veterans), Pennsylvania, Philadelphia Couty, City of Philadelphia, S.D. 1, E.D. 611, page 2, line 13, National Archives Microfilm Publication M496, Roll 80.

[19]Original Civil War Navy Pension Certificate for George W. Douglass, Certificate # 19429, dated February 2, 1893, was in the possession of the late William Scott Chambers, 325 N.W. 95th Avenue, Plantation, Florida 33324.

[20]George W. Douglass, Civil War Pension Application File, Navy SO 33012, Navy SC 19429, Records of the Veterans Administration, Record Group 15, National Archives, Washington, D.C.

[21]Pennsylvania, Philadelphia City Death Certificates, 1803-1915, # 8854, Return of Death in the City of Philadelphia for Sarah C. Douglass, <<www.familysearch.org>>, downloaded December 7, 2016.

[22]Find-A-Grave Memorial # 173611903, Sarah (Collins) Douglass (no headstone photograph), added December 7, 2016, New Cathedral Cemetery, Philadelphia, Philadelphia County, Pennsylvania, <<www.findagrave.com>>.

Street.[23] His sister-in-law, Alice M. (Courtney) Douglass, a widow, was enumerated next door at 3344 Ludlow Street with the family of Annie Braden. On December 28, 1900, George W. Douglass died of pneumonia at the Presbyterian Hospital.[24] He was buried with his wife in New Cathedral Cemetery, Section F, Range 5, Plot 21.[25] His pension payments terminated on February 12, 1901. To date, no obituary has been found for him in the *Philadelphia Public Ledger* or the *Philadelphia Inquirer*.[26]

CHARLES G. DOUGLASS

The second child of Henry G. Douglass (Sr.) was Charles G. Douglass.

SERVICE IN THE CIVIL WAR. Charles G. Douglass enlisted in the United States Navy on March 20, 1860, the same day as his older brother, George W. Douglass.[27] He served aboard the U.S.S. Powhatan, the U.S.S. Octorara, and the U.S.S. North Carolina as a coal heaver (the same job category as his older brother). He was discharged on April 10, 1863, in New York.

MARRIAGE TO ALICE M. COURTNEY. After he was discharged from the Navy, Charles G. Douglass married Alice M. Courtney. They were married on February 18, 1864, at the Nazareth Methodist Episcopal Church.[28] The marriage was performed by the Rev. Charles Hill

---

[23]1900 U.S. Census (population), Pennsylvania, Philadelphia County, City of Philadelphia, Ward 27, E.D. 662, page 4B, line 71, National Archives Microfilm Publication T623, Roll 1469.

[24]Pennsylvania, Philadelphia City Death Certificates, 1803-1915, Volume 2, p 333, # 13408, Registration of Deaths in the City of Philadelphia for George Douglass, <<www.familysearch.org>>, downloaded December 7, 2016.

[25]Find-A-Grave Memorial # 173611727, George W. Douglass (no headstone photograph), added December 20, 2016, New Cathedral Cemetery, Philadelphia, Philadelphia County, Pennsylvania, <<www.findagrave.com>>.

[26]Notice of Official Death Returns, *Philadelphia Inquirer*, Sunday, December 30, 1900, Philadelphia, Pennsylvania, <<www.genealogybank.com>>, downloaded January 1, 2017, says: Douglas (sic), Geo., 63, 28, 1577 Chestnut.

[27]Charles G. Douglass, Civil War Pension Application File, Navy SO 25907, Navy SC 14475, Navy WO 13045, Navy WC 8599, Records of the Veterans Administration, Record Group 15, National Archives, Washington, D.C.

[28]Nazareth Methodist Episcopal Church Records, Charles G. Duglass (sic) to Alace (sic) M. Courtney, February 18, 1864, Genealogical Society of Pennsylvania, Philadelphia, Pennsylvania, Microfilm Roll XX368.

of 253 (sic) N. 13th Street.[29] Charles G. Douglass was listed as a carpenter in the Return of Marriages.

OCCUPATION. As shown in the Philadelphia city directories, Charles G. Douglass worked at a variety of occupations over the years:

1862	waterman, 3 Lancaster av ab 32d (his mother, Sarah, widow, was listed there, too).
1864	USN, Ludlow n 31st
1868	assistant assessor, 2920 Market, h. 3620 Locust, W.P.
1869	assistant assessor, 2920 Market, h. 3433 Ludlow, W.P.
1870	police, h 3433 Ludlow
1872	police, h 3433 Ludlow
1873	police, h 3433 Ludlow
1874	police, h 3639 Ludlow
1875	police, h 3625 Ludlow (his half-brother, Harry, was listed there, too).
1876	police, h 3625 Ludlow (his half-brother, Harry, was listed there, too).
1877	police, h 128 Chestnut Place, W.P.
1880	watchman, h 3657 Ludlow
1881	park guard, h 3657 Ludlow
1882	park guard, h 3657 Ludlow
1883	clerk, h 3657 Ludlow (his half-brother, Harry, was listed there, too).
1884	clerk, h 3657 Ludlow (his half-brother, Harry, was listed there, too).
1885	clerk, h 3657 Ludlow (his half-brother, Harry, was listed there, too).
1886	clerk, h 3657 Ludlow
1887	clerk, h 3657 Ludlow (his half-brother, Harry, was listed there, too).
1888	clerk, h 3657 Ludlow (his half-brother, Harry, was listed there, too).
1889	watchman, 3657 Ludlow (his half-brother, Harry, was listed there, too).
1890	clerk, h 3657 Ludlow (his half-brother, Harry, was listed there, too).
1891	clerk, h 3657 Ludlow (his half-brother, Harry, was listed there, too).

LIFE IN PHILADELPHIA. Much like his older brother, Charles G. Douglass spent most of his life in West Philadelphia. In the first enumeration of the 1870 census, he was enumerated with his wife and her brother as follows:

Douglass, Chas.	29 M W	Police Sergeant	b. in Penna.
-, Alice	27 F W	Keeping House	b. in Penna.
Courtney, John	20 M W	Machinist	b. in Penna.[30]

Based on information contained in the second enumeration of the 1870 census, their street

---

[29] 1864 Philadelphia Marriage Returns for the Rev. Charles Hill, 253 (sic) N.13th Street, Methodist Episcopal Church, [First Quarter], Charles G. Douglass (24) to Alice Courtney (22), February 18, 1864, Philadelphia City Archives, Philadelphia, Pennsylvania.

[30] 1870 U.S. Census (population), First Enumeration, Pennsylvania, Philadelphia County, City of Philadelphia, Ward 27, page 75, National Archives Microfilm Publication M593, Roll 1445.

                    Appendix F

address appears to have been 3433 Ludlow Street.[31]

In the 1880 census, Charles G. Douglass was enumerated with his wife and his niece as follows:

3657 LUDLOW STREET:

Douglass, Charles	W M 41	Policeman	b in Penna.
-, Alice	W F 38 wife	Keeping House	b in Penna.
Collins, Ida	W F 8 niece		b in Penna.[32,33]

CIVIL WAR PENSIONER. Even though Charles G. Douglass could not be located in the 1890 veterans schedule, he received a pension for his service in the United States Navy during the Civil War. He began receiving the pension as of January 16, 1891, at a rate of $12.00 per month payable quarterly. His pension terminated with his death.[34]

DEATH OF CHARLES G. DOUGLASS. Charles G. Douglass died on December 31, 1892, from exhaustion due to excessive mental strain. He was working as a bookkeeper at the time of his death and living at 3646 Warren Street.[35] He was buried at Mount Moriah Cemetery in Section 204, Lot 537.[36,37] His obituary appeared in the *Philadelphia Public Ledger* on Monday,

---

[31] 1870 U.S. Census (population), Second Enumeration, Pennsylvania, Philadelphia County, City of Philadelphia, Ward 27, page 219B, National Archives Microfilm Publication M593, Roll 1443.

[32] 1880 U.S. Census (population), Pennsylvania, Philadelphia County, City of Philadelphia, Ward 27, E.D. 570, page 45C, sheet 5, line 44, National Archives Microfilm Publication T9, Roll 1186.

[33] The identity of Ida Collins is unclear. She is believed to have married Thomas Nolan. If this conclusion is correct, her death certificate dated April 19, 1941, states she was born on February 14, 1873, her father's name was Robert Collins, and her mother's name was unknown. She was buried in Holy Cross Cemetery. How Ida Collins came to be Charles G. Douglass' niece remains a mystery.

[34] Charles G. Douglass, Civil War Pension Application File, Navy SO 25907, Navy SC 14475, Navy WO 13045, Navy WC 8599, Records of the Veterans Administration, Record Group 15, National Archives, Washington, D.C.

[35] Pennsylvania, Philadelphia City Death Certificates, 1803-1915, Return of a Death in the City of Philadelphia for Chas. G. Douglass, <<www.familysearch.org>>, downloaded December 7, 2016.

[36] Mount Moriah Cemetery Burial Records, Genealogical Society of Pennsylvania, Philadelphia, Pennsylvania, reviewed on May 21, 2001, shows: Charles Douglass, aged 53 years,

 Appendix F

January 2, 1893. It read as follows:

> DOUGLASS - On Dec. 31st 1892, CHARLES G. DOUGLASS.
>
> The relatives and friends also Phoenix Lodge No. [36] O.S. of P. and employees
> of Phila. Gas Works are invited to attend the funeral on Tuesday afternoon at 2
> o'clock from his late residence 3646 Warren st. Int. at Mount Moriah.[38]

WIDOWHOOD OF ALICE (COURTNEY) DOUGLASS. After the death of her husband, Alice (Courtney) Douglass applied for a Civil War widow's pension. It was approved and her widow's pension began on January 11, 1893 at a rate of $8.00 per month payable quarterly.[39] She never remarried. She was enumerated in the 1900 census at 3344 Ludlow Street next door to her brother-in-law, George W. Douglass, a widower, who was living at 3346 Ludlow Street.[40] She was enumerated in the 1910 census at 173 N. 36th Street with the family of Henry Brothers. Her relationship to Henry Brothers was that of a roomer and her occupation was that of a servant.[41]

DEATH OF ALICE (COURTNEY) DOUGLASS. Alice Maria (Courtney) Douglass, the daughter of James Courtney and Julia Mooney, died of atheroma on May 14, 1914, while living at 4213 Aspen Street.[42] Her obituary appeared in the *Philadelphia Public Ledger* on Saturday,

---

Section 204, Lot 537.

[37]Find-A-Grave Memorial # 82857565, Charles G. Douglass (no headstone photograph), added January 2, 2012, Mount Moriah Cemetery, Philadelphia, Philadelphia County, Pennsylvania, <<www.findagrave.com>>.

[38]Obituary of Charles G. Douglass, *Philadelphia Public Ledger*, Monday, January 2, 1893, p. 4 and Tuesday, January 3, 1892, p. 4, Library of Congress, Washington, D.C.

[39]Charles G. Douglass, Civil War Pension Application File, Navy SO 25907, Navy SC 14475, Navy WO 13045, Navy WC 8599, Records of the Veterans Administration, Record Group 15, National Archives, Washington, D.C.

[40]1900 U.S. Census (population), Pennsylvania, Philadelphia County, City of Philadelphia, Ward 27, E.D. 662, page 4B, sheet 4, line 68, National Archives Microfilm Publication T623, Roll 1469.

[41]1910 U.S. Census (population), Pennsylvania, Philadelphia County, City of Philadelphia, Ward 24, E.D. 493, page 91, line 37, National Archives Microfilm Publication T624, Roll 1397.

[42]Death Certificate of Alice Maria Douglass, May 14, 1914, Philadelphia, Philadelphia County, Pennsylvania, Philadelphia City Death Certificates, 1803-1915, <<www.familysearch.org>>, downloaded December 7, 2016.

Appendix F

May 16, 1914. It read as follows:

> DOUGLASS - On May 14, 1914, Alice M., widow of Charles Douglass.
> Funeral on Monday at 7:30 A.M. from 4213 Aspen St., West Phila. High
> Requiem Mass at our Mother of Sorrows Church at 9:00 A.M.[43]

She was buried with her husband at Mount Moriah Cemetery, Section 204, Lot 537.[44,45]
They never had any children.[46]

JOSEPH H. DOUGLASS

The third child of Henry G. Douglass (Sr.) was Joseph H. Douglass.

MARRIAGE TO LINEY (CLEW) REIBSAM.[47] On August 11, 1876, Joseph H. Douglass
married Liney (Clew) Reibsam, the daughter of Jeremiah and Maria (Goldey) Clew and the
widow of Henry Howard Reibsam.[48,49] They were married at the Nazareth Methodist Episcopal
Church, which was the same church where Joseph's older brother, Charles G. Douglass, was
married in 1864 and where Liney Clew married her first husband in 1867. Their marriage was
performed by the Reverend Sylvester Chew of 252 (sic) N. 13th Street. Joseph H. Douglass was

---

[43]Obituary of Alice M. Douglass, *Philadelphia Public Ledger*, Saturday, May 16, 1914, p.
15 and Wednesday, May 20, 1914, p. 16, Library of Congress, Washington, D.C.

[44]Mount Moriah Cemetery Burial Records, Genealogical Society of Pennsylvania,
Philadelphia, Pennsylvania, reviewed on May 21, 2001, shows: Alice Marie (sic) Douglass, aged
71 years, Section 204, Lot 537.

[45]Find-A-Grave Memorial # 82857586, Alice Marie (Courtney) Douglass (no headstone
photograph), added January 2, 2012, Mount Moriah Cemetery, Philadelphia, Philadelphia
County, Pennsylvania, <<www.findagrave.com>>.

[46]1910 U.S. Census (population), Pennsylvania, Philadelphia County, City of
Philadelphia, Ward 24, E.D. 493, page 91, line 37, National Archives Microfilm Publication
T624, Roll 1397 says: 0 children; 0 living.

[47]This surname is spelled *Reibsam* or *Riebsam*, interchangeably.

[48]1850 U.S. Census (population), Pennsylvania, Philadelphia County, Philadelphia, South
Mulberry Ward, page 290A, National Archives Microfilm Publication M432, Roll 815.

[49]Marriage of Henry H. Riebsam (sic) to Liney Clew, June 26, 1867, Nazareth Methodist
Episcopal Church, Philadelphia, Philadelphia County, Pennsylvania, Pennsylvania and New
Jersey, Church and Town Records, 1708-1985, <<www.ancestry.com>>, downloaded January 8,
2017.

34 and his wife was 28. Both were born in Philadelphia and residing in Philadelphia at the time of their marriage. Joseph H. Douglass was working as an augermaker.[50,51]

OCCUPATION. Joseph H. Douglass appears in the Philadelphia city directories at the following locations:

1863	augermaker, Ludlow n 31st
1867	augermaker, h 2139 Locust
1868	toolmaker, h r Ludlow n S 31st (his mother, Sarah, widow Henry, was listed there, too).
1869	augermaker, h Ludlow c S 32nd W.P.
1870	blacksmith, h 3431 Ludlow
1872	blacksmith, h 3431 Ludlow
1873	blacksmith, h 3431 Ludlow AND fireman, h S. 37th c Ludlow
1874	fireman, h 4005 Ludlow
1876	liquors, h S. 36th c Ludlow
1877	liquors, h S. 37th c Ludlow
1878	liquors, h S. 37th c Ludlow
1879	liquors, h S. 37th c Ludlow
1880	liquors, h 3112 Market
1881	liquors, h 3112 Market
1882	liquors, h 3112 Market
1883	liquors, h 3112 Market
1884	liquors, h 3112 Market
1885	liquors, h 3110 Market
1886	liquors, h 3112 Market
1888	liquors, h 3220 Market

LIFE IN WEST PHILADELPHIA. Much like his older brothers, Joseph H. Douglass lived in West Philadelphia for much of his life, but he has been difficult to identify with certainty in the 1870 census schedules. In the first enumeration of the 1870 census, he *may* appear in West Philadelphia as follows:

Douglass, Jos.	24 (sic) M W	Augermaker	b in Maryland (sic)
-, Mary	22 F W		b. in Penna.
-, Harry	5 M W		b. in Penna.[52]

---

[50]1876 Philadelphia Marriage Returns for Reverend Sylvester Chew, Methodist Episcopal Church, 252 (sic) N. 13th Street, Second Quarter, Joseph H. Douglass (34) to Liney Riebsam (sic) (28), August 11 (sic), 1876, Philadelphia City Archives, Philadelphia, Pennsylvania.

[51]Nazareth Methodist Episcopal Church Records, Joseph H. Douglass (34) to Liney Riebsam (sic) (28), August 14 (sic), 1876, Genealogical Society of Pennsylvania, Philadelphia, Pennsylvania, Microfilm Roll XX368.

[52]1870 U.S. Census (population), First Enumeration, Pennsylvania, Philadelphia County, City of Philadelphia, Ward 27, page 77, National Archives Microfilm Publication M593, Roll 1445.

While his occupation appears to be correct, he seems to be listed with a wife named Mary and a child named Harry; his age is understated by about four years; and his birthplace is erroneously listed as Maryland. It is possible that the census enumerator may have erred or, at a later time, the information from two separate listings may have been accidentally merged when the enumeration schedule was prepared. Either way, Joseph H. Douglass is not presently known to have been married prior to his marriage to Liney (Clew) Reibsam who was listed separately with her first husband and son in the 1870 census.[53]

In the second enumeration of the 1870 census, Joseph H. Douglass *may* appear as follows at 3138 Market Street:

       Douglass, J.H.   30 M[54]

Six years later, on August 11, 1876, Joseph H. Douglass married Liney (Clew) Reibsam the widow of Henry Howard Reibsam.[55,56,57] Thereafter, she and her young son, Henry Howard Reibsam, lived with Joseph H. Douglass where the family was enumerated in the 1880 census as follows:

---

[53]1870 U.S. Census (population), First Enumeration, Pennsylvania, Philadelphia County, City of Philadelphia, Ward 10, page 259B, National Archives Microfilm Publication M593, Roll 1359, Household of Henry H. Reibsan (sic).

[54]1870 U.S. Census (population), Second Enumeration, Pennsylvania, Philadelphia County, City of Philadelphia, Ward 27, page 190, National Archives Microfilm Publication M593, Roll 1443.

[55]Obituary of Henry Howard Reibsam (sic), *Philadelphia Public Ledger*, Tuesday, September 3, 1872, Philadelphia, Pennsylvania, <<www.genealogybank.com>>, downloaded January 8, 2017.

> REIBSAM (sic) - On Sunday, Sept 1st, of consumption, HENRY HOWARD REIBSAM (sic), in the 28th year of his age. Funeral on Wednesday, Sept. 4th, from the residence of his sister, 1817 Ridge avenue, tomorrow at 2 o'clock P.M., precisely.

[56]Mount Moriah Register of Interments, Pennsylvania and New Jersey, Church and Town Records, 1708-1985, says: 18837 Robinson (sic), Henry H., 28 years, September 4, 1872, Section 41 Plot 23 [588-1/4], <<www.ancestry.com>>, downloaded January 10, 2017.

[57]Registration of Deaths in the City of Philadelphia for Henry H. Reibson (sic), September 1, 1872, Pennsylvania, Philadelphia City Death Certificates, 1803-1915, FHL Microfilm Roll 10036999, <<www.familysearch.org>>, downloaded January 8, 2017. Also, Return of Death in the City of Philadelphia - Physician's Certificate for Henry H. Reibson (sic), September 1, 1872, Pennsylvania, Philadelphia City Death Certificates, 1803-1915, FHL Microfilm Roll 2021566, <<www.familysearch.org>>, downloaded January 8, 2017.

       Appendix F

Douglas (sic), Joseph	W M 40	Saloonkeeper	b. in Penna.
-, Liney	W F 32 wife		b. in Penna.
-, Howard	W M 11 son (sic)		b. in Penna.[58]

DEATH OF LINEY (CLEW) REIBSAM DOUGLASS. Five years later, on September 15, 1885, Liney (Clew) Reibsam Douglass died of phthisis pulmonalis (i.e., consumption), the same disease that took the life of her first husband, the late Henry Howard Riebsam.[59] She was buried in a Clew family plot in Mount Moriah Cemetery.[60] To date, no obituary has been found for Liney (Clew) Reibsam Douglass.

Sadly, her only child, Henry Howard Reibsam also died of consumption on February 18, 1892.[61] He was buried in Mount Moriah Cemetery probably in the same plot as his mother.[62] The third victim of the scourge of consumption (i.e., tuberculosis), he was only 23 years old, single, and working as a butcher at the time of his death. His obituary read as follows:

> REIBSAM (sic), On the 18th inst., H. Howard, son of the late Howard and Caroline Reibsam (sic), in the 28th year of his age. The relatives and friends of the family are respectfully invited to attend the funeral, on Sunday afternoon, at 1 o'clock, from the residence of his uncle, George H. Hartman, 115 Elwyn street. Interment at Mt. Moriah Cemetery.[63]

---

[58] 1880 U.S. Census (population), Pennsylvania, Philadelphia County, City of Philadelphia, Ward 24, E.D. 568, page 2D, line 18, National Archives Microfilm Publication T9, Roll 1186. Howard Douglass is his step-son, Henry Howard Reibsam.

[59] Pennsylvania, Philadelphia City Death Certificates, 1803-1815, Return of a Death in the City of Philadelphia for Liney Douglass, September 15, 1885, Philadelphia, Philadelphia, Pennsylvania, <<www.familysearch.org>>, downloaded January 8, 2017.

[60] Mount Moriah Register of Interments, Pennsylvania and New Jersey, Church and Town Records, 1708-1985, says: 41938 Douglass, Liney, 38 years, September 18, 1885, Section 204 Plot 690 S.L., <<www.ancestry.com>>, downloaded January 10, 2017.

[61] Pennsylvania, Philadelphia City Death Certificates, 1803-1815, Return of a Death in the City of Philadelphia for H. Howard Reibsam (sic), February 18, 1892, Philadelphia, Philadelphia, Pennsylvania.

[62] Mount Moriah Register of Interments, Pennsylvania and New Jersey, Church and Town Records, 1708-1985, says: 54648 Reibsam (sic), Howard, 23 years, February 21, 1892, Section 204, Lot 696 (sic), Middle grave, <<www.ancestry.com>>, downloaded January 10, 2017.

[63] Obituary of H. Howard Reibsam (sic), *Philadelphia Inquirer*, Saturday, February 20, 1892, Philadelphia, Pennsylvania, <<www.genealogybank.com>>, downloaded January 8, 2017.

DEATH OF JOSEPH H. DOUGLASS.   In 1894, nine year after the death of Liney (Clew) Reibsam Douglass, Joseph H. Douglass married Martha Bell.[64] They were together at their home the night he died, September 11, 1895. Sadly, Joseph H. Douglass took his own life having endured unemployment, poverty, eviction, and the death of almost every family member he dearly loved.[65,66] His obituary read as follows:

> DOUGLASS - Suddenly, on September 11, 1895, Joseph H. Douglass. The relatives and friends, also Fire Relief Association, P.F.D., are invited to attend the funeral service, on Saturday afternoon, at 2 o'clock, at his brother's residence, 886 North Forty-three-and-a half street. Interment.[67]

He was buried in Mount Moriah Cemetery from the home of his half-brother, Henry G.

---

[64]Marriage of Joseph H. Douglass to Martha Bell, 1894, Marriage Licenses # 70077, Philadelphia, Pennsylvania, Marriage Index, 1885-1951, <<www.ancestry.com>>.

[65]News Story, *Philadelphia Inquirer*, Thursday, September 12, 1895, Philadelphia, Pennsylvania, <<www.genealogybank.com>>, downloaded January 18, 2012, reads as follows:

> HE WAS OUT OF WORK - Poverty Drove Joseph H. Douglass to Take His Life
> Poverty and his failure to get work drove Joseph H. Douglass, aged 55, of No. 1501 Fillmore street, to suicide on Tuesday night. When his wife awoke yesterday morning she found him lying dead on the floor of one of the lower rooms. There was an empty vial labeled: "carbolic acid" in the closet, and a glass from which he drank the poison was on the mantelpiece. A note which Douglass had evidently written just before he took the poison read as follows: "Please let my brother Harry have all to say, and he will give satisfaction to all."

[66]News Story, *Philadelphia Inquirer*, Friday, September 13, 1895, Philadelphia, Pennsylvania <<www.genealogybank.com>> downloaded January 18, 2012, reads as follows:

> The suicide of Joseph H. Douglass, aged 55, of No. 1501 Fillmore street, who poisoned himself with laudinum on Tuesday night after he and his wife had received notice that they were to be evicted for nonpayment of rent, was investigated [at an inquest held yesterday by Deputy Coroner Dugan]. The jury decided that he had taken his life while temporarily insane.

[67]Obituary of Joseph H. Douglass, *Philadelphia Inquirer*, Saturday, September 14, 1895, Philadelphia, Pennsylvania, <<www.genealogybank.com>>, downloaded January 18, 2012.

Douglass (Jr.), 886 North 43½ Street.[68,69]

CATHARINE A. DOUGLASS

The fourth child of Henry G. Douglass (Sr.) was Catharine A. Douglass. She was his only daughter.

EARLY DAYS IN WEST PHILADELPHIA. As shown in the first enumeration of the 1870 census, Catharine A. Douglass, who was always known to everyone as Kate, was still living at home with her mother, Sarah, her brother, Uncle Harry, and her aunt, Mary Ashton:

Douglass, Sarah	56 F W		b in New Jersey
-, Kate	23 F W	Sales Lady	b in Penna.
-, Harry	18 M W	App to Augermaker	b in Penna.
Ashton, Mary	57 F W	At home	b in New Jersey[70]

Based on information contained in the second enumeration of the 1870 census, their street address was 7 Steinmetz Place.[71]

It is unclear where Kate and Uncle Harry lived after their aunt, Mary Ashton, and their mother, Sarah (Ashton) Douglass, died on December 30, 1870, and July [20], 1871,

---

[68]Return of Death in the City of Philadelphia - Physician's Certificate for Joseph H. Douglass, September 11, 1895, Pennsylvania, Philadelphia City Death Certificates, 1803-1915, <<www.familysearch.org>>, downloaded December 7, 2016.

[69]Funeral Home Record for Jos. Douglass, 1501 Fillmore Street, September 11, 1895, Oliver Bair Funeral Home, Philadelphia, Philadelphia County, Pennsylvania, Pennsylvania and New Jersey, Church and Town Records, 1708-1985, <<www.ancestry.com>>, downloaded January 8, 2017.

[70]1870 U.S. Census (population), First Enumeration, Pennsylvania, Philadelphia County, City of Philadelphia, Ward 27, page 75, National Archives Microfilm Publication M593, Roll 1445.

[71]1870 U.S. Census (population), Second Enumeration, Pennsylvania, Philadelphia County, City of Philadelphia, Ward 27, page 141B, National Archives Microfilm Publication M593, Roll 1443, says:

#7 [STEINMETZ PLACE]

Douglas (sic), C. (sic)	60 (sic) M (sic)
-, C.	22 F
-, H.M. (sic)	15 M
Ashton, M.	70 (sic) F

respectively.[72,73] Initially, she and Uncle Harry, are likely to have joined their half-brother,
George W. Douglass, who was living at 9 Steinmetz Place in 1874. According to the 1875 and
1876 Philadelphia City directories, they seem to have lived at 3625 Ludlow Street with their half-
brother, Charles G. Douglass during those years.

In 1880, Kate and Uncle Harry were enumerated with Charles E. and Catharine
(Douglass) Kennedy. Catharine (Douglass) Kennedy was their father's sister. Her husband,
Charles E. Kennedy, was the son of Robert and Ann (Vanarsdale) Kennedy and the grandson of
Andrew and Elizabeth (Potts) Kennedy.[74] In 1880, they were enumerated as follows:

836 UNION STREET

Kennedy, Cha's	W M 64	Navy Yard	b. Pa.
-, Catharine	W F 62 wife	H. Keeper	b. Pa.
-, Andrew	W M 31 son		b. Pa.
-. Jos. D.	W M 17 son	Milk	b. Pa,
Green, Mary L.	W F 42 daughter		b. Pa.
-, Mary	W F 17 grand d	Lithograph Ofc.	b. Pa.
Douglas (sic), Cath.	W F 30 niece	Lithograph Ofc.	b. Pa.
-, Henry	W M 26 nephew	Augermaker	b. Pa.[75]

MARRIAGE TO WILLIAM P. McLAUGHLIN. Kate A. Douglass married William P.

---

[72]Obituary of Mary Ashton, *Philadelphia Public Ledger*, Monday, January 2, 1871,
Philadelphia, Pennsylvania, <<www.genealogybank.com>>, downloaded January 1, 2017

> On the 30th ult, MARY ASHTON in the [60th] year of her age. The relatives and friends
> of the family are respectfully invited to attend the funeral from her sister's residence, Mrs.
> Sarah A. Douglass, No. 7 Steinmetz Place, West. Phila. this (Monday) afternoon at 2
> o'clock.

[73]Obituary of Sarah Douglass, *Philadelphia Public Ledger*, Friday, July 21, 1871,
Philadelphia, Pennsylvania, <<www.genealogybank.com>>, downloaded January 1, 2017.

> On the [20th] inst., Mrs. Sarah Douglass, wife of the late Henry G. Douglass in
> the 53rd year of her age.

> The relatives and friends of the family and also the [Siloam] Lodge No. 11 [N of
> L] are respectfully invited to attend the funeral from her late residence, No. 7
> Steinmetz Place, West Phila., on Sunday at one o'clock. To proceed to Mount
> Moriah Cemetery.

[74]Kathryn Chambers Torpey, *Colonial and Revolutionary Kennedy Families from
Southeastern Pennsylvania*, (Alexandria, Virginia: Torpey Books, 2015), p. 59

[75]1880 U.S. Census (population), Pennsylvania, Philadelphia County, City of
Philadelphia, Ward 25, E.D. 496, pages 203B-203C, lines 48-50 & 1-5, National Archives
Microfilm Publication T9, Roll 1183.

McLaughlin, a carpenter, on September 30, 1885.[76]

MONTGOMERY COUNTY, PENNSYLVANIA. In their later years, William P. and Kate A. (Douglass) McLaughlin appear to have moved to Rockledge, Montgomery County, Pennsylvania where William McLaughlin worked as a carpenter. Kate's maternal aunt, Hannah (Ashton) Trainer was living with them at the time of the 1900 census. They were enumerated as follows:

64 CENTRAL AVENUE

McLaughlin, William C. (sic) Head		W M M Sep 1853 46 Carpenter	b. Pa,
-, Kate C. (sic)	Wife	W F M Jan 1850 50	b. Pa.
Trainer, Hannah	Aunt-in-Law	W F W May 1821 70 Dressmaker	b. Pa.[77]

Ten years later, the couple was still living in Rockledge where they were enumerated as follows in the 1910 census:

37 CENTRAL AVENUE

McLaughlin, Wm. P.	Head	W M M 54	Carpenter	b. Pa.
-, (sic)	Wife	W F M 63		b. Pa.[78]

According to both census enumerations, they never had any children.

DEATH OF WILLIAM P. McLAUGHLIN. William P. McLaughlin died of mitral regurgitation and bronchitis in Rockledge, Montgomery County, Pennsylvania, on March 31, 1915.[79] According to his death certificate, he was 61 (sic) years old. His obituary appeared in the *Philadelphia Inquirer* on Thursday, April 1, 1915, as follows:

> McLAUGHLIN - On March 31, 1915, at his late residence, 37 Central Ave., Rockledge, PA, WILLIAM P. McLAUGHLIN, husband of Kate A. McLaughlin (nee Douglass) in his 62nd year. Relatives and friends, also Waverly Castle, No. 13 KGE are invited to attend his funeral services on Saturday at 1:30 P.M. precisely at Bethany Baptist Church, Rhawn St., Fox Chase, Philadelphia.

---

[76]Marriage returns, 1860-1885, Filed by Person Performing the Ceremony, Returns: 1885, 3rd quarter (James I. Good) -- 1885, 4th quarter -- Misfiled returns, Philadelphia, Philadelphia County, Pennsylvania, FHL Microfilm Roll 1769296, <<www.familysearch.org>>.

[77]1900 U.S. Census (population), Pennsylvania, Montgomery County, Rockledge, E.D. 195, page 4A, lines 6-8, National Archives Microfilm Publication T623, Roll 1442.

[78]1910 U.S. Census (population), Pennsylvania, Montgomery County, Rockledge, E.D. 62, page 6B, lines 77-78, National Archives Microfilm Publication T624, Roll 1377.

[79]Death Certificate for William McLaughlin, March 31, 1915, Rockledge, Montgomery County, Pennsylvania, Pennsylvania, Death Certificates, 1906-1964, <<www.familysearch.org>>.

Interment Lawnview Cemetery. Remains may be viewed on Friday after 7 P.M.[80]

DEATH OF KATE A. (DOUGLASS) McLAUGHLIN. Kate did not live long after her husband died. She was always particularly close with her brother, Uncle Harry, so she appears to have gone to live with him and his wife, Aunt Lizzie (Reitze) Douglass, after her husband died. It was at their home in Gloucester City, Camden County, New Jersey, that she seems to have had a stroke. It must have been a bad stroke because she was hospitalized for ten months and twenty-six days at the Cumberland County Hospital for the Insane in Hopewell Township, Cumberland County, New Jersey. It was there that she died of apoplexy on July 26, 1917.[81,82]

Her obituary appeared in the *Philadelphia Public Ledger* on Saturday, July 28, 1917, and on Sunday, July 29, 1917, as follows:

McLAUGHLIN - July 27, KATE A. McLAUGHLIN (nee Douglass), widow of
William P. McLaughlin. Relatives and friends invited to funeral services, Mon.,
1 p.m., brother's residence, Henry G. Douglass, 15 Thompson st., (sic) South
Gloucester, N.J. Int. private, Lawn View Cem. Friends may view remains at
cemetery chapel.[83]

BURIAL OF WILLIAM P. AND KATE A. (DOUGLASS) McLAUGHLIN. William P. and Kate

---

[80]Obituary of William P. McLaughlin, *Philadelphia Inquirer*, Thursday, April 1, 1915, p. 7.

[81]Dr. Jeanette L. Jerger, *A Medical Miscellany for Genealogists*, (Bowie, Maryland: Heritage Books, 1995), p. 7, defines apoplexy as a condition resulting from an apoplectic fix (i.e., a stroke) characterized by paralysis or limitation in the ability to control body movements, with or without loss of consciousness, and often leaving the affected individual in a chronic state of debilitation.

[82]Death Certificate for Kate A. McLaughlin, July 26, 1917, Hopewell Township, Cumberland County, New Jersey, State of New Jersey - Bureau of Vital Statistics, New Jersey State Archives, Trenton, New Jersey.

[83]Obituary of Kate A. McLaughlin, *Philadelphia Public Ledger*, Saturday, July 28, 1917, p. 17 and Sunday, July 29, 1917, p. 8.

(Douglass) McLaughlin are buried together in the same plot in Lawnview Cemetery.[84,85] Also buried in that plot are Uncle Harry and Aunt Lizzie (Reitze) Douglass.[86,87]

A single large headstone marks the location of their burial. The inscription reads as follows in it's entirety:

MacLAUGHLIN (sic)

1853 WILLIAM P. 1915

HIS WIFE

1847 KATE A. 1917

1854 HENRY G. DOUGLASS 1932

According to cemetery records, Kate (Douglass) McLaughlin and Aunt Lizzie (Reitze) Douglass jointly owned the plot at Lawnview Cemetery.[88]

HENRY GRAFE DOUGLASS

The fifth child of Henry G. Douglass (Sr.) was Henry Grafe Douglass who was known to

---

[84]Find-A-Grave Memorial # 158990177, William P. McLaughlin (headstone photograph), added March 6, 2016, Lawnview Cemetery, Rockledge, Montgomery County, Pennsylvania, <<www.findagrave.com>>.

[85]Find-A-Grave Memorial # 158990121, Catherine Ashton (Douglass) McLaughlin (headstone photograph), added March 6, 2016, Lawnview Cemetery, Rockledge, Montgomery County, Pennsylvania, <<www.findagrave.com>>.

[86]Find-A-Grave Memorial # 158990535, Henry Grafe Douglass (headstone photograph), added March 6, 2016, Lawnview Cemetery, Rockledge, Montgomery County, Pennsylvania, <<www.findagrave.com>>.

[87]Find-A-Grave Memorial # 158990837, Elizabeth M. (Reitze) Douglass (no headstone photograph), added March 6, 2016, Lawnview Cemetery, Rockledge, Montgomery County, Pennsylvania, <<www.findagrave.com>>.

[88]Letter dated February 18, 1997, from Karen L. Crawford, Lawnview Cemetery, 500 Huntingdon Pike, Rockledge, Pennsylvania 19046 regarding burials in Lot 340, Fox Chase Lawn Section, belonging to Kate A. McLaughlin (deceased) and Mrs. Harry Douglass.

                    Appendix F

all his nieces and nephews as Uncle Harry. He was born on July 9, 1854.[89,90]

EARLY DAYS IN WEST PHILADELPHIA. When Uncle Harry was still a toddler, his father, Henry G. Douglass (Sr.), appears to have gone West to seek his fortune. He died there of marasmus on November 25, 1858, and was buried in the Stockton State Hospital Cemetery.[91] It is unclear how soon thereafter Uncle Harry's mother, Sarah (Ashton) Douglass, found out her husband was dead, but she was listed in the 1861 Philadelphia city directory as Sarah Douglass, widow of Henry, living at Chestnut above Moore.[92]

As shown in the first enumeration of the 1870 census, Uncle Harry was still living at home with his mother, Sarah, his sister, Kate, and his aunt, Mary Ashton:

Douglass, Sarah	56 F W		b in New Jersey
-, Kate	23 F W	Sales Lady	b in Penna.
-, Harry	18 M W	App to Augermaker	b in Penna.
Ashton, Mary	57 F W	At home	b in New Jersey[93]

---

[89]Affidavit of Applicant for Marriage License # 51028, April 19, 1892, (Henry G. Douglass & Lizzie Reitze), City of Philadelphia, Philadelphia City Archives, Philadelphia, Pennsylvania says his date of birth was July 9, 1854.

[90]Death Certificate for Harry Douglass, June 10, 1932, Lakeland, Gloucester Township, Camden County, New Jersey, State of New Jersey - Bureau of Vital Statistics, New Jersey State Archives, Trenton, New Jersey says his date of birth was July 30, 1853.

[91]Death of Henry Douglass, November 25, 1858, Stockton, San Joaquin County, California. Henry Douglass, Stockton State Hospital Commitment Register 1852-1862, p. 346, California State Hospital Records, 1856-1923, <<www.ancestry.com>>, downloaded January 2, 2017.

> Henry Douglass - Committed by M. C. Blake Co. Judge of San Francisco. Is a
> native of Penn. 42 yrs of age, says that he is married. Has been insane two
> weeks, cause of insanity unknown. Has no property. Admitted June 2[d] 1858.
> Died Nov 25th of marasmus. Grave No. 22. New G. Yd.

[92]Letter dated October 21, 1999, from the late Josephine Thompson Marshall, 121 Reillywood Avenue, Haddonfield, New Jersey 08033-2201 says, in part, that she once found a newspaper clipping stored in a small jar at her grandmother's house that said Uncle Harry's father died in California (somewhere just outside of San Francisco).

[93]1870 U.S. Census (population), First Enumeration, Pennsylvania, Philadelphia County, City of Philadelphia, Ward 27, page 75, National Archives Microfilm Publication M593, Roll 1445.

Based on information contained in the second enumeration of the 1870 census, their street address was 7 Steinmetz Place.[94]

Within a year, Uncle Harry and Kate lost both their aunt, Mary Ashton, and their mother, Sarah (Ashton) Douglass, who died on December 30, 1870, and July [20], 1871, respectively.[95,96] Initially, he and Kate, are likely to have joined their half-brother, George W. Douglass, who was living at 9 Steinmetz Place in 1874. Then, according to the 1875 and 1876 Philadelphia City directories, they seem to have lived at 3625 Ludlow Street with their half-brother, Charles G. Douglass during those years.

In 1880, Uncle Harry and Kate were enumerated with Charles E. and Catharine (Douglass) Kennedy. Catharine (Douglass) Kennedy was their father's sister. Her husband, Charles E. Kennedy, was the son of Robert and Ann (Vanarsdale) Kennedy and the grandson of Andrew and Elizabeth (Potts) Kennedy.[97] In 1880, they were enumerated as follows:

---

[94]1870 U.S. Census (population), Second Enumeration, Pennsylvania, Philadelphia County, City of Philadelphia, Ward 27, page 141B, National Archives Microfilm Publication M593, Roll 1443, says:

```
#7 [STEINMETZ PLACE]
        Douglas (sic), C. (sic)      60 (sic) M (sic)
        -, C.                        22 F
        -, H.M. (sic)                15 M
        Ashton, M.                   70 (sic) F
```

[95]Obituary of Mary Ashton, *Philadelphia Public Ledger*, Monday, January 2, 1871, Philadelphia, Pennsylvania, <<www.genealogybank.com>>, downloaded January 1, 2017

> On the 30th ult, MARY ASHTON in the [60th] year of her age. The relatives and friends of the family are respectfully invited to attend the funeral from her sister's residence, Mrs. Sarah A. Douglass, No. 7 Steinmetz Place, West. Phila. this (Monday) afternoon at 2 o'clock.

[96]Obituary of Sarah Douglass, *Philadelphia Public Ledger*, Friday, July 21, 1871, Philadelphia, Pennsylvania, <<www.genealogybank.com>>, downloaded January 1, 2017.

> On the [20th] inst., Mrs. Sarah Douglass, wife of the late Henry G. Douglass in the 53rd year of her age.

> The relatives and friends of the family and also the [Siloam] Lodge No. 11 [N of L] are respectfully invited to attend the funeral from her late residence, No. 7 Steinmetz Place, West Phila., on Sunday at one o'clock. To proceed to Mount Moriah Cemetery.

[97]Kathryn Chambers Torpey, *Colonial and Revolutionary Kennedy Families from Southeastern Pennsylvania*, (Alexandria, Virginia: Torpey Books, 2015), p. 59

836 UNION STREET

Kennedy, Cha's	W M 64	Navy Yard	b. Pa.
-, Catharine	W F 62 wife	H. Keeper	b. Pa.
-, Andrew	W M 31 son		b. Pa.
-. Jos. D.	W M 17 son	Milk	b. Pa,
Green, Mary L.	W F 42 daughter		b. Pa.
-, Mary	W F 17 grand d	Lithograph Ofc.	b. Pa.
Douglas (sic), Cath.	W F 30 niece	Lithograph Ofc.	b. Pa.
-, Henry	W M 26 nephew	Augermaker	b. Pa.[98]

OCCUPATION. Uncle Harry initially worked as an augermaker and later as a fireman. His big break came on April 15, 1885, when through sheer luck or dogged determination he was appointed to the position of hoseman for the Philadelphia Fire Department.[99] His first assignment was with Engine Company Number 30 located at the rear of 3546 Germantown Avenue. In 1886, he was reassigned to Engine Company Number 16 located at 51st and Lancaster Avenue. On June 23, 1896, this engine company relocated to a new station on Belmont Avenue below Girard Avenue.

During this time, Uncle Harry appears in the Philadelphia city directories at the following locations:

1882	augermaker, h 836 Union
1883	organmaker (sic), h 3657 Ludlow
1884	angermaker (sic), h 3657 Ludlow
1885	augermaker, h 3657 Ludlow
1886	knitter (sic), 3210 St, James pl
1887	fireman, h 3657 Ludlow
1888	fireman, h 3657 Ludlow
1889	fireman, 3657 Ludlow
1890	fireman, h 3657 Ludlow
1891	fireman, h 3657 Ludlow
1892	fireman, h 806 N 46th

With the exception of 1882, 1886, and 1892, Uncle Harry appears to have lived with his half-brother, Charles G. Douglass, during most of this ten year period.

MARRIAGE OF UNCLE HARRY AND AUNT LIZZIE. Uncle Harry probably met Aunt Lizzie through his half-brother, George W. Douglass who was married to Sarah (Collins) Douglass.

---

[98]1880 U.S. Census (population), Pennsylvania, Philadelphia County, City of Philadelphia, Ward 25, E.D. 496, pages 203B-203C, lines 48-50 & 1-5, National Archives Microfilm Publication T9, Roll 1183.

[99]Letter dated September 1, 1999, from F.F. Daniel J. Kenney, Archivist, Historian, Fireman's Hall, 147 N. 2nd Street, Philadelphia, Pennsylvania 19106-2010.

                                        Appendix F

Aunt Lizzie had married Edward Collins, the said brother of Sarah (Collins) Douglass, on November 7, 1882. It was an unhappy marriage and the couple divorced on October 3, 1891.[100] Uncle Harry and Aunt Lizzie were then married April 25, 1892, by the Reverend William Tracy, Minister of the Gospel at Christ Memorial, a Reformed Episcopal Church.[101] The church was located on the corner of Chestnut and South 43rd Street.[102]

MARRIED LIFE TOGETHER. After they were married, Aunt Lizzie moved from South Philadelphia to 886 N. 43-½ Street in West Philadelphia where Uncle Harry lived because he needed to be close to the firehouse where he worked as a fireman. A year later, Aunt Lizzie's mother, Lucy (Devlin) Reitze, as well as Aunt Lizzie's brother, John, and sister, Josephine, also moved to West Philadelphia. After Aunt Lizzie's brother and sister were married, Uncle Harry, Aunt Lizzie, and Aunt Lizzie's mother, Lucy, moved to 4242 Lancaster Avenue.[103]

When Uncle Harry was not working as a fireman, he is said to have been active in Republican politics.[104] He also may have been a member of the Vesper Boat Club located at # 10 Boathouse Row in Philadelphia where a plaque is said to hang on the wall of the club that lists his name as one of the founding fathers.[105]

After Uncle Harry retired from the Philadelphia Fire Department on August 1, 1905, he and Aunt Lizzie moved to Gloucester City, Camden County, New Jersey, where they bought a

---

[100]Elizabeth M. Collins v Edward J. Collins, CP # 3, January Term 1891, Case # 31, Court of Common Pleas of Philadelphia County, Certifications Unit, Room 266, City Hall, Philadelphia, Pennsylvania 19107.

[101]Affidavit of Applicant for Marriage License # 51028, April 19, 1892, (Henry G. Douglass & Lizzie Reitze), City of Philadelphia, Philadelphia City Archives, Philadelphia, Pennsylvania.

[102]1892 Philadelphia city directory.

[103]1900 U.S. Census (population), Pennsylvania, Philadelphia County, City of Philadelphia, Ward 24, E.D. 568, page 1B, line 88, National Archives Microfilm Publication T623, Roll 1466.

[104]Obituary of Henry G. Douglas (sic), *Camden Courier Post*, Monday, June 13, 1932, p. 2.

[105]Conversation on August 12, 1995, with David H. Marshall, Jr., 121 Reillywood Avenue, Haddonfield, New Jersey 08033-2201.

large house at 15 Thompson Avenue which they owned free and clear.[106,107] Having made their home in Gloucester City, Uncle Harry continued to be involved in local Republican politics.[108,109]

DEATH AND BURIAL OF UNCLE HARRY. Uncle Harry died from uremia on June 10, 1932, just seventeen days after Aunt Lizzie admitted him to the Camden County Mental Hospital in Lakeland, Gloucester Township, Camden County, New Jersey.[110] He was 78 years old and in the end stages of chronic nephritis. Despite her best efforts, Aunt Lizzie, who was 69 years old, was no longer able to take care of him at home.[111]

Uncle Harry's obituary appeared in the *Camden Courier Post* on Monday, June 13, 1932. It read as follows:

> HENRY G. DOUGLAS (sic) - The funeral of Henry G. Douglas (sic), husband
> of Mrs. Elizabeth Douglas (sic), active in Republican politics, will be held
> tomorrow afternoon at his late home, 15 Thompson avenue, Gloucester. Burial
> will be in Lawnview Cemetery, Fox Chase, Philadelphia. He died Friday. His
> wife was a former member of the Gloucester Board of Health.[112]

Uncle Harry was buried at Lawnview Cemetery in a plot that had been purchased jointly

---

[106]Letter dated September 1, 1999, from F.F. Daniel J. Kenney, Archivist, Historian, Fireman's Hall, 147 N. 2nd Street, Philadelphia, Pennsylvania 19106-2010.

[107]1910 U.S. Census (population), New Jersey, Camden County, Gloucester City, Ward 2, E.D. 98, page 7B, line 61, National Archives Microfilm Publication T624, Roll 1872.

[108]Conversation on September 14, 1999, with the late Josephine Thompson Marshall, 121 Reillywood Avenue, Haddonfield, New Jersey 08033-2201.

[109]1930 U.S. Census (population), New Jersey, Camden County, Gloucester City, Ward 3, E.D. 117, page 4A, line 48, National Archives Microfilm Publication T626, Roll 1323.

[110]Death Certificate for Harry Douglass, June 10, 1932, Lakeland, Gloucester Township, Camden County, New Jersey, State of New Jersey - Bureau of Vital Statistics, New Jersey State Archives, Trenton, New Jersey.

[111]Conversation on April 14, 1997, with the late Josephine Thompson Marshall, 121 Reillywood Avenue, Haddonfield, New Jersey 08033-2201.

[112]Obituary of Henry G. Douglas (sic), *Camden Courier Post*, Monday, June 13, 1932, p. 2.

by his sister, Kate A. (Douglass) McLaughlin, and Aunt Lizzie.[113]

DEATH OF AUNT LIZZIE. Aunt Lizzie continued living at 15 Thompson Avenue until about 1935. Then, she appears to have converted her house into a multi-family rental property and moved about a mile away to 821 Middlesex Street, Gloucester City, Camden County, New Jersey. There she became a lodger in the home of Albert and Delcinia Slater.[114] Later, she is said to have transferred the title to her house in Gloucester City to the Presbyterian Homes of New Jersey in exchange for life care after which she moved to the Presbyterian Home in Belvidere, Warren County, New Jersey. Eventually, she transferred to the Presbyterian Home in Haddonfield, Camden County, New Jersey, where she died on April 14, 1961, at the age of 97, her ambition to live to be one hundred years old thwarted by a fatal attack of auricular fibrillation.[115]

Her obituary appeared in the *Camden Courier Post* on Saturday, April 15, 1961. It read as follows:

> DOUGLASS - On April 14, 1961, Elizabeth, widow of Harry G. of the Presbyterian Home, formerly of Gloucester, N.J. Relatives and friends of the family are invited to attend the funeral services on Monday at 1:30 p.m. at Stretch Funeral Home, 8 Kings Highway, West Haddonfield. Interment at Lawnview Cemetery, Fox Chase, PA.[116]

Aunt Lizzie was buried at Lawnview Cemetery in the same plot as her husband, Uncle Harry, and her in-laws, William and Kate A. (Douglass) McLaughlin. Her name was not added to the large headstone that marks the grave.

---

[113]Letter dated February 18, 1997, from Karen L. Crawford, Lawnview Cemetery, 500 Huntingdon Pike, Rockledge, Pennsylvania 19046, regarding burials in Lot 340, Fox Chase Lawn Section, belonging to Kate A. McLaughlin (deceased) and Mrs. Harry Douglass.

[114]1940 U.S. Census (population), New Jersey, Camden County, Gloucester City, Ward 1, E.D. 4-41, page 4A, line 31, family 77, National Archives Microfilm Publication T627, Roll 2321.

[115]Death Certificate for Elizabeth Douglass, April 14, 1961, Haddonfield Borough, Camden County, New Jersey, State Department of Health of New Jersey, Trenton, New Jersey

[116]Obituary of Elizabeth Douglass, *Camden Courier Post*, Saturday, April 15, 1961, p. 13.

Descendants of Henry G. Douglass

Generation 1

1. **HENRY G.**[1] **DOUGLASS** was born in 1816 in Philadelphia, Pennsylvania. He died on 25 Nov 1858 in Stockton, San Joaquin County, California. He married (1) **MARGARET TROUT** on 29 Mar 1835 in Philadelphia, Pennsylvania. She was born in 1816. She died on 09 Jun 1845 in Philadelphia, Pennsylvania. He married (2) **SARAH ASHTON**, daughter of father Ashton on 19 Feb 1846 in Philadelphia, Pennsylvania. She was born in 1817 in New Jersey. She died on 20 Jul 1871 in Philadelphia, Pennsylvania.

Henry G. Douglass and Margaret Trout had the following children:

    i.   GEORGE W.[2] DOUGLASS was born in Jan 1837 in Philadelphia, Pennsylvania. He died on 28 Dec 1900 in Philadelphia, Pennsylvania. He married Sarah C. Collins, daughter of John Collins and Rose on 31 Mar 1865 in Philadelphia, Pennsylvania. She was born in 1842 in Philadelphia, Pennsylvania. She died on 23 Oct 1898 in Philadelphia, Philadelphia County, Pennsylvania.

    ii.   CHARLES G. DOUGLASS was born in 1840 in Philadelphia, Pennsylvania. He died on 31 Dec 1892 in Philadelphia, Pennsylvania. He married Alice Maria Courtney, daughter of James Courtney and Julia Mooney on 18 Feb 1864 in Philadelphia, Pennsylvania. She was born on 12 Oct 1842 in Philadelphia, Pennsylvania. She died on 14 May 1914 in Philadelphia, Pennsylvania.

    iii.   JOSEPH H. DOUGLASS was born in 1843 in Philadelphia, Pennsylvania. He died on 11 Sep 1895 in Philadelphia, Pennsylvania. He married (1) LINEY CLEW, daughter of Jeremiah Clew and Maria Goldey on 11 Aug 1876 in Philadelphia, Pennsylvania. She was born in 1847 in Philadelphia, Pennsylvania. She died on 15 Sep 1885 in Philadelphia, Pennsylvania. He married (2) MARTHA BELL in 1894 in Philadelphia Pennsylvania.

Henry G. Douglass and Sarah Ashton had the following children:

    iv.   CATHARINE A. DOUGLASS was born on 05 Feb 1847 in Philadelphia, Pennsylvania. She died on 26 Jul 1917 in Hopewell Township, Cumberland County, New Jersey. She married William P. McLaughlin, son of Daniel McLaughlin on 30 Sep 1885 in Philadelphia Pennsylvania. He was born in Sep 1853 in Pennsylvania. He died on 31 Mar 1915 in Rockledge, Montgomery County, Pennsylvania.

    v.   HENRY GRAFE DOUGLASS was born on 09 Jul 1854 in Philadelphia, Pennsylvania. He died on 10 Jun 1932 in Lakeland, Gloucester Township, Camden County, New Jersey. He married Elizabeth M. Reitze, daughter of Christopher Reitze and Lucy S. Devlin on 25 Apr 1892 in Philadelphia, Pennsylvania. She was born on 01 Dec 1863 in Philadelphia, Pennsylvania. She died on 14 Apr 1961 in Haddonfield, Camden County, New Jersey.

Appendix G

INDEX

INDEX

INDEX

9 781978 137097